RAW MEMORY

Isabelle Wesselingh and Arnaud Vaulerin

RAW MEMORY

Prijedor: an 'Ethnic Cleansing Laboratory'

Preface by
Elie Wiesel

Foreword by
Paul Garde

Translated by
John Howe

SAQI

in association with
The Bosnian Institute

British Library Cataloguing-in-Publication Date
A catalogue record of this book is available from the British Library

ISBN 0-86356-528-X
EAN 9-780863-565281

©Isabelle Wesselingh and Arnaud Vaulerin, 2005
Translated for this edition by John Howe
Translation © The Bosnian Institute (London), 2005
Originally published as *Bosnie: la mémoire à vif*, Buchet Chastel (Paris), 2003

This edition first published 2005

Saqi Books
26 Westbourne Grove
London W2 5RH
www.saqibooks.com

in association with
The Bosnian Institute
14/16 St Mark's Road
London W11 1RQ
www.bosnia.org.uk

Contents

Preface

This is a collection of personal accounts of recent events, and it is painful. Worse than that, it is shaming. It refers to a tragedy and a scandal that could have been avoided. It should be clearly stated, shouted from the rooftops: a minimum of moral courage, a single sign from the world community of solidarity with martyred Bosnia, just a little less hesitation and cowardice, could have saved innumerable human lives. But more or less everywhere, for political reasons that remain inadmissible, an attitude of hypocritical indifference had been adopted towards victims who were beyond our frontiers, out of sight and out of mind.

Everywhere, on every level, people blamed someone else. In Europe people said that nothing could be done without America. In Washington, the line was that it was a European concern. The United Nations waited with inexhaustible patience for the dust to clear. While the murderers controlled by Slobodan Milošević, Ratko Mladić and Radovan Karadžić went on filling the mass graves around Srebrenica and Omarska.

I visited one of these accursed places at the end of 1992, soon after the start of the 'ethnic cleansing'. In the evening, at Banja Luka: prisoners like ghosts, terrorized, haggard, starving. 'What can we do to help you?' They smelt of fear. Fear of asking for help.

Later I had a conversation with one of the regime's political leaders. He told me that as a Jew I ought to understand his people and their wish to get rid of the other ethnic group. I replied: 'No, the Jew in me cannot understand. We've been living alongside others for two thousand years now.' He was surprised by this but not convinced.

After the Dayton accords had been signed thanks to the intelligence and energy of Ambassador Richard Holbrooke, President Bill Clinton sent me on a fact-finding mission to the refugee camps in Albania and Macedonia. From morning to night I would go from tent to tent, family to family, questioning men and women on their ordeals: systematic humiliation, refined torture, rapes and massacres without end. No one got to the end of his account. They would break down in tears. So I told myself that our task would be a simple one: to speak about them and for them. It is for us to ensure that their tears are remembered.

The title of this book is well chosen, and should serve as a summons and a warning. *Bosnia: Living Memory* is not a parenthesis, a closed file. Readers will certainly find punishment in it as well as crimes.

But let us also bear in mind the incontrovertible fact that the culpable silence around Rwanda facilitated the horrors of Srebrenica. It has been said, we all know, that neutrality only helps the killer, never his victims. As for the present, is it too late to expect true reconciliation, in Bosnia and more specifically in Prijedor, between former adversaries and enemies, and above all between their children? People have a right to hope, they are worthy of it just as they have a duty to the painful truth of memory.

Certainly, these testimonies demonstrate in remarkable fashion the devastating force of racial, ethnic and religious hatred, and its consequences; but the reader will also find in them the possible promise of something that might be called: solidarity in the face of destiny.

Elie Wiesel

Foreword

One piece of news follows another, the drama that gripped the masses yesterday is today forgotten: that's how it is with public opinion. Bosnia remained unknown except to a handful of specialists until 1992. Then, for three tragic years, it was on the front page: the horrors taking place there, revealed through irrefutable evidence and first-hand accounts, aroused general indignation, accompanied here and there by real acts of solidarity from individuals and associations, but for a long time the governments of the major Western countries seemed indifferent to them. Eventually, after 1995, with the ending of armed conflict, the written and electronic media stopped talking about this country whose unfortunate inhabitants, on whom such pity had been lavished, seemed to have fallen back into obscurity. And it has already become respectable to cast doubt on the emotions of thirteen years ago, to wonder whether the facts were really so terrible, the guilty really so guilty and the victims so innocent; to suggest that it's all over now and the passivity of the great powers was justified after all. In other words revisionism, masquerading as hard-headed opposition to an allegedly politically correct 'mainstream view', has started working on public opinion, to the great satisfaction of the small groups that never stopped giving credence to the aggressors' justifications.

The great merit of Isabelle Wesselingh's and Arnaud Vaulerin's book is that it extracts us from these metropolitan arguments, so far removed from the realities, to put us very concretely in touch with everything that the inhabitants of this country have been through and are living still. For their fieldwork the authors chose a specific region, the town of Prijedor and its environs. This municipality has the sad privilege of having undergone in the spring and summer of 1992 a particularly systematic 'ethnic cleansing' of its Bosniak (or 'Muslim') inhabitants, hitherto the majority population by a small margin, along with their Croat fellows, by Serb forces, and of being the site of three of the worst internment – perhaps the word is 'concentration' – camps, Omarska, Keraterm and Trnopolje. Since that time it has been part of the 'Republika Srpska', a Serb-ruled part of Bosnia.

We are thus taken to very real places, town and village, plain and mountain, to meet men and women of all communities, Bosniak, Serb and Croat, all named and highly individualized: living individuals who speak to us, and the dead whose friends, and sometimes whose enemies, speak for them. Research on them is pursued from all angles. We find abundant and detailed accounts from victims or witnesses, collected at the time of the events. There are also eloquent extracts from testimony provided since, notably to the International Criminal Tribunal for former Yugoslavia at The Hague: for the contradictory depositions to the Court by victims and accused, and the findings of the meticulous inquiries carried out by the tribunal's investigators and embodied in the charges, are an inexhaustible source of documentation, ignored or virtually so by the media, but freely available – thousands of pages of it – from the Internet.

Most importantly, though, these documents concerning the past are rounded out by the personal research of the authors who, ten years after the events, revisited Prijedor itself, where Serbs who participated in or witnessed those events are still living, and to which some of the Bosniaks and Croats who were their victims – about 20 per cent, we are told – have returned; as well as other parts of Bosnia and elsewhere, to interview refugees driven from the region.

This enables us to see that 'ethnic cleansing' is a process that continues over time, and whose multiform traces, material but more especially psychological, can never be erased for either the victims or the perpetrators: the 'living memory' of the title. Of course there was the paroxysm of violence and cruelty in 1992, those few months whose description, filled out by new testimonies and recent discoveries, plunges us into horror once again: 'The bodies have holes in their skulls, limbs lopped off at the joints, their throats cut...' There was all that led up to these exactions, the brainwashing carried out by the Serb media to demonize the victims by attributing intentions to them: 'You're one of those who are massacring Serb children,' a Serb soldier said brusquely to a civilian who had just been arrested, on hearing his Muslim names.

But there are also the long-term consequences, which the authors' enquiry, carried out in 2002, exposes through a multitude of subtle observations. They make us understand the feeling of insecurity that dogs returning refugees, in particular their unease at having to live in a place where their former persecutors are still effectively in charge and their own sufferings are denied. We are shown the courage of some, who are confronting the situation with their heads high and trying to re-establish themselves, but also the resignation of some others. Above all we are made aware of the unsaid, the discourse of denial, of evasion of responsibility, of justification of the policies followed, which is universal among those guilty of exactions, supported by the more or less total complicity of their community and still encouraged today by the local media. The international authorities supposed to be supervising Bosnia are often guilty of naivety, sometimes being taken in by this discourse of denial and even lavishing honours on individuals whose hands are dripping with blood; coordination between their different executive bodies, and between them and the judicial authorities in The Hague, leaves a lot to be desired. It is enlightening to read this incisive critique of the multiple linkages and mechanisms, both local and international, of the heavy machinery that emerged from the Dayton accords. Memory plays no part in that. But only memory, only the shared, public and impartial recognition of an undeniable truth, can heal wounds and make reconciliation possible. Such anyway is the authors' conviction, supported by numerous historical examples.

This book, filled with a multitude of past atrocities and compelling current observations of truth, and completed by a severely impartial analysis, makes a mockery of much of the fashionable current debate on the subject, based on ideological *a priori*. By celebrating memory it tries to dissipate our tendency to forgetfulness, and it deserves every success.

Paul Garde

To the Reader

I still have in memory the images of the Keraterm, Omarska and Trnopolje camps, which appeared during the torpor of the summer of 1992. I have been unable to forget the articles of Roy Gutman, the American journalist who discovered those camps and thus saved lives.[1] Those images and those words recalled the words of my grandfather, who had once given me a short description of the opening of the Nazi camps at the end of the second world war.

I remember the silence of the Srebrenica woman in Leslie Woodhead's film *A Cry from the Grave*, who is searching fruitlessly for some trace of her disappeared son and husband. The same silence that oppressed me one summer evening in the hills above Prijedor.

I have never found the answer to an enigma that troubles me and will not go away: how do people get to the point of breaching the bonds of locality, friendship or even family to start massacring their neighbours?

I cannot help fearing that forgetfulness will slip into the interstices of the speeches of conciliation and end as the only winner after the years of war in Prijedor and throughout Europe.

Those images, that silence, that enigma and that fear have stayed with me for eleven years now. They are the reasons for this book.

A. V.
Paris, May 2003

* * *

Prijedor: after six hours of mountain road there it is, before my eyes on an April evening. Prijedor, a town I am seeing for the first time but that I feel I know already. I have heard it being talked about for long hours in a courtroom of the International Criminal Tribunal for former Yugoslavia at The Hague. I have listened while the inhabitants described their uneventful lives, and then the sudden lurch into madness, on an April day that perhaps looked like this one, eleven years ago in 1992. As a journalist covering the trials in that court, I heard those men and women recount the merciless campaign of ethnic cleansing mounted by the Serb nationalists: the sacking of all non-Serbs from their jobs, their internment in camps around the town, the tortures, the executions, the expulsions. I heard the incomprehension in their voices when they recalled a neighbour, a pupil or colleague, who overnight had turned into one of their persecutors.

For months at a time I was unable to get these stories, and the questions they raised, out of my head. The questions had germinated soon after the beginning of the conflict in 1992 and arisen continuously during numerous subsequent visits to Bosnia. How can people of the same country, the same town, who have lived together for centuries, arrive at such a point?

How does a person suddenly become capable of torturing a former classmate or murdering him in cold blood, merely for some difference of origin? The idea of going to Prijedor became more insistent by the day. I had a need, which Arnaud shared, to spend time talking to the people of that town, not just for a short interview on the hoof but on the contrary for long conversations extending over several months.[2] I also wanted to see how people resume, or rather continue, their lives in a place known to the outside world only through the terrible images that emerged in the summer of 1992, showing that the camps had returned to Europe, with their miserable groups of skeletal detainees behind barbed wire.

'The war's over, no one's interested in Bosnia now,' said some. Nevertheless the conviction that here, in the post-war period, was exactly where some of the most interesting stories could be found, kept nagging at me, would not leave either of us in peace. How are the shattered links between fellow-inhabitants reconstructed? Why do some survivors of the horrors of the camps decide to return to Prijedor to live without the thirst for vengeance? Why do others prefer exile instead? How do the Serbs of the town and the region deal with this painful recent past and the crimes committed in their name? What has the justice process deployed in The Hague achieved for those it should be serving in the first instance: the victims of former Yugoslavia?

Those eighteen months spent between Prijedor and The Hague supplied a lot of answers, a few marvels, disappointments, anger and the certainty that the denial and refusal to admit crimes discernible in many Bosnian Serbs is a continuing obstacle to durable peace. Just as the Dayton peace accords have done little more than ratify most of the divisions resulting from the conflict. Without recognition of the crimes committed, Bosnia remains in the grip of a cold war.

That return to Prijedor also strengthened the feeling that the war had not just been 'a Balkan freak show',[3] as the American journalist Peter Maass rightly points out. Before the lurch into insanity, the inhabitants of Prijedor and Bosnia-Herzegovina were living lives identical to our own. This does not make their sufferings any more or any less terrible than those of people from more distant cultures, like the hundreds of thousands of Rwandan and Cambodian victims of genocide or similar. But their relative proximity can make us understand that the mechanisms of hatred, divisive media propaganda and the manipulations of some politicians, the things that occurred in former Yugoslavia, could lead to conflict anywhere in the world, not just over there but here too.

I. W.
The Hague, May 2003

PART ONE

At the Heart of the Ethnic Cleansing

Will the night last much longer?
Jorge Semprun, *Le grand voyage*

We are nearly there. For a few kilometres more, the road runs along the river Sana, softly following the meandering watercourse across a gently undulating plain, green and wooded. Round a last curve, and the road stretches ahead, dead straight and rigid, with the Hotel Prijedor rising at the end of it. Flying the white, blue and red standard of the Bosnian Serbs, the imposing greyish block of concrete and glass, an architectural legacy of the Tito years, recalls similar buildings in small towns all over the Balkans. In the hope of attracting tourists, a leisure centre has been added at the foot of the building, on the bank of the river. In spring the inhabitants, and occasional passing tourists, go there to keep cool, swim and play water sports. In summer, people picnic there to the song of frogs, in autumn walk with their families.

Immediately after crossing the bridge the road enters Prijedor from the south in a leafy, residential area.[1] The road takes a 90-degree turn to the right, then passes in front of the freshly repainted Orthodox church with its neat churchyard. A bed-and-breakfast hotel, three blocks of flats, the cinema, a few cafés and then the first car park, the beginning of the 'administrative quarter'. Broad velvety lawns in front of well-maintained buildings, with restricted parking. On the left the town hall, a wide functional two-storey building; on the right Prijedor police headquarters, well guarded. In the morning this office district is the scene of permanent activity, which in the afternoon spreads to the cafés and big shops placed behind the town hall, at the crossing with a street lined with trees shading wide pavements. There is loud music, and in summer the terraces are packed as the inhabitants meet at midday and late in the evening. At first sight Prijedor does not present the appearance of a deprived and wounded community.

Ten-storey buildings stand all around. Nearby, at the edge of a quiet district of detached houses, is the Mira biscuit factory founded in 1928, one of the last remaining major enterprises in the centre of town: it employs nearly six hundred people. A hundred metres away, the railway station and a big parking area for buses. After a traffic light, the road passes under a railway bridge and forks to the right. A long bend through a mixed residential area leads into the road to Banja Luka, capital of the Bosnian Serb entity (RS),[2] fifty-five kilometres to the east.

Prijedor, a town of 112,000 inhabitants in north-western Bosnia, reveals slightly more of itself to visitors on foot. Start from the tourist office, in the corner of an ancient building. Most of its business is the sale of package holidays abroad and bus tickets for the big towns of Croatia, Serbia and of course Bosnia. A sort of 'green', family-oriented and 'historical' tourism is promoted there in a rather diffident and old-fashioned way: the tourist brochure dates from October 1985. It contains faded bucolic images of women in traditional costume and 'typical' dwellings, hunting and fishing scenes and an account of the National Liberation struggle during the Second World War.[3] What people say has not changed much either, even the younger shopkeepers. 'You ought to go into the hills and see the cliffs on Mount Vlašić, it's lovely up there. Our region's green, there's lots of forest,' the owner of a bar-restaurant says. 'And there's the river too. You can go swimming there in summer when it's hot. It's nice, you shouldn't miss it.'

Next door the Patrija department store is just about ticking over. A massive block with faded red facades and empty display windows, it sits beside the roundabout at the beginning of Prijedor's main street: Peter-I-the-Liberator Street, named after the Karađorđević monarch who ruled a kingdom in which for the first time all Serbs lived in a single state, and who supposedly liberated Bosnians, Croats and Slovenes from Habsburg domination.[4] This is the heart of the town, an artery lined with offices, houses and shops, with side streets leading to the market, the lorry park, town services and administrations, dilapidated housing estates and the suburb of private houses. The passers-by are peasants from the nearby countryside, beggars, office workers from the council administrations, youths, the unemployed, the retired.

Pedestrianized, rectilinear and central, the street is Prijedor's display window, the place for meetings, strolling and shopping. The biggest food and clothes shops are found there, along with stalls selling pirate CDs and sunglasses and small kiosks selling newspapers, lottery tickets and contraband cigarettes. Windows dressed in fusty obsolete style alongside boutiques and hi-fi shops whose displays might be anywhere in Europe.

People go there in couples or groups or families. Children play on the house doorsteps and in the stairwells. Teenagers drink coke, eat ice cream, listen to music and watch foreign TV programmes in bars. Older people sit on terraces or beside scraggy flowerbeds sipping coffee or beer. In the evening and at weekends, this traffic takes on a ceremonial aspect, becomes a parade, like surf on a beach: from top to bottom and bottom to top the street is patrolled and occupied as an essential place for living. It is where people go to show off new clothes, try out new makeup, enjoy the admiration aroused by a good figure ...

The atmosphere is a mixture of nonchalance and enjoyment of life. Prijedor at such moments shows a face that seems banal, ordinary, almost like anywhere else and free from dramas. You could leave straight away taking this impression of a peaceful, well-organized, well-behaved, protected township, as if it was simply a place not exactly forgotten but slumbering in the depths of a country, a market town with all the attributes of 'normality'. But if you stay, the impression does not survive for long.

ONE

'Everything Seemed Calm, then Suddenly it Was all Turned Upside Down'

It has been there for months, painted in black letters on a white wall for all to see in Peter I Street, and in English too, as if addressed to the international community: 'Radovan Karadžić, Serb hero'. *Hero* is also the uncompromising title of a dubious biography of Ratko Mladić, displayed on the counter of a bookshop a hundred metres away. Calendars bearing the effigies of these two promoters of Greater Serbian nationalism were still on sale in the street early in 2004. But Karadžić and Mladić, respectively ex-political leader and ex-military chief of the Bosnian Serbs, have been indicted since 1995 by the International Criminal Tribunal for former Yugoslavia (ICTY) for war crimes, crimes against humanity and genocide committed between 1992 and 1995. The charges concern exactions perpetrated in Prijedor, a town with the sad distinction of having served as an ethnic cleansing laboratory at the beginning of the war in April 1992. The raw facts are these: several hundred deaths, perhaps several thousand, since there are nearly three thousand unexplained disappearances according to associations of the families concerned; and the opening of three internment camps on the periphery of Prijedor, in council buildings and factories. For nearly four months torture, rape and mass murder were practised at Omarska, Keraterm and Trnopolje. Then in August 1992 Roy Gutman's articles in the American paper *Newsday*, followed by images from the British TV company ITN, exposed the reappearance of 'the camps' in Europe.

Thirteen years on, the town wants to bury this recent past. One thing that helps is that it was relatively little damaged in the fighting. Unlike many

Bosnian towns (Mostar, Sarajevo) and some of its own surrounding settlements (Hambarine, Kozarac, and further to the south Ključ and others), Prijedor has virtually no bullet-pocked walls, blackened burned-out buildings, shell-damaged roofs. All such traces have been carefully erased. The 'cleansing' has also had a devastating effect on people's memories.

It is very hard work to get confirmation that the piece of waste land covered with thick grass in the middle of town is where the mosque used to be.[1] Equally hard to get directions to the old town (essentially Muslim) that once occupied a small island between the Berek watercourse and the river Sana. In 1992 it was shelled, then razed. A market, illegal shacks and a few new houses occupy the place now. Nature too has moved back into this no man's land., Officially, there have been no great indelible crimes here; no three-and-a-half-year siege as in Sarajevo, no massive and unforgettable genocidal murder as at Srebrenica in July 1995. Almost nothing, almost forgotten.

As if to excuse themselves, some claim that the past has not been forgotten: and to prove it, a monument has been raised to 'all the victims of the war'. The thing really exists, facing the town hall of course. But it is in doubtful taste to put it mildly: it takes the form of an Orthodox cross, when the majority of victims at Prijedor were Bosniaks,[2] mainly Muslim by religion, followed by Croats, mostly Catholic, and only then, a long way behind, by Orthodox Serbs. While aware of 'the burden of events', Nada Ševo, mayor of Prijedor and a member of the moderate nationalist Independent Social Democratic Party (SNSD), prefers to cut this sort of discussion off at the roots: 'On principle, I'm going to reduce the number of monuments to victims. There's something wrong with talking endlessly about the past and never about the future. I was a teacher for twenty-eight years, and learned to look to the future from young people.'

Muharem Murselović would like to look to the future too, but not without having confronted the past. The ex-president of Prijedor's municipal assembly[3] is still refusing to turn the page. He knows that from his sister's house you can see the chimney of the Keraterm ceramics factory, where several thousand men were interned between May and August 1992. Many were beaten and tortured there, and some murdered. Nor is he unaware that when he goes to the RS national assembly in Banja Luka his route passes close to the notorious Omarska internment camp. He spent sixty-eight days there, saw the majority of his friends and colleagues – Bosniaks like him, and Croats – die there, and himself came close to death. He cannot bring himself to pretend not to recognize the former war criminals, torturers, camp guards and ideologues of ethnic cleansing who are often to be seen parading up and down Peter I Street. That is where he lives. He can be found there every evening at about six. After a short siesta he takes his coffee at the Accord, a bar on the ground floor of his building. From his table there he observes his fellow-citizens and looks them searchingly in the eye.

Muharem Murselović was born in Prijedor on 24 November 1947. His parents were restaurant owners and caterers. After catering studies and a few years of teaching, he followed in his family's footsteps. The Mursel establishment (his nickname), which he had opened in 1978, was in the centre of town. It was frequented mainly by Bosnian businessmen, but people came from elsewhere in Yugoslavia to sample a cuisine that was both typically local and European. In Peter I Street, then still Marshal Tito Street, he owned a snack bar selling quick meals, which also served as a café. As a private businessman in a socialist economy, he was led to set up a political group with an eye to the first free elections, in 1990. The Private Initiative Party was thus formed by entrepreneurs anxious to defend their own interests, and Muharem Murselović was elected to the Prijedor municipal assembly as one of its representatives. In 1992 he decided to close his restaurant and sell the building to invest in a new establishment. But the fallout from the war in neighbouring Croatia and the first stirrings of political crisis in Prijedor put an end to all his plans: the town was seized by force on the morning of 30 April 1992.

Murselović is a short, slightly balding man with a reserved and discreet manner. He speaks firmly, precisely, often certain of his ground; his gaze is direct and sometimes hard. This determined but solitary individual exudes an almost imperious dignity and strength of character, as if his confident bearing and frank gaze were themselves a sort of revenge tinged with pride. A way of asserting 'I'm still alive, I'm still here', his nephew repeatedly points out. He certainly is still present. He invites interlocutors into the first floor of his house. He never refuses to talk to them. He works closely with the ICTY and often gives interviews to journalists, as this evening in Prijedor and many times at The Hague. His personal story symbolizes and summarizes the experience of many non-Serb inhabitants. It is entangled with the events that have left their mark on Prijedor. Before starting he opens the office window which gives onto the street. 'You see the Hotel Balkan, opposite? That's where I was imprisoned on 30 May before being interned at Omarska.' Then he sits with his back to the window and starts to talk.

First Arrest

'On the morning of 23 May, alone in the house, I was watching the Serb TV news from Banja Luka. It was about seven o'clock. Suddenly the TV said: "A group of extremists at Kozarac [a mainly Muslim village twelve kilometres from Prijedor] admits to having been financed by a very well-known restaurateur called Murselović." Terribly shocked to hear my name being bandied about on TV, I called the police straight away, told them the information was false and asked for an explanation. The policeman who answered the phone didn't know anything and told me not to worry. All the same, I went to the police station to ask for the news item to be corrected. They kept saying: "If we need anything from you, you'll know soon enough." Half an hour after I got back to the office I heard my name being called in the street. I opened the window and saw two policemen one of whom was Bato Kovačević, from the Prijedor station. They told me to accompany them there.

'Until twelve-thirty I stayed on the second floor and the police told me I was under arrest. Then I was taken to the ground floor and put in what must have been a sobering-up cell for drunks. There I found several people I recognized: Ilijaz Musić, a physics teacher and official of the SDA (Democratic Action Party);[4] Mehmed Turšić, head of the taxation department; Dr. Željko Sikora, a young Croat medical man; a fellow called Juso Šerić, a businessman employed by the Naftagas company; and a young restaurant worker. Half an hour after me the current president of the municipal assembly, Muhamed Čehajić, was also put in the cell. We wondered why we were there, since we were all civilians.

'Meanwhile the policemen were loading and unloading their weapons and firing live rounds into the courtyard, sometimes in the direction of our building, while shouting repeatedly: "They're Ustashe (name used by fascist Croat militias during the second world war),[5] they all ought to be killed." So we stayed clear of the windows and spent the night under those conditions.

'On the morning of 24 May I was taken to see Inspector Krneta, who had questioned me the previous day. He told me: "The Crisis Staff has denied the TV news item." That reassured me, but I stayed in that office until four or five in the afternoon. Then the head of the police investigation department, Ranko Mijić, whom I was to see later at Omarska and still pass in the street in Prijedor, informed me that I was going to be released but was to stay in touch with the police. At about five or six o'clock I was finally let out.'

Second Arrest

'On 30 May, between eleven and midday, the police came back to arrest me.

A local resident, Ranko Vujasinović, who was wearing police uniform, told me to take refuge in the Hotel Balkan across the road from my house. With most of my Serb and Bosniak neighbours, some of them elderly, I therefore crossed the road and went into the café where we stayed at least three or four hours. We waited there without knowing what to do. We heard a lot of shooting. Then we were split up: on one side the Serbs, on the other all the Croat and Muslim men aged under sixty, who were told to line up. We were led to buses. There were about twenty-five people in mine.

'A barber who knew this Vujasinović asked him where we were going. The young policeman beat the old man up before saying to the driver: "Take this shit away." The bus drove off, then stopped at the crossing between the town hall and the police station. An officer got in. I asked him where he thought he was taking us and why we were in this bus. He shrugged and said he didn't know. Another policeman whom I knew allowed me to get off the bus to seek information. A soldier, not from Prijedor, asked my name. When I said I was called Muharem Murselović, he seemed astonished. "You're one of the people massacring Serb children. Get back on the bus!" He struck me in the small of the back and I jumped into the bus. He followed me: "You're the people who want to massacre our Serb children, lie down on the floor!" We all lay down. The bus drove off. After half an hour, passing through Saničani and Tomašica, we arrived at Omarska, near the mine. That was on 30 May 1992. I stayed there until 6 August.'

Omarska

'The room I was put in was called Mujo's room (after a prisoner at the camp), placed just behind the restaurant and normally used as a locker-room. The lockers had all been moved to one side. I stayed there for virtually the whole of my detention, apart from a few days living on the *pista* (a strip of tarmac the detainees followed to get to the "refectory"). The room measured about fifteen metres by twelve. At first there were no more than fifteen of us, but the numbers rose to two hundred, and on to five hundred, packed in rows like sardines. There I found Muhamed Čehajić, president of the municipal assembly. A Catholic priest from Ljubija, Stipo Šošić, was there too. So was a Croat music teacher, Ivica Peretin.

'I also spent two or three nights in a place called the Garage, alongside Mujo's room, at the end of my detention at Omarska. I never went to the White House or the Red House.[6] In the Garage there were between a hundred and fifty and a hundred and seventy people. Among us was a woman[7] called Hajra. Women I knew there included a Prijedor judge, Nusreta Sivac, an economist, Mugbila Beširević, an office-worker at the mine, Sadija Avdić, and Velida Mahmuljin, a teacher and member of the SDA. These last two I have never seen again.

'The conditions of detention were inhuman. We slept on the bare tiles. It was a privilege to have a bit of cardboard or paper. We were supposed to get one meal a day, but you couldn't really call it a meal. Generally it was rotten wormy stuff, beans or potatoes drowned in watery soup. In groups of thirty, we were given a very short time, less than three minutes, to run from the *pista* to the kitchens, get our food, bolt it down and return the plates and cutlery.

'We were regularly beaten on the way back, for slipping on oil and water that the guards had poured on the floor. Our drinking water wasn't clean, and a lot of us had dysentery and stomach pains. Some were so ill that they couldn't help evacuating their bowels in the room packed tight with detainees.

'I was among the last in my room to be interrogated. It was thirty days after my arrival. My first "interrogation" lasted between thirty and forty minutes. I was not beaten that time. Their questions didn't have much sense.

'Once, I was beaten on the *pista* where we had formed the habit of sitting after our meal. The guards could get at us there. Šimo Kević, who was wearing an army uniform, came up to me saying: "Look, it's Mursel who used to persecute Serb children when he worked at the school." I hadn't been working at the school for fourteen years, but he remembered me. So the guards grabbed hold of me and started laying into me with lengths of cable and batons longer than police truncheons. A blond policeman named Marmat was the worst of the lot. I was in a crouching position trying to protect myself; I was severely beaten on the head and shoulders before they turned on another detainee.

'Another time, coming back from the meal, a guard hit me in the ear and I slipped and fell to one knee: the pain was agonizing. He started hitting me with a fat cable while I was down there. After about fifteen minutes of this I tried to get up, he continuing to hit me the while, and someone came to help me. When the guard saw the state I was in, he said: "OK, he's useless!" and abandoned me. Immediately afterwards two other men were requisitioned for some task. They were taken away and never seen again.

'I was beaten up when I was in the toilets too. I was squatting when guards knocked on the door. "Oh! A Balija, a Turk, you're cleaning yourself." That day I had some ribs broken, so badly that for two months I had trouble breathing and eating. "Interrogations" went on all day: one heard the thud of bodies thrown against walls or floors, screams mixed with heartbreaking groans, unbearable to us listening from the floor below. Afterwards, victims would be carried to our room to die, for example Zijad Ziko Mahmuljin, an economist and president of the town's executive council. He died less than two hours after a so-called interrogation. There was also a man called Esef Crnkić, an engineer at the Omarska mine, who was robust and strong: he came back from an interrogation session black and blue all over his body. We put damp compresses on his wounds for two days. Then suddenly big and small bumps, blisters, appeared all over his body: it looked horrible and indicated that his liver and kidneys were ruptured. He died very quickly.

'A small yellow truck used to come for the bodies in the early afternoon, and would stop by the White House where dead bodies were left. The daily number varied from five to thirteen. We could often see these bodies in the morning from our room only thirty metres away.

'One morning we were called out and crammed into buses. There must have been a hundred people in mine. We had to lie down on top of each other. We were forbidden to sit on the seats. Before we left, the guards gave us stale food. Some detainees were ill and unable either to go to the toilets or to control their bowels. Then the guards turned on the heating in the bus and closed the doors and windows. As you can imagine, the heat in early August was unbearable. As I suffer from diabetes I tried to get as close as possible to a window to lick off traces of moisture. I believe that day was the worst of my life, except for those I spent in the Garage at Omarska.'

Manjača

'After a long wait at Omarska, lying down all the time, we realized that the bus was heading for Banja Luka. The journey was extremely unpleasant. We went through a lot of villages whose inhabitants shouted and threw things at us. During the journey the guards walked about on our backs and insulted us; they tried to make us sing Serb nationalist songs.

'At about ten o'clock at night we understood that we had arrived at Manjača. It was a former JNA camp where people had gone for training before the war. The bus stopped at the entrance. The guards put the heating on again and we spent the night like that. Men got hold of several detainees whom they beat and murdered. At six the next morning we were parched, filthy and stinking. An elderly man of my acquaintance, Mr Edo Crnalić, was dragged off the bus. Once outside he was beaten up. Then his lifeless corpse was thrown back into the bus on top of the other detainees.

'I was held at Manjača until 14 or 15 November 1992, when a first convoy organized by the International Committee of the Red Cross (ICRC) for the oldest detainees, those born before 1951, left Manjača. The travel conditions were a good deal more humane than the ones I was used to. We passed through Banja Luka on the way to Nova Gradiška in Croatia, then Karlovac.'

Exile and Return

After living as a refugee at Opatija, in Croatia, Muharem Murselović was allowed to live in Germany. In February 1994, straight after the Washington accords which ended the war between Bosniaks and Croats by creating a Croat-Muslim federation, he decided to join the Bosnian Army at Travnik. When the Dayton accords were signed in November 1995 his battalion was at Sanski Most, around thirty kilometres from Prijedor. He was demobilized on 15 February 1996.

Since then Muharem Murselović has resumed his political activities. His old party, the Private Initiative Party, having been dissolved, he became a member of the Party for Bosnia-Herzegovina. He was elected to Prijedor municipal assembly in 1997, again in 1998 and again in 2000, when he also became president of the assembly. In April 2003, however, he resigned from this last function in protest against the decision by the municipality to choose a Serb nationalist symbol as its emblem. A deputy in the RS national assembly, he stood in the municipal elections of 2 October 2004 and was again elected to Prijedor municipal assembly.

Thirteen years after his internment, Muharem Murselović is determined never to leave his town again. He has the posture and abilities of a classic oppositionist, but he is alone and isolated in a town and a region anxious to forget the events of the war. Despite everything Muharem Murselović means to remain a living memorial to that past, and a lookout.

He has lost most of his friends, as the town has lost nearly all its Bosniak and Croat intelligentsia. So if only for them, he carries on the fight against 'nationalism' and 'fascism' and continues to 'work against oblivion'.

'I would never have imagined that the Serbs could go so far against civilians. Everything seemed calm, then suddenly it was all turned upside down.'

There Was Once a Country …

'Life changed utterly in less than twenty-four hours, overnight,' confirmed another survivor, Emir Beganović.[1] The night referred to was that of 30 April 1992 when the nationalist Serbs of Bosnia, backed by paramilitaries and troops from Serbia, seized control of Prijedor. On the fringes of western Europe, armed troops had simply overthrown municipal authorities elected two years earlier. After taking power they started to subject the Croats and Muslims of Bosnia, and those Serbs who tried to oppose them, to a régime of terror and effective apartheid.

Although the lives of the Bosniak and Croat inhabitants of the town were transformed overnight, surprising them with a nightmarish awakening, it is now well known that the martyrdom of Prijedor was the outcome of an operation that had been planned long in advance by its backers and executants, and had its origins in the disintegration of Yugoslavia.

Yugoslavia: A Precarious Structure

Yugoslavia was born in 1918 at the end of the First World War. At the time the new state was called the 'Kingdom of Serbs, Croats and Slovenes'. In 1929, King Alexander I Karađorđević ended the democratic system and proclaimed his personal dictatorship. The country was officially renamed Yugoslavia.

In 1940, just after the Nazi invasion of France, Yugoslavia came under strong pressure from Hitler who wanted to recruit it as an ally. The country's position made it strategically important for the conquest of the Balkans.

The regent Paul eventually signed a pact with the Führer on 25 March 1941. Angered by what they saw as an unacceptable alliance and encouraged by the British, Serb officers organized an army coup d'état that overthrew Prince Paul and installed a new government. Although the latter quickly confirmed the pact, Hitler responded by bombing Belgrade and Germany and Italy invaded Yugoslavia on 6 April 1941.

Reactions to the German and Italian invasion varied. Many Croats saw it as an opportunity to detach themselves from the embrace of Yugoslavia, and Mussolini's protégé Ante Pavelić proclaimed an 'Independent Croat State' (NDH) with the backing of the Axis occupiers. The new régime established laws that discriminated violently against the two million Serbs living on the territory of the NDH, which included also Bosnia. Some were even made to wear a white armband to show that they were Serbs, in an echo of the yellow star Jews were forced to wear by the Nazis.[2] Ante Pavelić's Ustashe imprisoned Jews, Serbs and all its opponents in concentration camps. One of the most sinister and best known of these was Jasenovac in eastern Croatia, a few dozen kilometres from Prijedor.

In occupied Serbia two resistance movements quickly appeared: the Chetniks and the Partisans. The Chetniks (whose name signifies 'armed band') were loyal to the royalist government, and anti-communist. The movement was led by Draža Mihailović and treated all non-Serb peoples as its enemies. The communist-led Partisans were quickly defeated in Serbia, but their resistance grew elsewhere, above all at first in Bosnia. The massacres of Serbs perpetrated by the Germans and the Ustashe were often answered by Chetnik massacres of Bosniaks and Croats. The Partisans, commanded by the Croat Josip Broz, alias Tito, were inspired by communist principles and welcomed all the Yugoslav nationalities with open arms. Although the majority of recruits to the Partisan forces were initially Serbs from Bosnia and Croatia, the movement had an all-Yugoslav leadership and included Croats, Bosniaks, Slovenes and Montenegrins. Partisan tactics consisted of waging as many actions against the occupant as possible. By the end of the Second World War, Tito had managed to liberate the entire national territory, whereupon he took charge and ruled the country with an iron hand for the next thirty-five years.

Under the 1946 Constitution the Federal Republic of Yugoslavia comprised six republics (Bosnia-Herzegovina, Croatia, Macedonia, Montenegro, Serbia and Slovenia), corresponding to the six peoples it embraced. The two main non-Slav populations were accommodated with autonomous provinces, Kosovo (Albanian majority) and Vojvodina (large Hungarian minority). This structure enabled the diversity of nationalities inside Yugoslavia to be properly recognized for the first time. While an enormous advance on the pre-war monarchic régime, however, it was counterbalanced in practice by the absence of freedom within Tito's totalitarian system.

'Any debate on questions of nationality was practically impossible, and potential reformers and oppositionists reduced to silence',[3] writes Paul Garde, a leading expert on Yugoslavia. 'With the passage of time all the peoples were to become discontented, the Serbs at seeing their national unity broken up, the Croats because their cultural specificity was denied, the Albanians at being deprived of the status of a nationality with its own republic...' he adds, emphasizing that everyone imputed the injustice they thought they had suffered to collusion between the régime and the neighbouring people or peoples.

In 1948, wishing to retain his autonomy in the shadow of the Russian 'big brother', Tito broke with Stalin. Yugoslavia followed its own course inside the communist bloc, opening its frontiers to West European visitors and partially restoring private property. But the political system remained as authoritarian as ever and trials of dissidents continued.

In 1974, with the republics pressing to have their interests considered more seriously, a new Constitution was adopted. It incorporated a measure of decentralization: henceforth the six republics and two autonomous provinces were sovereign, with a right of veto over decisions by the federal government.

After thirty-five years during which the expression of national discontents had been repressed, Tito's death on 4 May 1980, and the severe economic crisis afflicting the country, freed people to put their demands and sharpened passions. In accordance with the provisions of the 1974 Constitution, no one was appointed to succeed Tito. The role of head of state would be filled by one of the members of the collective presidency, consisting of representatives of the six republics and two autonomous provinces, under a system of annual rotation.

A 'Defender' for the 'Beleaguered' Serbs

One man in particular was able to profit from the resurgence of national thinking and the weakness of the system: Slobodan Milošević. The former Serbian president, who has been on trial since 12 February 2002 before the International Criminal Tribunal for former Yugoslavia (ICTY) in The Hague, was at that time just a communist apparatchik devoid of all charisma. Although he had become head of the Serbian League of Communists, he sensed that

Serbian nationalism could serve him as a springboard to power. In 1986, a memorandum written by some intellectuals at the Belgrade Academy of Sciences and Arts complained that Serbs were being exploited in Yugoslavia despite their sacrifices during the Second World War, and issued a strident call for the 'defence of Serb interests', under alleged threat from the other nationalities. This text was described as a call 'for a new fratricidal war and a new bloodbath' by one Belgrade journalist, Alexander Đukanović. While other Serb leaders denounced the document as a 'requiem for Yugoslavia', Slobodan Milošević maintained a complicit silence.

He then began brandishing the spectre of a threatened Serb population. He used the media to indoctrinate public opinion and spread the belief that Serbs had been massacred by Kosovo Albanians. Frustrated by the economic crisis, the population turned to this new leader who was promising to 'protect' it.

On 28 June 1989 a million Serbs gathered to hear Milošević, the new president of Serbia, deliver a speech commemorating the 600th anniversary of the battle of the Field of Blackbirds, a few kilometres from Prishtina, capital of Kosovo. The battle on 28 June 1389 had sealed the defeat of troops led by the Serbian Prince Lazar against the forces of the Ottoman Empire. Six hundred years later, the Serbs somehow acquired the impression that they were at last being avenged on the Turks, whom they now assimilated with the Albanians. In fact Slobodan Milošević had just succeeded in modifying the 1974 Constitution to withdraw its autonomous status from Kosovo. Segregation measures were imposed on the Albanian population of the province.

In January 1990, the Fourteenth Congress of the League of Communists of Yugoslavia was due to assemble the leaderships of all the Republics in Belgrade, to try to find a new and more democratic model for the country. The Serbian delegates, under Slobodan Milošević's orders, blocked all the democratization proposals put forward by the Slovenian delegates, who eventually walked out. Somewhat to the surprise of the Serbian president, they were followed by the Croatians, while the Bosnians, the Macedonians and the Yugoslav People's Army (JNA) delegation voted to adjourn the sitting. The Yugoslav communist party, the only thing holding the federation together, had just disintegrated.

After the first free elections in 1990, Slovenia and Croatia proclaimed their independence on 25 June 1991. The JNA intervened in Slovenia but the war lasted only a few days (27 June to 3 July 1991): Slovenia was of small importance to Slobodan Milošević because virtually no Serbs lived there. In Croatia, though, tension had risen when a group of local Serbs proclaimed a 'Serb Republic of Croatia' on 28 February 1991, with the support of the federal army, in defiance of the elected government in Zagreb.

On 8 October that year Croatia and Slovenia both ratified their independence. The ancient port of Dubrovnik on the Adriatic coast, officially classified as a world heritage site, was besieged and quite heavily shelled by the JNA, manned largely by Serbs and Montenegrins. In Slavonia (eastern Croatia) the town of Vukovar, a symbol of Croatian resistance, fell on 19 November 1991. Federal troops and Serb paramilitaries massacred civilian evacuees in the hospital. Vukovar was one of the first brutalized towns in the conflicts that would now spatter much of Yugoslavia with blood: Slovenia (1991), Croatia (1991–95), Bosnia (1992–95) and then Kosovo (1998–99).

Disintegration of the Ethnic Mosaic of Bosnia-Herzegovina

Slightly bigger than Switzerland at 51,000 square kilometres, Bosnia-Herzegovina is a mountainous territory crossed by rivers whose names – Neretva, Una, Sana, Bosna, Drina – have been the delight of local poets and composers down the centuries. It was occupied by the Ottomans for four hundred years before coming under Austro-Hungarian dominion in 1878. In 1918 Bosnia joined the 'Kingdom of Serbs, Croats and Slovenes'. Three intermingled populations, Serbs, Croats and Muslims (Bosniaks), had been living side by side for centuries in what can only be called a mosaic.

According to the 1981 census, the last to give complete figures, Bosnia-Herzegovina then had a population of 4.3 million of whom 39.5 per cent declared themselves Muslims (44 per cent in 1991), 32 per cent said they were Serbs (31 per cent in 1991) and 18.3 per cent said they were Croats (17 per cent in 1991), while 7.9 per cent declared that they were Yugoslavs and 0.3 per cent Montenegrins.[4] All are of Slav descent and have spoken the same language (known after the mid 19th century as Serbo-Croat) for centuries.

The first free multi-party elections, which took place between 18 November and 9 December 1990, gave the majority of votes to the three nationalist formations: the Party of Democratic Action, SDA (Muslim), Radovan Karadžić's Serb Democratic Party (SDS) and the Croat Democratic Union (HDZ). Despite their divergent views on the future of Bosnia as part of Yugoslavia, the three political organizations came together to form a government. The alliance was only skin-deep, however.

Constant harping in the Belgrade media on atrocities committed by the Croat Ustashe during the Second World War was aimed at arousing fear in the Serb populations of the other Republics, including Bosnia. The objective of the manoeuvre, which was supported by the SDS, was to 'arouse the fears of Serbs everywhere and in the end to have them seek protection within a Greater Serbia' stretching from Kosovo to Croatia with its capital in Belgrade, according to the ICTY judges in their arguments supporting the conviction of a war criminal from the Prijedor region.[5]

In Bosnia-Herzegovina, this idea started to gain ground with a segment of Serb opinion soon after the elections. With the support of Slobodan Milošević, the psychiatrist and mediocre versifier Radovan Karadžić set about organizing the secession from Bosnia of the Bosnian Serbs, in the hope of later attachment to Serbia. From 1990 onward, a well-oiled and meticulously-planned operation was working to establish a parallel Serb administration that would not be answerable to the Sarajevo authorities.

In April 1991 the municipalities controlled by Serbs formed an association, ostensibly to promote economic and cultural links. In reality, nationalist leaders were already starting to establish parallel police forces composed exclusively of Serbs.

In September 1991 a number of 'autonomous Serb regions' (*Srpska autonomna oblast*: SAO) were proclaimed on the territory of Bosnia-Herzegovina: on the fringes of north-western Bosnia around Banja Luka (a region also known as Krajina); in Romanija, the mountainous zone to the east of Sarajevo; and in eastern Herzegovina, on the frontier with Montenegro. It is important to note that these autonomous zones all included areas of very mixed population. To nationalist Serbs, the Croats and Muslims were an obstacle to the establishment of a Greater Serbia that would have to be got round in one way or another.

In Sarajevo, Croats and Muslims were becoming anxious about these developments. The war being waged by Belgrade in Croatia was causing bad feeling between the Serbs enrolled in the JNA and their Muslim and Croat colleagues who were refusing to go and fight in what they saw as an operation in support of 'aggression'. On 15 October 1991 the Bosnian parliament proclaimed the sovereignty of the Republic. The Serb deputies rejected the decision and nine days later set up a parallel assembly.

In the autonomous Serb territories the Yugoslav army, dominated by Serbs and Montenegrins, was building up its forces. The nationalists were setting up parallel administrations in municipalities they did not yet control. In November the SDS organized a plebiscite on the following question: 'Do you agree with the decision of 24 October 1991 by the Parliament of the Serb People in Bosnia-Herzegovina for the Serb people to remain in a common State of Yugoslavia with Serbia, Montenegro, SAO Krajina, SAO Slavonia, Baranja and Western Srem and all others wishing the same?'[6] Serbs were virtually the only voters, some of them under threat.. 100 per cent answered positively according to the official results. As the threat of war loomed closer by the day, Europe demanded that a referendum be held before it would recognize Bosnian independence.

On 9 January 1992, the supporters of Karadžić proclaimed a 'Serb Republic of Bosnia-Herzegovina' which, they said, would be put into effect if the international community recognized the independence of Bosnia-Herzegovina. The referendum on independence took place on 29 February and 1 March 1992, and was boycotted by most Serbs. To discourage the rest, Radovan Karadžić's men threatened people and closed down polling stations in constituencies they controlled. Of the 62 per cent of voters casting a vote, more than 99 per cent favoured independence. Shortly after the results were announced, armed Serb militants barricaded all the roads into Sarajevo, cutting the town off completely. Thousands of the city's inhabitants, including many Serbs, organized a peaceful mass demonstration. The SDS dispersed it by firing live rounds close overhead.

On 6 April the European Economic Community officially recognized Bosnia-Herzegovina's independence. The same day more than sixty thousand people again took to the streets of Sarajevo, demonstrating for peace. Radovan Karadžić's men fired from the rooftops into the crowd, consisting of people opposed to their schemes and proud of Bosnia's multi-ethnic character. A girl student was killed. The Bosnian war had begun.

'If war was going to break out in Bosnia, it would undoubtedly be bloodier than it would be anywhere else,' wrote Paul Garde in March 1992. In the three years from 1992 to 1995 the war killed up to a quarter of a million people, and sent more than three million others down the road to exile.

The old multi-cultural city of Sarajevo was placed under siege, immersing its inhabitants in what ICTY prosecutor Geoffrey Nice described as 'a mediaeval hell'.[7] Dug in on the mountains that surround the city, Radovan Karadžić's forces shelled and sniped at will randomly killing passers-by, children at play, women fetching water, the elderly.

While their rulers were in Maastricht signing the treaty consolidating the European structure, the inhabitants of the twelve EEC countries watched in disbelief as a brutal and bloody war erupted on their continent. The papers were stuffed with accounts of whole towns 'cleansed' of their populations by force, mass rape, repeated shelling of civilians, detention camps. The European and American governments remained apathetic and unable to stop the massacres.

On 11 July 1995 the Bosnian Serb forces led by Radovan Karadžić and Ratko Mladić captured the Bosniak enclave of Srebrenica in eastern Bosnia, a zone the United Nations had undertaken to protect. Over the next few days more than seven thousand men, Muslims, were murdered in cold blood.

The Srebrenica massacre, the worst to have occurred in Europe since the Second World War, finally got a reaction out of the Western countries. On 14 December, after American mediation, the Dayton peace agreements were signed between the three parties giving birth to the new Bosnia-Herzegovina. It was formed out of two entities: the Federation with 51 per cent of the land area and Republika Srpska, the Bosnian Serb entity, with 49 per cent.

THREE

Prijedor: an 'Ethnic Cleansing Laboratory'

After Banja Luka, Prijedor is the second largest town of Republika Srpska. In three years of war the ethnic makeup of the town's population changed radically. This was the result of a policy of ferocious ethnic cleansing put in place at the beginning of the conflict in 1992. In 1991, the municipality of Prijedor counted 49,000 Muslims and nearly as many Serbs (47,745) out of a total population numbering 112,470 inhabitants. These two groups represented 44 per cent and 42.5 per cent respectively of the town's total population. By 1995, after the war, only 1 per cent of the Prijedor population was Muslim, while 89 per cent were Serbs. It had lost more than 43,000 Muslim inhabitants and virtually all its Croat residents.[1]

This drastic fall in the number of Croats and Muslims was not the result of accident or the product of voluntary migration. It resulted from a 'deliberate policy' of persecution devised and carried out by Radovan Karadžić's Serb nationalists. 'The main purpose of the Serbian manoeuvres in Prijedor municipality was "ethnic cleansing" of the non-Serbs to secure a homogeneous Serbian district', wrote the UN expert Hanne Sophie Greve in a report to the Security Council dated 28 December 1994.[2] In fact Prijedor was of crucial importance to the adherents of a Greater Serbia. The municipality, as she had already pointed out, 'is clearly located inside any corridor that Serbs could want to clear between Serbia proper and the Serbian-occupied Croatian Krajina'.[3]

Ethnic cleansing went on from the first beginnings of the war. The methods used in this Krajina city were to reappear later in numerous towns seized by Serb nationalists. Radoslav Brđanin, president of the Crisis Staff of the 'autonomous Serb region' of Banja Luka, which included Prijedor, in 1992 proposed 'three stages of ridding the area of non-Serbs: 1 creating impossible conditions that would have the effect of encouraging them to leave of their own accord, involving pressure and terror tactics; 2 deportation and banishment; and 3 liquidating those remaining who would not fit into his concept for the region'.[4] In the view of Radoslav Brđanin, '2 per cent was the upper tolerable limit on the presence of all non-Serbs in this region.'[5]

First Rumblings

Before the 1990 elections Prijedor lived the life of a peaceful provincial city. 'Many witnesses speak of good intercommunal relations, of friendships across ethnic and coincident religious divides, of intermarriages and of generally harmonious relations', write the judges in the Duško Tadić trial. A café manager from the village of Kozarac in the municipality of Prijedor, Tadić in 1997 was found guilty in the first instance of exactions committed against civilians at the Omarska camp. 'Frankly, no one was bothered about who was a Serb, a Croat or a Muslim. Someone was a friend or colleague, that was all,' says Nurka, a teacher now in exile in the US. The first tensions started to show during the elections. Mirsad Mujadžić, a former SDA municipal councillor, remembers proposing to the SDS and HDZ a common poster to be displayed during the campaign bearing the text: 'We will continue to live side by side as we did in the past'. Intended to underline the possibility of peaceful coexistence, the poster was displayed in zones of Muslim and Croat majority. But although it had agreed in principle, the SDS did not put it up in the zones of Serb majority.[6]

In the poll of 18 November 1990 the Serb, Croat and Muslim nationalist parties got most of the votes and managed to reach an understanding over the distribution of posts. The SDA obtained that of president of the municipal assembly (at that time equivalent to mayor), which went to Muhamed Čehajić, with Milomir Stakić of the SDS as vice-president. Negotiations over the rest stalled, however. The SDS, which had come second, demanded 50 per cent of the managerial posts with the other parties sharing the other half. More logically that should have gone to the SDA, which had polled the most votes. To end the stalemate the SDA eventually gave way to the SDS demands. But 'the Serbs tended to block proposals made by Muslims or Croats in the assembly in Prijedor. The Serbs more or less tried to obstruct the work of the assembly as such'. The SDS continued to block discussions to protect the current situation, in which 'the Serbs held almost 90 per cent of the key positions.'[7]

Quite apart from the rowdy debates in the municipal assembly, the proximity of the fighting in Croatia breathed a cordite-smelling wind across the town. Prijedor Serbs were enrolled to go and join the fighting. After a first favourable response, Muslims and Croats refused to support what they saw as an aggression.[8] Numerous soldiers came home from the front and started walking about the streets of the town.

'When the soldiers came back after twenty days at the front, there was a lot of shooting and exchanges of fire. The Serb soldiers were armed. The weapons were brought back from Croatia. It was said that Bosnia had the biggest concentration of weapons. Prijedor started to live in an atmosphere of mistrust. People were scared. The Croats in the town were publicly condemned and blamed for not taking part in the fighting. That was an uncertain time for all the citizens of Prijedor,' remembers Muharem Murselović.

In this menacing atmosphere, the SDS walked out of the municipal assembly in November 1991 and began setting up parallel police and administrative structures. The nationalists were already making their preparations and starting to weave their spider's web around Prijedor in the first months of 1992.

A Meticulously Planned Operation

'The Serbs took power in Prijedor municipality on 30 April 1992, after more than six months of careful planning', notes the UN report. The massacres committed there were the result of a specific, deliberate strategy. The inhabitants were aware of these manoeuvres but did not really take them seriously. 'We've always lived on pretty good terms,' they told themselves.

By November 1991, however, the principal leaders of what later became the Crisis Staff were putting the finishing touches to a detailed plan of attack. Interviewed in 1995 during a special broadcast by Radio Prijedor from the Ljubija mine, Simo Drljača, chief of police during the war, and two eminent members of the Serb parallel administration, Dr. Kovačević and Slobodan Kuruzović, confirmed that they had worked for months on the preparations for the seizure of the town on 30 April 1992. Their activities were guided from Banja Luka by Bosnian Serb leaders like Biljana Plavšić and Radovan Karadžić.

The Serbs were building up their military presence in the municipality from 1991 onward. But the nationalists had a quite serious problem: how to persuade the local Serb population, used to living on friendly terms with its Croat and Muslim compatriots, to help with the operation, or failing that keep quiet and not resist. The SDS knew the task would be difficult. In the 1990 elections the nationalist party had only obtained 28 per cent of the votes although 42 per cent of the voters were Serbs. Instead of supporting Karadžić and his sirens of nationalism, a large number of Prijedor Serbs had voted for the party led by Ante Marković, Prime Minister of what was still the Yugoslav federation.

In office from December 1988 to 1990, Marković had implemented a range of radical economic reforms to stabilize Yugoslavia. Before the elections he launched a multi-ethnic Reformist Party, an act that branded him a traitor in the eyes of nationalist Serbs. The party was officially founded at a congress held near Prijedor. In the Bosnian elections 90 per cent of local Serbs living in mixed families (about 12 per cent of the population) voted for Ante Marković.[9]

With the Serb vote thus divided, Alija Izetbegović's SDA got the biggest vote, making Prijedor the only town in Bosnia's Krajina region not controlled by Karadžić's party. This meant that it could not be incorporated into the self-proclaimed 'Serb autonomous region' of Krajina, which symbolized the pride of Serb militancy according to Misha Glenny, former BBC correspondent in Vienna:[10] a bitter pill for the local SDS leadership.

The local police chief, Simo Drljača, told a foreign observer after the seizure of Prijedor that Ante Marković was 'a vote thief'. But supporters of Radovan Karadžić would not accept defeat. 'Why was Prijedor the target of such a violent campaign?' wondered the ICTY prosecutor Nicholas Koumjian in April 2003. Perhaps because 'before, and immediately after the November 1990 multi-party election, the municipality remained an area of ethnic peace'. It was one of those places where people were on such good terms that it posed a particular challenge to those hoping to separate the different populations, those hoping to create hatred and division.[11] Aware of the difficulty of setting neighbours, former classmates and friends at each other's throats, the nationalists decided to resort to the propaganda weapon.

As soon as the war broke out in Croatia, Serb journalists working for Radio Prijedor went to the front escorted by the army, and without permission from their editor-in-chief Muharem Nezirević. 'They came back in uniform with stories far removed from reality, claiming that the Croats tried to make necklaces of Serb children's fingers,' Nezirević remembers.

Between 21 and 28 March 1992 the Serbs took control of the TV relay transmitter on Mount Kozara. During that time the inhabitants of Prijedor were unable to receive programmes from Sarajevo or Zagreb. Only the Belgrade stations were still visible. As Florence Hartmann recalls, 'since 1987, the Belgrade media had been steadily distilling a hysterical propaganda campaign for Serb nationalism'.

'The television broadcast endless programmes on the Second World War and massacres of Serb Partisans by Ustashe with Muslim help,' remembers a witness at Milomir Stakić's trial. Belgrade television made out that the Serb people were again under threat in Kosovo, Croatia and Bosnia. Instead of talking about the shelling of Dubrovnik or the massacres at Vukovar, the media in the Yugoslav capital showed images of Serb civilians fleeing from alleged massacres. 'Overwhelmed by allegations and atrocious images of massacres by a propaganda that inverted reality to the point of comparing the situation of the Serb people to that of the Jews during the Second World War, the population backed Slobodan Milošević's criminal scheme or sank into indifference and apathy,' Florence Hartmann adds.

In Prijedor, these references to the Second World War did in fact have a certain impact on the Serb population. The town had been annexed by the Croat fascist régime at the time and become the scene of a campaign of savage exactions. 'A large number of Serbs were killed by the Ustashe, taken en masse to the camp at Jasenovac for extermination or expelled from their houses in furtherance of a systematic campaign of persecution,' writes the historian Robert Donia.

After the seizure of Prijedor on 30 April 1992, the propaganda went into top gear. The local media were controlled by nationalist Serbs. The editor-in-chief of the weekly paper *Kozarski Vjesnik* was Mile Mutić, a member of the Crisis Staff. 'Mile Mutić can be considered the father of falsification where the history of Prijedor is concerned,' remarks the writer and journalist Rezak Hukanović, quoted in a report on human rights.[12] Radio Prijedor fired its Muslim editor-in-chief, Muharem Nezirović, and replaced him with Zoran Baroš, a Serb.

These media accused the Muslims of wanting to establish an Islamic state. Simo Drljača could thus assert with a straight face that the Muslims and Croats 'have been preparing for twenty-two years to annihilate the Serbs'. The radio broadcast false news items alleging the discovery of arms caches and the arrest of armed Muslim extremists planning to exterminate the Serbs. Much coverage was given to a story that a Croat doctor had been castrating new-born Serb infants and forcibly sterilizing Serb women. 'What with the constant brainwashing to which people were subjected by the media, it didn't take long for someone to cross the line of no return and behave in a way no one could ever have imagined in the past,' remarks Rezak Hukanović. 'It was truly amazing to watch the chameleon-like transformation of people one knew, even former friends, into faithful lackeys of the new authorities.'[13]

The results of this mutation were often extremely sad and dispiriting. Muharem Murselović was arrested by his neighbour, then beaten up by a former pupil. Nurka recounts that not one of her Serb neighbours, 'whom we had known and associated with for years', had lifted a finger to protect her and her children from their Serb attackers. Rezak Hukanović was brutally beaten by someone he knew well, one Saponja, a member of Bosna Montaža football club. At Omarska, Keraterm and Trnopolje prisoners were beaten by their former teachers, murdered by their old customers, robbed by their ex-colleagues.

There were, however, a few cases of resistance. Two Serb women were arrested and interned at Omarska for objecting to the treatment of their non-Serb neighbours at the hands of soldiers and reservists. 'Not all the guards were bloodthirsty and full of hatred, there was a small number of good Serbs,' Rezak Hukanović writes. He singles out the case of Željko, known as Džigi, who always tried to slip the prisoners food and news from outside. Nisad, a survivor of Trnopolje camp, recounts that a Serb former colleague helped him escape the horrors of Omarska by arranging for him to be transferred to Trnopolje, where conditions were less harsh.

But most of the Serbs who tried to oppose the ambient hysteria were sent to the front at Derventa or Gradačac. One Prijedor Serb, a soldier during the wars in Croatia and Slovenia, had deserted when conflict broke out in his own region, explaining: 'They arrested one of my Muslim friends when he was out fishing. They put him in one of the concentration camps saying he was planning to kill Serbs. But he didn't have any weapons and he wasn't trying to get any. No, he was just fishing.' After his desertion his family was threatened and made the object of frequent searches. Despite these isolated acts of resistance, however, a large part of the Serb population of Prijedor was hypnotized and, like the population of Serbia itself, sucked into a vortex of insanity.

The Mysterious 'Crisis Staff'

Awakening on the morning of 30 April 1992, Nurka and her husband, both schoolteachers, and their two children found Serb troops posted on the roof of their apartment house. 'Every evening they sang Chetnik songs and drank. Sometimes they would start shooting, people were scared,' Nurka remembers.

Just a stone's throw from their building, people on their way to work could not help noticing the white, blue and red of a Serbian flag flying above the rectangular block of the town hall. Serb soldiers and paramilitaries guarded the entrance.

'When I got up that morning the restaurant staff told me there were a lot of soldiers in town, more than usual,' Muharem Murselović recalls. 'One of the women told me that checkpoints had been set up in the town and she had been stopped ten times. "I can't make out what's going on," she said. It was seven in the morning. I went into the pedestrianized street outside my house and saw troops all over the place. The radio announced that the SDS had seized power because it could no longer bear to watch the SDA leading the municipality to economic disaster. That was a bit cynical, since the SDA hadn't been alone at the controls. It had been sharing power with the SDS. I was shocked.'

The wide-eyed inhabitants found sandbag emplacements at major road junctions and in front of the banks. Yugoslav army soldiers sat behind them with machine guns. Wall posters announced that the SDS had taken power in Prijedor, their text signed by a mysterious 'Crisis Staff'. A doctor from Omarska village, Milomir Stakić, introduced himself as president of this new institution set up by the Serb putschists. Among the more influential members of the Staff were former Prijedor schoolteacher Slobodan Kuruzović, the chief of police Simo Drljača, another doctor, Milan Kovačević, local SDS chief Šimo Mišković and Srđo Srdić, a dentist and close associate of Radovan Karadžić.

The non-Serb inhabitants of Prijedor experienced an immediate sharp decline in their living conditions. The new authorities decreed a curfew between ten at night and six in the morning. 'During the night there was so much shooting that you couldn't sleep, and that helped strengthen the climate of fear,' Muharem Murselović remembers.

When the surprise wore off, people went to work as usual. The Croat and Muslim employees of all the state enterprises were asked to go home and not come back: they were sacked. At the Mira biscuit factory, one of the biggest in former Yugoslavia, the Croat managing director was replaced by an SDS Serb, Ranko Topić, who still has the job today. The elected mayor of Prijedor, Muhamed Čehajić, was stopped by Serb soldiers when he tried to get into his office. They told him he was no longer entitled to enter the building since the Crisis Staff was now in power. All the Croat and Muslim officials in the municipality were thrown out in similar fashion.

The new authorities cut off the telephone lines of non-Serbs and switched off parts of the electricity network. The bank accounts of Croats and Muslims were frozen. Non-Serbs had to get travel permits just to go from Prijedor to one of its surrounding villages.

Prijedor's two main news media, the weekly paper *Kozarski Vjesnik* and Radio Prijedor, 'both became, almost immediately after the Serbian takeover, mouthpieces of the new Serbian leaders, or rather the latter took control over these media,' notes Hanne Sophie Greve. They endlessly criticized the Muslims and Croats and accused them of trying to prepare a genocidal attack on the Serbs. The historian Noel Malcolm believes that the power of propaganda should not be underestimated: 'Having travelled widely in Bosnia over fifteen years, and having stayed in Muslim, Croat and Serb villages, I cannot believe the claim that the country was forever seething with ethnic hatreds. But having watched Radio Television Belgrade in the period 1991–2, I can understand why simple Bosnian Serbs came to believe that they were under threat, from Ustasha hordes, fundamentalist jihads or whatever. As the independent Belgrade journalist Miloš Vasić put it to an American audience, it was as if all television in the USA had been taken over by the Ku Klux Klan: "You must imagine a United States with every little TV station everywhere taking exactly the same editorial line – a line dictated by (KKK leader) David Duke. You too would have war in five years." '[14]

It is hardly surprising that some were conditioned by this propaganda into shouting in the street that 'all Muslims and Croats ought to be slaughtered'.[15] 'Sometimes,' Muharem Murselović says, 'Croats and Muslims travelling by bus were taken off the vehicle and killed.'

Roundups, Armbands and Ultimatums

The Serbs organized the collection of the few weapons still in Muslim hands and consolidated their presence. Paramilitary troops led by Arkan and Vojislav Šešelj, notorious for their cruelty in Croatia, arrived in the town in May (as confirmed by an SDS official on Radio Prijedor[16]).

Violence was then unleashed during the latter part of May 1992. On the 22nd, an incident at a roadblock manned by Muslims in the village of Hambarine, six kilometres from Prijedor, was to serve as the pretext for an attack by the new authorities. The incident, whose circumstances are contested and remain unclear, ended with two Serbs and a Muslim killed. The Crisis Staff issued an ultimatum to the inhabitants to deliver up a policeman who lived near the spot where the incident had occurred. The inhabitants – mostly Muslims – believed that the man had not been involved, and refused. At midday on 23 May, the Serb forces started shelling the farming village, set in a bucolic landscape of green hills. Shells rained down on the houses without pause for several hours. Then JNA troops and paramilitaries, supported by tanks, entered the hamlet. Each house was ransacked and its inhabitants arrested or killed. A handful of people escaped temporarily from these outrages by fleeing into surrounding woodland.

On 24 May it was Kozarac's turn to be attacked, after the village's poorly-armed police and defence units had refused to assure the new Serb authorities of their loyalty. As at Hambarine, the Serbs shelled the place heavily for several hours before sending in the infantry and paramilitaries. The houses were systematically looted and then torched, but most of those belonging to Serbs were left intact by the troops. They dynamited the mosque but left the Orthodox church untouched. 'We could never have imagined they'd go so far,' says one of the inhabitants, Ibrahim Kulielović, a Muslim married to the daughter of a Serb-Muslim couple. Like all the inhabitants he was forced to walk to one of the camps the Serbs had just opened. Arbitrary roadside executions were a feature of the march. Ibrahim was sent to Trnopolje, a detention centre established in a former school. 'From there I was able to watch my village burn,' he recalls. Kozarac was reduced to rubble.

Prijedor's turn came on 30 May. After a failed attempt to retake the town mounted by a handful of non-Serb men, the Stari Grad (Old Town) quarter, the majority of whose inhabitants were Muslim, was shelled. Radio Prijedor broadcast a message ordering Muslims and Croats to hang a white flag from their houses. Roundups began.

The journalist and poet Rezak Hukanović wrote later: 'Saturday, May 30, 1992. A sunny day. Djemo (author's pseudonym) didn't wake up until around 9.30. Actually, it was the deafening sound of shooting outside that woke him up ... That night he had played cards very late at his cousin Fadil's place and ended up staying over, along with the rest of the family... Djemo drank his usual morning coffee. He lit a cigarette and took a few drags... Alma had gone over to their place to make breakfast. Soon she came back and put the food on the table... Djemo drew the curtain a little and saw two armed men with face masks cautiously approaching the main entrance of the building, crouching down, with their fingers on the trigger. Just then there was a heavy thump on Fadil's door. It opened, and Djemo turned to see another soldier exactly like the ones he had just seen across the road. He stood by the door with his rifle aimed right at them. "Got any weapons?" he demanded. They were petrified.

'"You deaf or what?" By now he was shouting. "Got any weapons or not?"

'"No, brother," Fadil was the first to speak. "We don't."...

'With a look of utter disbelief, the soldier walked around the room, without lowering his rifle for even a second; he kept it aimed at the table and everyone sitting around it. "You've got to get out of here," he said, as if they were under his command ... Brandishing his rifle, he motioned to Djemo and Fadil to go out ... The children were crying.'[17]

Rezak Hukanović was taken to the police station with several dozen neighbours caught like him in the roundup. After summary interrogation he was taken by bus to Omarska camp.

The same scene was repeated all over town. 'All the people who had white flags on their houses were ordered to report to the Balkan hotel. When they got there, the Serb army and police separated the men from the women and children. The men aged between eighteen and sixty were put in buses,' remembers Azedin Oklopčik.[18] A number of Muslim and Croat men were assembled near the Radio Prijedor building. 'Ten men shot by the Serbs had been left lying in the road nearby,' recalls another inhabitant who prefers not to be named. The arrests and roundups continued in the weeks that followed, emptying Prijedor of most of its non-Serb inhabitants. The ones who remained were required to wear a white armband.

Bus after bus, dozens of them, drove people to the three camps set up by the Serbs: Omarska, a former mine, Keraterm, a ceramics factory, and Trnopolje, a secondary school.

Three Concentration Camps: the Summer of 1992

'An orgy of infernal persecution': that is how the ICTY judges chose to describe the events that occurred in the Omarska detention camp. This was the camp where the Serb forces had chosen to intern the non-Serb elite of Prijedor: judges, teachers, intellectuals and political leaders, including the ousted mayor Muhamed Čehajić. Thousands of individuals passed through the dungeons of Omarska. The conditions there were horrifying: an insufficient diet of rotten food, torture, beatings with rifle butts and baseball bats, summary executions.

Keraterm, the former ceramics factory on the edge of Prijedor, was used to intern more than fifteen hundred men not belonging to the intelligentsia in equally horrible conditions. Women, children, old men and a few younger ones were shut in a school at Trnopolje, a country village to the east of Prijedor.

In August 1992 the international community discovered the horror of the camps. Images of the starving emaciated bodies of the detainees opened the eyes of the outside world to the ethnic cleansing being carried out, most notably by the forces of Radovan Karadžić and Ratko Mladić, with the support of Slobodan Milošević.

After the existence of the camps became known, the surviving detainees were transferred to Muslim-controlled zones or to Croatia. Nevertheless two hundred and twenty-eight prisoners, due to be exchanged, were executed on the edge of a cliff in the Mount Vlašić region in August 1992. Just twelve men managed to escape alive.

In 1994, given the scale of the persecutions being suffered by the few Croats and Muslims left in Prijedor, the International Committee of the Red Cross (ICRC) and the UN High Commission for Refugees (UNHCR) asked the Bosnian Serbs for permission to evacuate the remaining non-Serbs.

'What happened in Prijedor resembles genocide in that the aim of this criminal campaign was to destroy the Croat and Muslim communities of Prijedor. The crimes were committed to ensure that these two communities would no longer exist in Prijedor: their houses, their places of worship, were destroyed... The bodies of those who had been executed were even hidden to make sure that none of these people would have any reason for coming back: no house, no mosque or church, not even a grave where they could mourn their relations',[19] explained the prosecutor Nicholas Koumjian to the ICTY judges in The Hague.

Stakić was nevertheless acquitted of the charge of genocide on 31 July 2003. While recognizing that 'crimes were perpetrated on a massive scale' in Prijedor in 1992, the magistrates felt that they could not conclude with certainty that a genocide had been committed, or therefore that Milomir Stakić could have been responsible for it. The judges emphasized that the purpose of the SDS members had been to force non-Serbs to leave Prijedor but not to kill them all. But genocide, the crime of crimes, designates the destruction of a group, in whole or in part. 'The intention to displace a population is not equivalent to the intention to destroy it,' the magistrates pointed out, adding however that crimes against humanity and war crimes had been committed on a large scale in Prijedor.

'To be quite frank, when my parents told me what was going on in Prijedor in April 1992 I didn't believe them. I was in Sarajevo and I told myself this wasn't possible, some of my best friends were Serbs, we'd grown up together in Prijedor, all proud of the Partisans and the resistance to the Nazis ... But what my parents were saying turned out to be true. Even today, I still can't understand why they did it,' says Refik Hodžić, who ran the ICTY communications programme in Bosnia until the end of 1993.

Perhaps the clearest indication of what was going on in Bosnian Serb heads during the war comes from Biljana Plavšić, a one-time Bosnian Serb nationalist who now regrets her actions. In a historic confession to the ICTY, made in December 2002, she started by admitting the existence of an ethnic cleansing plan and thus became the first high-ranking Serb leader to admit awareness of systematic criminality on the Serb side. She tried to explain the madness that seized her and her fellows by referring to the Serbs' obsessive fear of again becoming the victims they had been during the Second World War: 'Why didn't I see the truth sooner? The reason lies in the word fear, fear that renders people blind. Driven by this obsession never to be reduced to the status of victims again, we allowed ourselves to become makers of victims … We violated the first duty of every human being: to control oneself and respect the dignity of others,' Mrs. Plavšić affirmed in a declaration to her judges on 17 December 2002.

Today the figure for those missing and presumed dead at Prijedor stands at around three thousand individuals.[20] To the prosecutor at The Hague tribunal, Carla Del Ponte, Prijedor is an example of Slobodan Milošević's genocidal policy in Bosnia. Thirteen years after 'the camps', the deeds that occurred in this town could still contribute to the conviction of a former head of state for genocide, one of the gravest crimes in international law.

PART TWO

The Prijedor Triangle

The horror of the camps is born and grows out of this discovery,
that some men have been capable of deciding that the destiny of
other men is to have a destiny no longer.

Agnès Lejbowicz, *La philosophie du droit international –*
l'impossible capture de l'humanité

As the door of the guard hut opened a voice boomed out of it, firm and pompous; and the vituperations of Slobodan Milošević echoed across the site of Omarska to lose themselves in that lifeless place under a thin, deadening rain. A surreal moment. On this 27 September 2002, the men guarding the mine complex spent most of their working day glued to the television, watching the trial of Serbia's former strong man in The Hague. For two days now, the International Criminal Tribunal had been examining the role of the Belgrade supremo during the war in Bosnia. The head of the security guards refused to give his name, but thought fit to assert that 'at last we're going to hear the whole truth about the war': from Milošević of course. Straight from the horse's mouth.

Today it was raining in Omarska. Neat and sleepy, with its lovely Orthodox church built of dark wood, the village lies off the main road from Banja Luka to Prijedor. The Rudnik Ljubija mine complex lies still further off the road, on the far side of the village which has a large Serb majority. After three hairpin bends and the bridge over the railway, the main entrance appears flanked by a huge and imposing building of red corrugated iron and an ornate Orthodox church with a graveyard.

To get into the place you have to have permission. A day earlier the mayor of Prijedor and his staff had promised to arrange access to the former camp. Owing to some reluctance somewhere, or a failure to cooperate, some crucial telephone calls had not been made, and the visit was cancelled at the last minute for what Nada Ševo's woman assistant called 'material reasons'. But the manager of the iron mine, Ranko Cvijić, a man with a baritone voice, square spectacles and an apparatchik-like manner, eventually opened all doors with a simple phone call. On his orders, one of the guards raised the main barrier and invited us to follow his sports car. From the north, the internal road leads into a vast broken plain littered with mineshafts, deserted quarries and derelict buildings.

FOUR

Omarska, End of the Line

The huge, decrepit red building blocks the view. To get round the rusting corrugated-iron mastodon you have to drive along a tarmac track, pass under some pipework and a loading ramp. Round another corner and the road runs straight ahead: nearly three kilometres of dead straight tarmac running alongside a seized and rusting conveyor belt through a desolate landscape of scrub and waste. A gloomy and sinister link that conjures up ghastly images of the Nazi camps, that awful one-way semiotic of a single track ending in a full stop. At the end, lost in the vast landscape, three buildings stand clustered around a fourth, much bigger and higher structure. On a vast parking area, potholed and bumpy, the giant ore trucks and bulldozers used for open-cast mining lie rusting in all weathers.

In this space covering several hectares, the property of the Rudnik Ljubija state mine, a few metres from an open-cast quarry and several mineshafts, a detention camp was operated by the Serb political and military forces from 25 May to the end of August 1992.

Return of 'the Camps'

On 2 August 1992 the American journalist Roy Gutman revealed the existence of Omarska by publishing an article based on the testimony of former detainees who had just been released.[1] His story caused something of a stir. Radovan Karadžić, in London for yet another peace conference, was mobbed by journalists and vigorously questioned from all sides. In the end the leader of the Bosnian Serbs invited journalists to come and see for themselves that 'there isn't a single camp being run by Bosnian Serbs'. A news team from the British ITN company, accompanied by *Guardian* and *Observer* journalist Ed Vulliamy, took him at his word and hustled their way through reluctant, obstructive Serb forces to reach Omarska on 6 August. Their articles and images alerted the world to the reappearance of camps in Europe less than fifty years after the end of the Second World War, and compelled the Serbs to open them – albeit slowly and reluctantly – to journalists and humanitarian teams.[2] Not without some hasty attempts at damage limitation: the Omarska camp had been cleaned up beforehand, food had been distributed along with beds and blankets, and some of the detainees had been moved to other camps by bus or train.

Several thousand individuals had passed through this camp, where the conditions of existence had been more horrific than in any other prison or detention centre in Bosnia. According to several inquiry reports, notably the one by Louis Joinet of the UN Commission for Human Rights,[3] the prisoners were divided into three groups. Group A, 'to be watched closely and executed when the opportunity arises', included doctors, businessmen, teachers, judges, lawyers, well-known sporting stars, clergy, journalists (especially the ones who had tried to set up a free radio station after the 1990 elections), etc. Group B consisted of so-called prisoners of war, held with a view to later prisoner exchanges; some members of this group were transferred to group A. In Group C, finally, were internees not regarded as dangerous 'to the Serb people'. These were generally released after a month or two of internment. Some of this group were selected to be shown to the media during the first visits to the camps.

The majority of the detainees were Bosnian Muslims and Croats, but a number of Serbs who had tried to protect the Muslims and opposed the exactions were also imprisoned. 'Up to three thousand prisoners, men for the most part, were detained at Omarska at any one time, but at least thirty-six or thirty-eight women were also detained,' specifies the ICTY's verdict on one of the Omarska jailers Duško Tadić, condemned to twenty years in prison for war crimes and crimes against humanity at an appeal hearing in 2000. Kept out of contact with the male prisoners, these women were compelled to do the 'cooking' and other domestic services for the prisoners and guards. Most were subjected to rape, sexual abuse and torture. According to Nusreta Sivac, a former Prijedor judge who survived Omarska and who gave a long and detailed account of the way the camp was run, five women died there. But the total number of deaths is not known with any accuracy. What is known for certain is that several hundred inhabitants of the Prijedor region were starved, tortured, raped and murdered there. Infectious diseases, diarrhoea and dysentery were commonplace. Detainees suffered severe weight loss, up to 50 kilograms in some cases, and lasting neurological and psychological problems. Some Omarska survivors are still suffering from the tortures and torments inflicted on them in 1992.

In her report on Prijedor, Hanne Sophie Greve specifies that the camp was run by three groups of around thirty guards each, who kept the interior and the environs of the camp under surveillance. They worked in rotating twelve-hour shifts, with changeovers at seven in the morning and seven at night according to former inmates. In the words of the Human Rights Watch organization, '…forty-two interrogators were responsible for questioning the prisoners at Omarska. The camp was guarded by dozens of guards wearing both army and police uniforms. They were armed with AK-47s, other automatic weapons and rubber truncheons.'[4] Thirteen years after the events, it is known that Željko Mejakić, who gave himself up to the ICTY in July 2003, was the commandant of Omarska. He was seconded by Miroslav Kvočka and Dragoljub Prčac. Under them came the three team leaders Mladen Radić, Momčilo Gruban and Milojica Kos. All the members of this leadership group, some of whom have already been tried – others are scheduled for trial in the near future[5] – were fully aware of the conditions of detention inflicted on the prisoners for the simple reason that they themselves took part in acts of torture and murder, and tolerated the crimes committed even when they had not instigated them personally. In addition, 'paramilitaries or Serbs from the district were allowed to enter the camp, where they would insult, beat and kill prisoners', the ICTY investigators add. It is in this context that Dušan Knežević (nicknamed Duško Knežević or Duca) and Zoran Žigić were seen maltreating and murdering detainees.

Mirsad, an Omarska survivor,[6] described the climate in these words: 'They beat us with truncheons, baseball bats, bits of pipe, rifle butts and worst of all with a fat rubber hose weighted with metal at each end. They smashed people's heads with hammers.' Another Omarska internee, Edin Mrkalj, told the ICTY investigators: 'The barrel was in my mouth and I was receiving double blows with a rubber baton and with a metal spring. Now, a rubber baton, one can still survive, somehow manage it, but not a metal spring. My head was bursting, blood was bursting. It was awful. My teeth were breaking. Everything was breaking. I cannot remember exactly which blow was the last one. The last one was really terrible. I have a feeling that Duško Tadić at that moment had stepped backward. I do not know whether the barrel was out of my mouth at that moment or before that, but I received a terrible blow there and everything burst. I fell. I fainted.'[7] Other evidence collected by investigators for the Hague tribunal and the US government mentioned cases of castration, and Hanne Sophie Greve reports cases of bodies being incinerated.

The Refectory and the Offices

When you arrive, the nearest building is set slightly apart on the right. It houses the administrative offices where the women were imprisoned and where a lot of 'interrogations' were carried out, often in the daytime. The questions usually put to the detainees, over and over again, were: 'Who has weapons? Where were you when the shooting started? Who are the organizers of the resistance? Admit you're a Muslim extremist! Admit you organized a rebellion!'

On the ground floor are the showers and lavatories reserved for the women and camp personnel, and the refectory. Here the prisoners were given three minutes – a minute and a half when there were a lot of them – to swallow a thin broth or rotten food, clear the table and return plates and cutlery, and run back to their cells being beaten by the guards. Today the refectory is destroyed and the dining room strewn with debris and rubble. The building is abandoned, the lavatories and showers smashed, the offices locked and entry forbidden. From the broken bay window of the refectory you can see the White House.

The Two Torture Chambers

This single-storey building, surrounded by grass, was the scene of the worst exactions. Few emerged from it alive. It was 'the slaughterhouse'. People were taken there and stripped naked, beaten, tortured, literally massacred. Edin Elkaz was taken to a room in the White House with several other Bosniak soldiers. They could see people being flogged through a glass door. The guards were using pick-handles and iron bars, and concentrated on the head, genitals, spine and kidneys. Sometimes the victim's head would be smashed against a radiator. 'You could still see bits of flesh or brains there the next day,' Elkaz remembers. The worst torture was to place the prisoner against the wall and beat him with a cable. 'I think they killed at least fifty men that way,' he says. 'Every morning detainees would put the bodies on the tarmac outside the White House. Others would load the corpses into the small yellow truck which had just delivered the food to the camp kitchen. Four more would accompany the truck as an undertaker's crew, and none of these ever came back alive.'[8]

Today, this 'room is being used by the administration of the mining complex,' the caretaker says. In fact, although repainted and cleaned up, the five rooms of the White House, giving onto a corridor in which a puppy was playing when we visited it on 27 September 2002, are dirty and neglected, serving essentially as storerooms. In the first room, on the right, a battered desk sits against the wall facing a cupboard; in the second are two beds, three chairs and a desk; across the corridor in the third room, metal cupboards stand in the middle of the tiled floor. The windows look out onto waste land surrounded by barbed wire. The fourth room is locked.

When you emerge, the Red House stands on your right. Another single-storey building, this time of brick, it was used as a torture and execution chamber. Today it is closed for safety reasons: fuel and lubricating oil are kept there. On the day of our visit cats were sleeping peacefully on the windowsill.

The Hangar and the Pista

In the middle of this vast patchwork of tarmac, mud and rank grass stands the main concrete and corrugated iron hangar, facing north and south and standing some sixty feet high and three hundred wide. Crammed into its forty-odd rooms, on ground level and two higher floors, and its central hall, were nearly three thousand people. They were often too closely packed to be able to lie down. At night the guards would come to select people for 'interrogation', forced labour or execution. Today this huge dusty shed smells of used engine oil and shelters trucks, lifting and hauling machinery and the workshops for repairing and maintaining them. Many of the rooms are closed and disused, while others have been repainted and fitted out as locker-rooms and offices.

The hangar is surrounded by a huge, surfaced parking area. This is the *pista*, a broad area of tarmac that encircles and connects the buildings. When the guards were not throwing oil and water on the surface to make the prisoners slip and beating them, they would make them lie down there, in the midday sun or the middle of the night, and walk or jump on their bodies. Today trucks, piles of pipes, gigantic tyres, boring and extraction machinery lie there exposed to all weathers.

Over this industrial complex there reigns a comprehensive lethargy. Omarska is one of three sites (the others being Ljubija and Tomašica) exploited by Rudnik Ljubija, a vast mining enterprise spread over twenty-five hectares in all. It restarted a low rate of production in early 2003. But before anything else the boss of what was once a giant operation, Ranko

Cvijić, is anxious to point out that 'the mine had nothing to do with this past episode', what had happened was that 'the army requisitioned the plant and site'. And he goes on to underline hurriedly that he himself was not there during the war but in the army 'far away, from 1991 to 1996'. He is happier going into detail about the long and tortuous process of privatization being undergone by the mine, opened in 1916 by the Austrians. This is no time for the glorification of a prestigious past, the time at the end of the nineteen-eighties when Rudnik Ljubija with its five thousand workers could produce three million tonnes of iron ore a year. It had then been one of the biggest mines in Europe producing such high-grade ore. 'But today, although we're in profit (13.5 million Euros in 2001), we're only producing about ten per cent of the pre-war output', Ranko Cvijić admits. 'Since 1999 we've been working on getting production moving again,' he adds with rather muted optimism. 'We'll soon be able to take advantage of the rail network, which is also getting going. That's the background to the relaunch of Omarska.'

In April 2004 the steel magnate Lakshmi Mittal acquired 51 per cent of the equity of the Ljubija-Omarska mining complex in a joint venture with the Republika Srpska's Bosnian Serb authorities, which retain the other 49 per cent. Mittal, who was born in India and has British nationality, indicated that he wanted to resume ore production at the mine. Some of the associations of Omarska victims and survivors asked Mr. Mittal not to refurbish the mine without preserving some part of the buildings and site 'in memory of what happened here'.[9] Some wrote to the new owner expressing the hope that he would 'consider our request with compassion' so that the past would not be forgotten.

Noticeably irritated by the fuss, the company said through a spokesman that it would 'give close attention to all requests', adding that it was a 'major investor' in the region. Quoting an informed source, *The Guardian* said the company found itself 'in a difficult situation. The region is populated largely by Serbs; they are who we have to deal with, and we don't want to do anything that might upset them.'

A few days later Mittal's company, LNM, in a letter to the Editor of *The Guardian*,[10] pointed out that 'no remains have so far been found at the Omarska mines.' The letter went on: 'LNM is aware of the sad past of the surrounding area and is in conversation with international and Bosnian authorities regarding potentially building a memorial to commemorate those who lost their lives. LNM conducts its operations with the highest standards of integrity.'

FIVE

Trnopolje, a School Among Meadows

Take the main road back towards Prijedor. Nine kilometres later, a crossroads: Kozarac is signposted to the right, and the left turning leads to Trnopolje. But there is no sign, and the surfaced road peters out. The track leading to this small village is a rutted succession of potholes and craters devoid of tarmac. For its whole length the road is lined with houses randomly scattered on the bare plain. It takes more than half an hour to cover the five kilometres to the school, an L-shaped two-storey building surrounded by a small yard and two small paddocks.

Theatre, Barbed Wire, Iimprovised Sshelters

Here, most probably from 24 May 1992, a detention camp was opened following the ethnic cleansing of the village (more than half Muslim before the war) and the obliteration of the neighbouring settlement of Kozarac, twenty-six thousand inhabitants, mostly Muslims. 'The camp consisted of a two-storied former school building and what had been a municipal centre and attached theatre, known as the "dom". An area of the camp was surrounded by barbed wire,' notes the ICTY verdict on Duško Tadić.

Thousands of people were held at Trnopolje. A delegation of the International Committee of the Red Cross visiting the camp on 11 August 1992 counted about four thousand detainees.[1] Hanne Sophie Greve writes that the camp at one time had held nearly seven thousand individuals. Children, elderly people and local women comprised the bulk of the first group of detainees. The second group consisted of former prisoners from Omarska and Keraterm after the closure of those camps in late August. Many of these were subjected to 'special treatment': shut in the school, beaten and interrogated. The third group was composed of people who had voluntarily left their homes and added their names to the Red Cross lists in the hope of being able to leave the country, notes Helsinki Watch. The camp was under the command of Major Slobodan Kuruzović, a member of the Prijedor Crisis Staff who is still at large in the town today.

The living conditions were unpredictable and dangerous, but somewhat less terrifying and horrible than those at Omarska. The detainees were housed in the main building, under improvised tents and in old container trailers. No food was distributed to them. They were thus dependent on help from the local inhabitants among whom there were some notably courageous Serbs. They could try to leave the camp in search of food, but risked being attacked by the militiamen and soldiers who were more concerned with patrolling the neighbourhood than providing security inside the camp. Interrogations, beatings and summary executions were far less constant than at Omarska, but they did occur.

Nisad Jakupović lives in Nantes these days but returns periodically to Kozarac, where he has managed to recover possession of his house after endless difficulties. When the grey-bearded former miner and technician recounts his experiences his hands shake and his blue eyes fill with tears. 'I was interned at Trnopolje from May to September 1992. I saw a lot of deaths. Life was very harsh at the camp. People were beaten, whole families were killed. I saw a Serb kill a woman before my eyes. She had a baby in her arms. He left it alive. I don't know what became of it. All round the camp there were soldiers. I saw the camp commandant kill five or six youths beside the big lake (a few hundred metres south of the village).'

Rape as a Weapon

Although it is claimed that Trnopolje was a relatively open prison, especially in view of the presence of the local Serb Red Cross, one of its characteristics was a different reality: widespread and repeated rape. 'Girls aged between sixteen and nineteen were most at risk. Groups of soldiers would enter the camp in the evening, choose their victims inside the Dom and rape them,' the ICTY investigators note. A detainee testified to the numerous rapes that took place in the camp, having personally helped and treated some of the victims, the youngest of whom was barely twelve years old. Some women were subjected to gang rape.

S.S.,[2] a detainee from Trnopolje village, testified later: 'We spent the night in a big room at the school. They came at night with flashlights looking for a specific woman, my cousin, A.S. I was at her wedding one year ago. She had an eight-month-old baby and was still breast-feeding. When they came into the room, they were cursing Muslims. We knew these men, they used to be our neighbours.

> 'They asked for her (the cousin, A.S.) by name. Her mother and mother-in-law said she wasn't there. The soldiers threatened to put a bomb in the room. Her mother screamed: "Don't take her." The men said: "We want her, not you." She gave her baby to her mother and went out with the two soldiers. They were in their uniforms. She was outside for about three hours. When she returned she was stiff and frozen and in shock. They raped her and told her not to talk or they would kill her family.'

In a damning document, the Croatian academic Jadranka Čačić-Kumpes of the Zagreb Institute for Migration and Nationalities has charted all the dimensions of rape as a weapon of war, practised systematically throughout Bosnia in much the same way as at Trnopolje.[3]

'Commonplace' Return to Normal

At the very beginning of October 1992, after the expulsion of the remaining detainees, the camp was closed. A collective centre for Serb refugees was established on the ground floor in 1993, and the school was reopened in some adjoining rooms and on the first floor. By September 2002 the school had recovered the whole of the ground floor and the work of disinfection and redecoration was in hand. The walls inside the school were gaily painted in red, yellow and blue, with children's paintings on display. Pot plants had been placed on the staircase and in the classrooms. And the roof, severely damaged in a storm during the summer of 2002, had been repaired. The headmistress herself was supervising all the operations from her office on the first floor.

Milica Ivić, fifty-six, smart and energetic in her navy-blue suit, is pleased with the way things have returned to normal since her appointment in 1999. A member of the Serb nationalist SDS who nevertheless professes to be apolitical, her sole concern is for her two hundred and fifty-seven pupils aged between one and eight years, and her thirty teachers. Optimistic and peaceable, she enthuses over the encouraging numbers of Muslims returning to the village and the school. 'Trnopolje is one of the youngest areas in the region. Since 1999 the refugees have been returning, and parents have been coming to see if they could enrol their children at the school.' She exhibits the sort of religious multiculturalism that members of the international community find reassuring.

Milica Ivić is in a hurry to turn the page on a terrible recent past. One can hardly blame her for this although it is not something that can be done unilaterally. Her main objective remains the physical transformation of the site. 'Sometimes when I see a TV shot of the school when it was a camp, I feel a bit uneasy,' she admits. So she is working hard to advance one of the plans closest to her heart: 'To repaint the outside walls of the school in pink or red, because the present grey is a sad reminder of that camp business.' In the meantime she is hoping to have trees planted in the grounds and clear the site of all remaining 'political considerations'. In a similar spirit she is reluctant to see, or anyway show interest in, the monument to victims – Serb victims of course – in the form of an eagle with a poem in Cyrillic script by the Ukrainian poet Tarass Chevchenko, celebrating the glory of soldiers. It has been placed facing the Dom, ten metres from the school gates, at the side of the roadway. At the foot of the monument is a flowerbed, with a little chain to delimit and 'sacralize' the space with all due solemnity … the usual stuff.

SIX

Keraterm's Red Brick Chimney

As at Omarska, there is no official monument at Keraterm. It was the third camp to be opened in the region but ranks second in terms of horror. It lies on the same road as the other two, the strategic straight line that links Banja Luka with Prijedor. The first sign of the Keraterm plant is a tall chimney in the distance, built of red brick. Then, beside the last straight stretch of road into Prijedor, there appears a building of purple corrugated metal, a good hundred metres long, a steel gateway and a security hut set slightly back from the road. Apart from the colour of the building, the layout is strikingly similar to Omarska: the same division and use of space, the same proximity to the railway line and the same closed perimeter. However, Keraterm has no economic or juridical connection with the Rudnik Ljubija iron mine. Before the war the Keraterm factory, founded in 1987, produced tiles and ceramics.

Four Crammed Rooms

The rectangular building, aligned north and south, is quite low having only two floors. Entrance to the administrative offices, only a small section of the building, is from the south. A staircase climbs to three offices on the first floor. From there, a corridor leads to service and store rooms, the refectory (virtually a copy of the one at Omarska) and kitchens and some locked rooms. A further extension of the corridor leads on to the warehouses and machine shops.

In this place more than fifteen hundred people were held. Reserved for male detainees only, Keraterm was opened apparently on 25 May 1992, but did not start to function fully until the 31st. It was closed some time in the middle of August, after the revelation of the camps' existence by the international press and the visit by the international Red Cross. Four rooms were used to hold the prisoners. Averaging about ten metres wide and up to twelve long, the rooms were very soon completely crammed, making it impossible for people to lie down and facilitating the spread of infections and epidemics. Each room had a dormitory head, a prisoner who served as a contact between the detainees, the heads of the three guard crews and the guards themselves. These were organized in groups of ten and worked twelve-hour shifts.[1]

Duško Sikirica, born in 1964, was not the camp commandant as had been claimed at first, but the head of security at Keraterm. The concrete administration of the camp was run from the Prijedor-II police post by Živko Knežević (today at large), under the overall authority of Simo Drljača, a member of the Crisis Staff who is now deceased. Sikirica took up his function at Keraterm on 14 June 1992 and performed it until 27 July. He was not ranked an NCO and his role only gave him very limited authority over his police-reservist colleagues.[2] He was backed by three team leaders who like him were tried before the ICTY in 2001. One was Damir Došen, today aged thirty-six. Between 3 June and the beginning of August he led a team of six to twelve men. At his trial before the Hague tribunal he was one of the very few accused to plead guilty of crimes against humanity. Another was Dragan Kolundžija, aged forty-three. He had worked as a guard at Keraterm before being put in charge of a team of men, which he led from the beginning of June until 25 July 1992. The third was Dušan Fustar, a former mechanic who gave himself up to the ICTY in January 2002. One of the forty-odd guards at Keraterm, Predrag Banović, was arrested with his brother in Belgrade in November 2001.

In addition to this guard staff, people from outside the camp would turn up, often at night as they did at Omarska, to join in the punitive expeditions, crimes and torture. They generally did what they liked. Two of these were Zoran Žigić and Dušan Knežević, free to come and go as they wished and murder people whenever they felt like it. It is for this reason that the conditions of detention at the factory were more or less comparable to those at Omarska: detainees were starved, parched, suffocated, tortured and summarily executed. More than one report mentions the disappearance of five or six people each night and the execution of two or three prisoners a day.

Also covered by the ICTY is the massacre that occurred on 24 July 1992. The investigators write: 'In the afternoon and evening, there were more soldiers than usual in the Keraterm camp. One witness has said that some were wearing the uniform of the former Yugoslav People's Army (JNA)... A machine gun was set up on a desk or table in front of Room 3 shortly before the massacre. At about 3 or 4 p.m. the detainees were taken into Room 3 and the doors bolted. Shortly after that gas was squirted into the room. Some prisoners tried to force the door to get out; the soldiers responded by firing bursts and volleys... the bullets passed through the windows and door and ricochetted about inside... The dead and wounded, some hundred and sixty to two hundred men in all, were taken away in a truck. Not one of the people taken away that morning has ever been seen again.' A second massacre took place on the morning of 26 July. About fifty men were mown down by submachine gun fire and the survivors finished off with pistol shots, according to Médecins sans frontières.

Suffocation and Social Fracture

Today, the Keraterm factory is on life support. Activity has not really taken off, and in early 2003 Keraterm was operating at only five per cent of production capacity. Stocks of tiles and bricks await delivery on palettes, the production machinery turns at just above idling speed. The managers are trying to put the best possible face on the effort involved in coming to terms with a very long and very byzantine process of privatization.[3] They seemed desperate to find a strategic partner and one or more big investors. Parts of the premises have been rented out to local enterprises: small carwashes, bodyshops and mechanics, metalworkers. Their workers supply what life there is in these vast echoing sheds, empty and frozen in time. The chief executive Staško Bajić and his predecessor Bogdan Mršić, working in tandem on their Mission Impossible, are pretty realistic. 'It's very tough here for an investor, even more so for a foreign company. The law changes every couple of days, the stuff we make isn't all that profitable, the Prijedor area is too shut off from the rest of the country, and anyway there's no money.' Accessible, open and caring, the two men fear the worst: closure, purchase of the plant by a big firm for use as a warehouse, most of all the social fracture that would result. 'Nothing is planned for the employees (Keraterm still had a hundred or so in 2003). No one has even considered a support programme.' So they are doing their best.

These two men take a sort of pride in exhibiting the industrial plant, underlining the strength and durability of the machinery and explaining the manufacturing process. They gave us free and confident access to their factory. Then, before we asked, Bogdan Mršić took us to the refectory and surrounding rooms. And dawdled there. And with an expression of distaste, explained that during the war the detainees had to queue there and hastily swallow some broth and a cube of bread. He recalled the images from the period, subsequently broadcast on TV and published by the ICTY. 'During the Second World War it was mostly Serbs who were shut in camps but this time, here, it was Serbs who imprisoned the Muslims and Croats and committed exactions.' He sighed. Later his successor at Keraterm used the word 'camp' for a place in which 'the Bosniaks were held'. Coming from a Serb these words signify an admission and recognition of the truth, the facts: something quite rare in Prijedor.

Back to the Nazi Past

Neither will go so far as to use the term 'concentration camp', however. The expression was the object of argument in 1992, and it still is. Given that all the euphemisms used by the Serb community when referring to the three camps can be rejected out of hand, the question then arises as to what terminology should be used to describe the reality of Omarska, Trnopolje and Keraterm. The analogy with the Nazi camps was made immediately in 1992, and there seems no doubt that it was this comparison which mobilized the international community and forced it to intervene, albeit pusillanimously and too late.[4] The Auschwitz survivor and Nobel Peace Prize laureate Elie Wiesel took President Clinton to task – in a sad irony of history – at the inauguration of the Holocaust Memorial Museum in Washington. 'Mr President,' he said, 'I cannot not tell you something. I have been in the former Yugoslavia last fall. I cannot sleep for what I have seen. As a Jew, I am saying that we must do something to stop the bloodbath in that country.'[5] Later, however, when asked at a press conference whether he could see 'any similarity between the ethnic cleansing in Bosnia and the Holocaust', the US president denied that there was any connection between the two events.

Thirteen years on, the parallel seems as real as ever. Madeleine Albright, Bill Clinton's Secretary of State from 1997 to 2001, revived those same memories in December 2002 during the three-day ICTY hearing to determine the sentence to be imposed on the former president of the Bosnian Serbs, Biljana Plavsic. 'It was obvious to everyone that what was happening recalled images of the Second World War. We saw images of these people being put in what can only be called a concentration camp.'[6]

Madeleine Albright was very well informed on the war in former Yugoslavia, but her comment needs to be inflected slightly. The three camps around Prijedor (there were many other, smaller ones elsewhere, like the one at Manjača, south of Banja Luka, where some of the Omarska prisoners were interned) were not identical. Despite the harsh conditions of detention and the horror of the killings that occurred there, it seems to be stretching a point to call Trnopolje a concentration camp.[7] This expression originated during the Boer War in South Africa between 1899 and 1902, but is primarily associated with the Nazi era and the Nazis' network of camps for forced labour, imprisonement and programmed mass murder. Trnopolje by these standards was a mere detention camp.

This argument is not devoid of significance. It is central to a long polemic that started in 1992 and is still going on, based on the image of a Bosniak prisoner called Fikret Alić who, emaciated and terrorized, was photographed through the barbed wire at the Trnopolje camp.[8] The British magazine *Living Marxism* declared in 1997 that there were no barbed wire fences round the camp, nor around the refugees filmed by the ITN TV news crew. It had to be explained once again that the camp was partly surrounded by barbed wire and that TV crews as well as journalists from AFP, *The Guardian* and *Libération* had indeed seen and filmed the reality. ITN eventually won its libel case against *Living Marxism*. Ed Vulliamy too had to return to this controversy in September 2002, during the trial of the former mayor of Prijedor, Milomir Stakić.

Being very cautious, one might use the expression chosen by the historian Jacques Rupnik, 'concentration or detention camp', for the heavily supervised detention and execution sites Omarska and Keraterm; or the terms 'ethnic cleansing camp' or 'ethnic purification camp' adopted by Bernard Kouchner in 1992, which describe the Bosnian reality including its specific features. It seems to us dubious to call Keraterm and Omarska 'death camps', as some UN experts and journalists did. This expression, which 'designates concentration camps conceived for the mass extermination of detainees',[9] refers almost exclusively to the Holocaust with its institutionalized and absolute character. We have no wish to get entangled here in the unending debate on the 'uniqueness of the Shoah' and the 'hierarchization of victims',[10] we want to describe the 1992 reality as accurately as possible, as Jean Kahn did at the time on returning from former Yugoslavia: the President of the Representative Council of Jewish Institutions in France had rejected the label 'death camps' as a designation for the three Prijedor camps. He too chose to use the term 'detention camp' while describing the full force of the 'ethnic cleansing' process.[11]

All these arguments and polemics cease at the gates of Omarska, Keraterm and Trnopolje. These three places are hermetically sealed. The past is forbidden there and worse still, so is remembering. Thirteen years after the events, the Serb community is still refusing to reopen that inevitably painful but nonetheless salutary chapter. Anxious to bury the past, it has turned its face stubbornly towards the future, unanimously fixated on the dire economic situation that currently serves as an absolute, usefully exclusive priority.

PART THREE

Two Parallel Worlds

Since the collapse of the Berlin wall, I have travelled a world where new walls are going up everywhere.

François Maspero, *Les Abeilles et la Guêpe*

As usual, Nada Ševo took her time that morning when she reached the subject closest to her heart.[1] Her discourse was well-honed. No interview with the mayor of Prijedor could conclude without some reference to one of the first priorities – if not the only priority – of her mandate: employment. With her measured delivery and smart, sober suit, today bearing a lapel pin of the Euro symbol, this approachable and moderate woman of fifty-three is a model of prudence, an ex-schoolteacher with an unparalleled talent for reassurance. Elected in April 2000, she made the employment question the basis of her whole sales pitch for the establishment of a 'climate of trust' between the inhabitants. The discourse is smooth, brisk, the essence of modern communication: 'The important thing is to create jobs, for returning refugees as well as the people who stayed. That's basic. I was a teacher for years and I want the youth of this town to have favourable conditions for living here, so they won't be tempted to leave in search of work.'

This theme, using the same phrases and the same pleading tone, recurs time and again, with imposing unanimity, in the talk of many of Prijedor's inhabitants, its local journalists and business community. It monoplizes conversations, it fills people's thoughts; above all it eclipses and relegates more sensitive and difficult matters.

Even the religious leaders echo this refrain. Outside the freshly-painted, well-kept Orthodox church Father Ranko, who boasts of being in close touch with his three or four thousand 'very devout' parishioners, speaks of the sad daily lot of citizens reduced to 'walking up and down the main street all day long and spending the evenings going from bar to bar in Prijedor'. No, he says, the problem here is 'lack of jobs and the standard of living.' He is an impressive man who looks and sounds the part of a priest, but he seems unaccountably more interested in the material problems of his flock than its spiritual welfare. The representative of the Catholic community (and the aid agency Caritas) is also keen to mention the primacy of the economy 'which is the only thing that can revitalize Prijedor'. He explains: 'If investors came and invested in the mine [at Ljubija, where a lot of Croats live], that could give a boost to the economy and everyone would be happy.' Neither is by nature a chatty man, but both are almost impossible to interrupt once they start listing the omnipresent difficulties of daily life.

SEVEN

A Serb Society Adrift

The discourse goes without saying. It combines all points of view. No one would dream of denying the difficulties or minimizing the scale of the problems, for the picture of the local economy is not a glittering one. The average unemployment rate is slightly over 50 per cent, far higher in some districts. Only eleven or twelve thousand people, out of a hundred and twelve thousand inhabitants, have jobs in the municipality. Ranko Stjepić, assistant in charge of the economy and an SDS member, gives these figures without much in the way of detail. He even admits to not having 'a complete picture' of the local economic situation, and refers without explanation to a 'grey economy'. To give an idea of a distressed situation over which he has little control, he states repeatedly and against all expectation that he 'has no budgetary line for economic affairs'.

A more meaningful diagnosis comes from the managers and occasional isolated entrepreneurs. What they produce, with a wealth of pessimistic detail, really boils down to an autopsy. 'This town is economically dead,' says Dragoslav Balaban, boss of a computer and software business. 'Nothing but brothels, café-bars and small boutiques.' He is well up in manager-speak. The firm, KI Sistemi, set up seven years ago, has twelve employees and turned over a million convertible marks (KM), roughly half a million euros, in 2001. His attitudes are very liberal and pragmatic. He denounces corruption, criticizes administrative foot-dragging and unwieldy business support policies, bewails the absence of enterprise culture. He expects nothing from the local authorities, preferring to put his time into establishing links with nearby towns and especially with the neighbouring countries Austria, Serbia and Croatia.

Isolated and somewhat out of step with other bosses, Dragoslav Balaban is a man seething with impatience and business projects.

From his grand conference room just down the road from the town hall Ranko Cvijić fills out the collective picture. Boss of the former mining giant Rudnik Ljubija, his reading is sombre and realistic. 'Before the war, you had two big companies in the area, Rudnik Ljubija and Celpak, the paper and cellulose factory. Celpak is no longer operating. We have been producing at only a tenth of our capacity since the end of the war. Of our thirteen hundred workers only seven hundred are actually working, the others are getting benefit. Only big companies can generate work for medium and small enterprises. But here the problems are serious and there are too many of them: the banking system has been completely destroyed, the political risk level is very high and the judicial apparatus too haphazard to create a climate of confidence. Nor have the international community's promises to unblock funds come to anything yet.'[1]

Head of the third biggest enterprise in the region, the Mira biscuit factory, Ranko Topić is more hopeful, counting on the opening of new markets in the Balkans and also in the US. At the helm since a few days after the takeover of Prijedor by Serb forces in 1992, he can point to some profit (27 million convertible marks – 14 million euros – in 2001) but would rather discuss the investments and new technologies he means to encourage. Proud of the unlikely and perhaps undeserved title of 'Best manager in Bosnia' for 2001, he says his aim is to 'preserve jobs and maintain the social climate'. His manner is urbane and his attitudes to the economic situation consciously neutral and objective. Another manager based on the Croatian frontier, tanned, expensively dressed and with the tough, Teflon grin of a Berlusconi, talks cheerfully if amateurishly about the slowness of privatization, apparently unconcerned by the risks of social damage.

The privatization process that launched the anarchic dismantling of former State companies could lead to the sacking of workers, if not on a massive scale, certainly in sufficient numbers to cause trouble in an extremely fragile post-war economy subject to all the prevailing uncertainties and risks. Suspect and roundabout, privatization is also slow partly because to avoid mass sackings, a lot of bosses are waiting for retirements and natural attrition to reduce staff numbers to a level that can be presented as efficient before selling the enterprises.

Besides, a lot of entrepreneurs and economic decision-makers are counting on time itself to do the healing. With near-perfect unanimity, they see the passage of time acting as a miraculous balm to revive economic activity from its moribund, suffocated state. Another factor presented as a semi-miraculous lifebuoy is the arrival of foreign investors. This constant leitmotiv among bosses is encouraged by the international community, which is as keen as they are to trumpet the priorities in the absence of actual results. Everyone, more or less, goes on about their 'special' contacts, their 'partnerships' and 'cooperation', their 'openness to Europe', but alas, without concrete results. In 2001, according to the International Monetary Fund (IMF), Republika Srpska's gross domestic product fell by 1.9 per cent, and Bosnia-Herzegovina was the country in East Europe receiving the lowest level of foreign investment.

These claims and these vain ambitions have Refik Hodžić, the former director of the ICTY's information programme in Bosnia, almost literally crawling up the wall. 'Just find me,' he challenges, 'a single foreigner likely to invest in this destabilized region, where war criminals walk about unmolested, the media are controlled by politicians and a large part of the population is in a state of collective amnesia about what's happened. Let me say this once and for all: there will be no economic stability if there's no justice for the victims.'

'There's Something Wrong with Talking Endlessly About the Past'

When the past is mentioned faces darken, manners become more perfunctory and people start looking at their watches. The loquacity and 'enlightened' opinions elicited by the economic situation start to disappear behind a growing lassitude and irritation. Ranko Topić's fixed smile vanishes abruptly. 'You can't compare the war period with the present day,' he snaps, 'and in any case I don't want to stray into political territory.' He refuses to admit that he is a member of the SDS. According to the ICTY investigators, company bosses like Ranko Topić, appointed by the Crisis Staff in 1992, were fully aware of the ethnic cleansing campaign, in fact were one of its essential mechanisms. Ranko Cvijić, who became director of Rudnik Ljubija after the war, has a slightly easier time: 'The people who did that [committed the war crimes in 1992] are crazy. And what happened then has nothing to do with the Rudnik Ljubija mine,' he says. Another manager, based on the Bosnia-Croatia frontier, simply dismisses those enormous crimes – the establishment of internment and torture camps for non-Serbs, the death or disappearance of thousands of victims, the deliberate destruction of houses, etc. – as 'the sort of things that happen in all wars'.

The mayor of Prijedor, Nada Ševo, hesitates for a few moments before getting annoyed: 'One thing there's something wrong with is talking endlessly about the past and never about the future. That past ought to be examined in The Hague, so that we can have done with it and this town can be left in peace.' But she is reluctant to go into detail on what the ICTY is doing. Somewhat surprisingly, religious leaders adopt a similar line. The Orthodox priest, Father Ranko, is pretty brisk as well: 'In general it's the politicians who like talking about the past, when really we ought to be interested concretely in the present and future.' More from fear of reopening painful wounds than any real desire to forget, Marijan Komljenović, who represents Caritas and the Catholic Croat community, wants to turn the page. 'We shouldn't go on talking about the past,' he says. Nor will he make much of the destruction of the Catholic church in August 1992 and the delays in rebuilding it, or of the exodus of Croats from the region, or of the repeated nationalist provocations during religious festivals.[2]

A retired local journalist, a Serb friendly to the Bosniaks who would not give his name, sums up the state of mind of a population given to ostrich-like behaviour and longing for tranquillity: 'The past must be forgotten so that people can live together without thinking about it all the time, as they did before the war. The politicians should free the people and admit their own errors.' He is unlikely to be widely heard, for the time is not really ripe for remorse let alone the examination of conscience.

Nevertheless, following the discussion of daily material problems and after the first reactions to the evocation of the past, the masks start to slip and the conversation gradually takes on a different complexion. The comments of the Serb community start to display an inclination to reexamine if not rewrite History, a wish to relativize the events, if not minimize them or deny them altogether. As if eight years after the end of the war, with the sharpest pain dulled, it had become almost legitimate to 'correct' the facts, to 'reframe' them or 'tone them down'.

On the local level Dušan Berić is undoubtedly one of the leading promoters of this rampant campaign. This economist by training and former director of the Republika Srpska lottery used to be the boss of the SDS nationalists in the Prijedor region, which extends from Banja Luka to the Croatian frontier, until 2004. That was when he was removed from his functions by the High Representative of the international community for 'obstructing the peace process', notably through his direct or indirect involvement in a support network for Radovan Karadžić. His party is the main political force in Republika Srpska and the biggest opposition group in the town's municipal council,[3] after having been one of the political mainstays of the ethnic cleansing. The SDS has infiltrated the mechanisms of administrations and enterprises, and its capacity to twist arms and make a nuisance of itself is considerable.

A tall man with a loud, confident delivery and a frank gaze, Dušan Berić receives visitors in his office decorated with a Serbian eagle, an Orthodox icon and a map of Bosnia in which the frontier between the two entities is heavily marked. This is a way of showing, as he repeats again and again, that 'institutional centralization' in Bosnia is out of the question and that Bosnia's Serb Republic must 'survive' against the 'Federation of Bosniaks'. He is a person made of certitudes: 'The insecurity of the Serbs, the provocations of the Bosniaks and their wish for vengeance, the endless complaints of the Muslims and the threat of dictatorship from them…' He goes on and on. Like Berić, the Bosnian Serbs fear most of all the disappearance of their entity and of their measure of autonomy, acquired through armed conquest.

A probing question on the reality of the internment camps during the war elicits a long and embarrassed silence punctuated by furtive sidelong glances. Then, after a first self-defensive reaction – 'I'm not personally bothered by these so-called concentration camps' – a smile gradually takes shape on Berić's cheerful face. He is about to give himself away. In the manner of one confiding a collusive anecdote, Dušan Berić murmurs: 'You know, I talked about these camps with Murselović. He said: "The first night they killed engineers; the second, doctors; the third, jurists." I replied: "But in that case, Mr Murselović, how did you manage to get out of it yourself?".' Dušan Berić bursts out laughing. He starts going on about 'the alleged missing persons of Prijedor' whose names and photos appeared in a book of post-war testimonies. 'I keep seeing most of these allegedly dead people in the street in Prijedor. You really shouldn't be taken in by the enormous Bosniak propaganda campaign,' he adds, unblinkingly, almost proud of the effect he is having.

The laugh subsides, the analysis is ready: 'No, really, contrary to what people say, there wasn't any criminal enterprise in Prijedor planned by the Serbs during the war,' asserts the head of the SDS, sweeping aside the detailed accounts of the facts assembled and compiled in numerous inquiry reports over nearly ten years. 'The Bosniaks haven't accepted the reality of the war or the fact that it's over. It may be true that a few Serbs sought revenge during that war, but there was a much bigger genocide of Serbs by Muslims at Sanski Most. In Kozarac the Muslims had started preparing the genocide of the Serbs. A list of Serbs to be liquidated was discovered in a mini-bunker. It was like 1942, during the Second World War at the Jasenovac concentration camp,' Dušan Berić blares, forgetting that that particular well-documented crime was essentially committed by Ante Pavelić's Ustashe.

The SDS boss wants to go further. He advances the idea that 'the first victims were Serb, they were killed by the Bosniaks in Hambarine', a village six kilometres south-west of Prijedor, adding that 'the twenty-six Serbs killed in the attack on the town hall' should not be forgotten. He is 'ashamed', he confesses, when he remembers that 'no one talks about the war veterans and their families any more, the way they used to do'. Boško Bajić, the vehement president of Ostanak (the association of Serb refugees from Croatia and the Federation), puts the finishing touches to this viewpoint: 'How can you live with people who accuse you of having committed a genocide? The ethnic cleansing story is false. It was invented by the Bosniaks.'

All Victims, all Guilty

In this way, little by little, the discourse of Serb victimization is gathering speed. It is frequently heard. It affirms a truth and conceals an ambition. For it is certainly true that the Serb population, too, suffered from the war, and is still suffering its economic and political consequences every day. According to Ostanak, more than twenty-five thousand Serbs from Croatia and the Federation are refugees in the Prijedor area, some in a state of total destitution. The townspeople are aware of the lack of resources, living as they do on small salaries often paid late. They can see the young graduates leaving, the firms laying off staff to prepare for privatization. And they are surprised and overwhelmed by the unexpected, large-scale reappearance of the refugees. Many of these, after making lives for themselves abroad, are returning from exile better educated and better trained than their countrymen. Some are richer too, having found work in western countries with higher wages and better living standards than Bosnia's. The Serbs are just beginning to realize that the nationalists in power since the end of the war have failed to solve their problems by the widest of margins, despite all the fine pre-election promises and speeches. So they grumble, and many feel that they are doomed to swell the ranks of the underclass.

So there may well be perfectly good reasons for the feeling that they are victims. In some cases, however, it serves as a smokescreen for the development of the idea that 'all are victims, all are guilty'. 'Alas! Crimes were committed on all sides,' Dušan Berić analyses. Mile Mutić, the media boss, local editorialist and avowed former propagandist whose name figures on several international lists of war criminals, shores up this assertion. 'The war arrived here because of the three nationalist parties, Serb, Croat and Bosniak (SDS, HDZ and SDA), who reached an understanding to destroy the socialist régime. But in the end nothing happened in Prijedor that wasn't committed in other towns as well.' Father Ranko raises the bidding: 'The guilt is shared between the three nationalities: the Serbs, the Muslims and the Croats.'

This is quite a neat and tidy concept. By delicate brushstrokes, it builds up the idea that an everyday, sad sort of 'normality' prevailed in the town during the war. 'I would have been just as ashamed if I'd lived in Zenica, Mostar or Sarajevo,' Mutić says, careful to name only towns in the Federation. In Prijedor, then, the evil was widespread and shared, as elsewhere; as elsewhere, troops fought each other and crimes were committed by the belligerent parties and criminals of every stripe; and as elsewhere, the civilian populations came off worst in the fighting. Neat, tidy, equal; except that back in 1992, the story had not really unfolded quite like that.

The hidden intention is to give Prijedor the image of a town like any other: nothing less, but most especially nothing more. The aim is not so much the frontal denial of history as its homogenization, its levelling-off. This wish is built around a number of representations. Among the population we were sometimes given a partially censored account of the truth: the town and its environs had been invaded by 'troops from outside the region', 'fascists' arriving from elsewhere to perpetrate crimes during the war. Thus, the troubles were in a sense imported. This point of view is aimed at laying the blame on the outside world and protecting, up to a point, the cohesion of the local community.

This logic also helps support the idea that the local Serb inhabitants cannot be associated as a group with the exactions committed. Father Ranko puts it very well: 'When the truth comes out, we can see that the blame is individual and doesn't rest on just one nation.' When the case of Prijedor is mentioned as being one of the nine places in which genocide was committed during the war, according to the indictment against Slobodan Milošević on Bosnia, the mayor puts in a plea for her town: 'I put a great deal of energy into showing the town in a different light so that it won't be associated with something bad,' Nada Ševo says. 'I'm doing my best to show that the inhabitants of Prijedor aren't genocidal.'

While it goes without saying that a whole community, let alone an entire people, cannot be held responsible for every crime committed in its name, the idea of total innocence is just as hard to swallow. The war and ethnic cleansing might conceivably have been dreamed up and planned without any input from Prijedor criminals, but they were certainly waged and practised by local people aided, it is true, by militias and troops foreign to the town. And it runs from top to bottom, from next door neighbour to the town mayor. Muharem Murselović described the participation of an acquaintance in his own arrest, as he recalled the role and involvement of the local Serb authorities in the seizure of the town in 1992, and the subsequent 'éliticide' or liquidation of leading citizens. In their own narratives,[4] Rezak Hukanović and

Kemal Pervanić described the way their Serb former schoolmates, colleagues, neighbours or friends had become committed to the war and taken part in crimes or acts of torture in the internment cmps. Other testimony relates that the camps were open to certain local inhabitants who would visit them 'to have a bit of fun'.

In Prijedor as in many other towns in Bosnia, part of the population, some of whose members are still at large and unprosecuted,[5] committed crimes and took part in the 'war effort', all in a climate of 'monstrous intimacy' (to use the journalist Ed Vulliamy's spot-on expression). In the analyses of Keith Doubt or Noel Malcolm,[6] the collaboration was sometimes under pressure, even the threat of execution made by militias and politicians keen to set the communities against one another, to destroy all the links of coexistence and tolerance based on centuries of living together, and above all, according to Michael A. Sells,[7] to spread through forced or voluntary enrolment a feeling of generalized guilt and thus create criminals.

Battle of Numbers, Conflict of Words, War of Memory

The temptation to rewrite history is strong and real. It opens the way for revisionism, fed by battles of numbers and quarrels over words. While the expression 'concentration camp' should be used carefully, one can hardly justify going to the opposite extreme and calling Keraterm, Trnopolje and Omarska simple 'collection centres', or 'assembly sites', or 'transit centres'.

These falsely neutral, genuinely revisionist expressions recur frequently in conversations with political leaders and economic decision-makers. They are accompanied by some curious descriptions of what went on in the camps during the war. 'People were assembled at Omarska to await departure to the destination of their choice,' explains one of the site's present security officials, before admitting a few minutes later that he was not present in the area during the war. Near the entrance to the camp, a couple of hundred metres from the gates to the mining complex through which the busloads of prisoners and truckloads of corpses were driven, you can hear the point of view of some rather surly garage men: 'Listen, the facts of what happened here have been exaggerated. The people who came here were better looked after than the ones who stayed outside. In the collection centre, which absolutely wasn't a concentration camp, there were more people saved than killed. They were brought here for their own protection and to find their families.'

A similar stifling logic is deployed to minimize numbers. Dušan Berić relativizes the number of disappeared people. Recurrent doubts are cast –

when it is not revised downward – on the figure for the number of people killed during the war, officially held to be several hundred, but not precisely established. You hear them on the lips of economic officials, coldly calculated words reeking of euphemism. If you ask Ranko Topić, the boss of Mira, what became of the three hundred staff members missing from the enterprise today, he tells you that 'those Bosniaks decided to leave town during the war'. He does not tell you that most of them were forced to leave and the rest are dead. Indeed he assures people that 'not a single employee died in the camps', contradicting the 1997 Human Rights Watch report and Hanne Sophie Greve's UN document.

It is hard to see what could change this outlook, especially since it has received indirect encouragement. On 3 September 2002, a commission of the Republika Srpska government published a report on the Srebrenica massacre of July 1995 which estimated the number of victims as no more than 2,000-2,500 Muslims, 1,800 of them combatants; independent investigations had already established that in fact more than 7,000 died, the majority civilians. The international community condemned the report as a 'depressing example of revisionism'. It aroused deep anger among Bosniaks, but all the Bosnian Serbs could manage was a half-hearted official denial: Mladen Ivanić, then RS prime minister, merely said that the report did not represent his government's position. But of course the harm had already been done. In the end, under strong pressure from the international community and its representative in Bosnia Paddy Ashdown, Republika Srpska set up a new commission of enquiry which, in 2004, recognized that the massacre had taken place and admitted its scale, for the first time accepting the figure of more than 7,000 victims.

This squabbling over numbers, casting suspicion and discredit on the established facts, has been accompanied by the deliberate appropriation of places and names. The 'Serbianization' of territory and nomenclature that began in 1992 has been maintained and pursued. Refugee organizations estimate that more than 40 per cent of the names of streets, squares and villages in and around Prijedor have been changed to embody national references. Thus, while the pedestrianized Marshal Tito Street has become Peter-I-the-Liberator Street, the village of Ostraluka just outside Prijedor with its thousand-odd inhabitants and handful of empty shops has been renamed 'Serb Sanski Most', twinning it imaginatively with the Federation town of Sanski Most (population sixty thousand). The Esad Midžić school in the centre of Prijedor, named after a famous Second World War Muslim Partisan, is now called after St. Sava, venerated by the Orthodox Church. Many of these changes were imposed during the war, but nothing has been done since that time to restore normality. It is not at all unusual for a returned refugee seeking an address under its old name to get a blank response from a resident who only knows the new one.

The authorities have also taken over the calendar to play on the symbolism of dates. Thus, the end-of-year celebration at Trnopolje school, formerly at the end of June, has been brought forward. Henceforth the headmistress, who has SDS connections, requests the pleasure of the presence of pupils' families on 24 May: the date on which Trnopolje camp was opened in 1992 to intern, torture and kill women and children. Until the beginning of the war Prijedor celebrated its annual festival on 16 May, the anniversary of the town's liberation at the end of the Second World War. Now the festival has been brought forward a few days to 30 April, the date in 1992 on which Serb nationalists seized the town by force. These changes caused trouble and set many people's teeth on edge, so much so that a municipal commission was set up in 2000 to consider further modifications. But so far nothing has been done to restore normality.

Worse still, a majority in the municipal assembly voted in April 2003 to adopt a symbol for the town of Prijedor consisting of the 'four esses', well known as a nationalist and Chetnik emblem.[8] The Chairman of the municipal assembly, Muharem Murselović, tendered his resignation following this decision, which he regarded as wholly unacceptable.

By altering names and shifting dates, the authorities were trying to appropriate the public space. They have also been attempting to 'sanctify' it. A photograph hung on walls inside Prijedor hospital is a memorial portrait of Milan Kovačević, known as Mico, the hospital centre director who died of a heart attack in The Hague on 1 August 1998, just after the opening of his trial on charges that included genocide. Facing the entrance to Trnopolje school, a monument to victims – *Serb* victims – has been built in the form of an eagle, its base carrying a poem in Cyrillic script by the Ukrainian poet Taras Shevchenko.

In this enterprise of occupying and demarcating territory the most coveted prize of all, without any doubt, is Prijedor town centre. It is a display window. In the space of a few years, in a three hundred metre radius bounded by the town hall, a secondary school and the main post office, no fewer than three monuments have appeared. 'All in honour of war victims,' town officials assure you with earnest sincerity. But it is worth taking a closer look.

There is a broad space in the heart of the administrative quarter. A long wall of polished granite, a covered way scattered with stone benches, and a monolith of stone and stainless steel. On its faces are written two dates: 1990-1995, followed by the names of victims: *Serb* victims. They were from the Rudnik Ljubija mine, which has itself placed a monument outside its main office to 'honour them', in the words of Ranko Cvijić who is reluctant to discuss the subject in detail.

With almost perfect symmetry, another 'mausoleum' has been erected two hundred metres away. Facing the town hall, at the end of a tarmac roadway leading from the town hall portico, stands a massive metal cross five metres high, pierced through its centre by a sort of 'wound' from which tragic outlines project. The symbolism is clunking: it will escape no one that the cross is an Orthodox one and the non-Serb communities will therefore find it difficult to identify with this allegedly ecumenical memorial. Just nearby, next to a secondary school in the middle of a green space, what the mayor describes as 'a cupola recalling the style and spirit of a Belgrade monument' has recently been completed. 'The remains of victims will be placed there,' Nada Ševo adds. On being asked whether *all* victims will be able to benefit from this vault, she has to admit that only Serbs will have that right, although she personally thinks that 'a victim is a victim, irrespective of any nationality considerations'.

On this subject the mayor of Prijedor is in a permanent state of ambivalence and embarrassment. Her views sound paradoxical to put it mildly. She has often claimed that she would like to 'reduce the number of monuments' and that she does not want 'Prijedor town centre to be turned into a cemetery'. Nevertheless, constructions of this sort have proliferated during her mandate despite the constantly mentioned financial difficulties and her own avowed wish to 'look towards the future'. Pressed about this, she argues that these particular monuments were incorporated in urban renewal plans adopted by her predecessors, so there was nothing she could do about them. However, Nada Ševo is not always so conscientious in defending earlier municipal decisions, an example being the violation of a deed of ownership signed by one of her predecessors at the town hall concerning the marketplace in the Old Town.[9]

It seems that what she really fears above all else is to have to confront the veterans, the nationalists, certain Serb politicians who would not fail to make their feelings known were she to get in the way of one of their monument projects. Nor would they be slow to react if a memorial to the non-Serb victims – a broad and large majority in the town and all around it – looked like seeing the light of day. But this is not something that is even being considered. She can just be persuaded, after a good deal of evasion and disclaimers, to consider the hypothesis of a structure in honour of *all* the victims. 'Let's be realistic, it will be a long time before we get a monument of that sort, if it's ever possible here, or in the rest of Bosnia. That's just the sort of scheme that takes one step forward, two steps back.' She brings the same level of enthusiasm to supervising the planned reconstruction of the mosque burned and then flattened in 1992, which has made a reluctant, halting start under heavy American pressure.

A Non-existent Civil Society

Once again, the mayor is counting on the aid of time as a healer. 'A lot of things should change in the mentalities created and conditioned during the war. The politicians need to become more mature to understand what's happened here. That takes time. We need to advance cautiously, build up a climate of trust and in particular avoid imposing decisions.'

The climate of fear that still reigns over the town is unlikely to speed the process. Nada Ševo recognizes this herself: 'The citizens of Prijedor are afraid of expressing their viewpoints in public.' At least on this point, she has the support of Angelina Femić, a Montenegro-born Serb and member of the Social Democratic Party (SDP, practically the only genuinely multi-ethnic party in Bosnia). 'There's a widespread fear of saying what one really thinks in public,' observes this lucid Prijedor teacher. 'During the war the only voice one heard was that of the SDS. Since the war the situation hasn't really changed. Access to genuinely pluralist media is limited. It will take time for people who have been subjected to this propaganda for so many years to look reality in the face. The Muslims and Croats of the Federation have better access to the foreign and especially European media. Another thing is that there are a lot of refugees or displaced people from rural areas in Prijedor. They've obtained houses in town and are afraid of losing them. This makes them very easy for the SDS to manipulate. The nationalists tell them that only they are defending these people's interests and enabling them to hold onto their houses in town. These displaced people from the Federation have been promised houses and land, they have been persuaded that they can stay here. It will be some time yet before the Prijedor Serbs can recognize what happened here during the conflict. SDS members are the only ones who say openly that they're nationalists, but actually there are a lot of others, especially in the police and judiciary.'

A fellow SDP member – also a Serb – said it publicly during an electoral meeting in September 2002: 'The nationalist parties will never admit Trnopolje, Omarska, Srebrenica. They lie about what happened. The people running Republika Srpska make out that none of it ever happened, they try to make people forget that crimes were committed. But we should make peace now by admitting what went on.' Rade Dženopoljac got more applause than any other speaker at the meeting. But there were only sixty or so people in the audience, nearly all SDP members, all convinced, but few and isolated.

So these days the population can only depend on itself when it needs to address questions concerning the past or politics, or even to discuss 'neutral' subjects like town management, leisure facilities and communal life. The individuals who could act as 'references', 'conduits' or 'mediators' have left, or have no desire to play such a role. The trade unions are very weak, the network of associations still undeveloped and the religions hermetically closed off. 'Before the war I used to have good relations with my opposite numbers from the other confessions,' Father Ranko explains. 'Now we have no contact. Not through any wish of mine. I've been here all along and in my view it's up to the people coming back to make contact with me. In any case, it's only to be expected that one has less to do with people who left, one has more in common with the ones who stayed. A time will come when the wounds will have healed. The international community may expect this to happen overnight, but that isn't the way it goes. The wounds are still fresh.' The other religious dignitaries are clearly not in a strong position and distinctly cool towards the Orthodox community. Catholics are very few in number, and the Muslims cautious and circumspect after two waves of attacks on their places of worship... in 2001 and 2002.

Among Serbs, the risk of being labelled a 'traitor' is ever-present, along with the related threats. 'I was accused of betraying the Serb cause. In 1998 they even organized a phoney prosecution against me. They told me I'd stolen some seed when I've never done anything like that. But the pressure's even heavier in the actual town of Prijedor,' remembers Milan Glusac. Glusac, who does not make an undue fuss about his own case, is a very calm and peaceable Serb farmer from the hamlet of Donja Vola on the left bank of the Sana. His offence had been to ignore all nationalist huffing and puffing and continue to associate with all the inhabitants of his village whether Serb or Muslim, to help returning refugees and work alongside Muslims, as he did before the war. These days Milan Glusac often walks with his Muslim friend Derviš Hadžić in the hills, where they feel happier and relatively free from pressures of one sort and another. But they are alone, and they are utterly atypical.

For on the lips of some leaders of opinion, explanation can swerve into menace. 'It's impossible to have representatives of all three nationalities in each of the entities. It's better to live separately and just promote sporting and cultural exchanges. If they try to unify Bosnia, there'll be another war,' says the president of the Serb refugees' association, Boško Bajić, with one eye on Prijedor and the other on the whole country.

Nor is the fourth estate in a position to take part in the emergence of a civil society and the establishment of a democratic and critical culture. Indeed the media in Prijedor have not even started to look at themselves clearly. Mile Mutić is the dispiriting model. His name appears in several reports of international inquiries into crimes committed during the war and the role played at that time by the organs of communication. His collusion with the Serb forces is incontestable and proven. Eleven years after the events this man, aged fifty-nine, is managing director af a group consisting of Radio Prijedor, the weekly paper *Kozarski Vjesnik* (print run 3,000 copies) of which he is editor in chief, and RTV Tele-Prijedor. In running *Kozarski Vjesnik*, Mutić has the help of Zoran Sovilj, a subtle and open-minded younger journalist whose nationalist viewpoint is neither exclusive nor aggressive towards the other communities. He would seem to represent a sovereignist and intellectual tendency, the disappointed heir of a Greater Serbian cultural tradition. He is critical of SDS and SDA activism. Asked for his version of the facts of 1992, he comes up with the theory of 'a town in the hands of a few individuals who damaged an entire community'.

His paper struggles to deliver believable information. Some of the articles are devoted largely to rumour, sources are seldom identified and pieces about dark plots produce an occasional sensation. Zoran Sovilj mentions threats delivered to his home where a bomb was planted in the spring of 2002. Fortunately it did not go off, but nor has any light ever been cast on these incidents. The editorial line, slippery and ambiguous, gibes at the international community. The week in June 2002 that the war criminal Darko Mrđa[10] was arrested in Prijedor and extradited to The Hague for trial, the paper carried the headline: 'Blood on the pavement, Mrđa at The Hague'. The body of the sub-headline continued: 'Many indications found of police cooperation with international community. Freedom purchased with intelligence given to the international community.'

With the same detachment and insouciance, Sovilj avoids following the trials in The Hague where some of those responsible for the ethnic cleansing, in particular people from Prijedor like the former mayor Milomir Stakić, have been and still are on trial. 'This isn't the sort of material that interests the population,' Mile Mutić says, straight-faced, adding: 'We don't get any information from The Hague, except what's on national television.' Evidently he has never heard of the press agencies covering the trials, or the ICTY website in Serbo-Croat. Zoran Sovilj is every bit as eloquent: 'No information is sent to us by the ICTY and it's difficult to know when the trials are due to start. We don't have a correspondent. We use the agencies when we can.' He ends by saying that 'the Serb population will accept the ICTY when it's convinced that this tribunal is impartial. But so far, and from following the Milošević trial on television, that's hard to believe.'

Željko Kopanja, editor in chief of the biggest independent daily paper in the Republika Srpska, *Nezavisne Novine* (fifteen thousand copies daily), is not all that surprised by remarks of this kind. In his office in the outskirts of Banja Luka he receives visitors seated, having lost both legs when a bomb was planted in his car on 22 October 1999.[11] He had just published the list of the two hundred and twenty-eight victims – detainees and inhabitants of Prijedor – of the massacre that took place on Mount Vlašić, near Travnik, in August 1992. 'It's hard doing journalism in this country. There are very few reliable sources. The media are often controlled by political parties. Propaganda is mixed with journalism and political affairs are mixed up with private life,' says this discreet and tenacious man. 'In any case, the readers buy papers that suit their ideas, and there are a whole lot of people who don't want to see reality or deal with the truth.'

Nezavisne Novine has just one correspondent in Prijedor. The big Sarajevo daily *Oslobođenje* also has one in this the second city of Republika Srpska. Besima Kahrimanović has inherited the job from her late husband. She is isolated. 'The influence of *Oslobođenje* is limited in Prijedor. Only a few dozen copies are sold each day. The local media,' she observes, 'never cover exhumations of bodies or the funerals of those exhumed, and take no interest in the ICTY trials.' Although she has not been overtly threatened, she is much criticized and feels she needs to be vigilant just in case. There is not much room for an autonomous press critical of the authorities and parties. In its last report on Bosnia the organization Reporters sans frontière notes that 'on 10 March 2001, an explosive device destroyed the car belonging to Rezak Fukanović, a Muslim Bosniak journalist and owner of the Prijedor television channel 101'.

In the prevailing climate, while the tensions persist, there is little to be expected from the religious communities, which have nothing to do with each other despite ecumenical declarations. And where bridge-building is concerned the same blockage affects the younger generations. Imprisoned by a conflict in which they played no part, they have also inherited the raw divisions between their elders: the worst of both worlds. Without having heard it, but through the naïve optimism natural to the young, they tend to echo Nada Ševo's discourse on the need for a happy future. 'In quite a few cases what's important comes down to one question: "Can you tell us how to get out of here and leave this town?" ' reports a woman representative of the international community in Prijedor. Their concerns are plain enough, leaving little room for doubt: how to find amusement, what to do for a living, where to go to meet each other, how to learn foreign languages. Their main objectives seem not just obvious but entirely reasonable: to wangle a job, go to Banja Luka or better still abroad, and forget all about Prijedor.

Rajko Macura, a man in his forties, presents himself as the organizer of the biggest and most 'genuine' local youth association, Svetionik. He talks about 'psychological counselling to address post-war trauma and help young people deal with these problems'. A glance at the list of activities shows that the reality is very different. Apart from a few conferences on the rights of young people, the bulk is made up of providing prepackaged services: language, dance and gymnastics courses, films, parties and sports.

When some of the young people, from different ethnic backgrounds, wanted to organize a pacifist demonstration after the serious incidents in Kozarac in September 2002, the idea was vetoed. The same 'wish for openness' was displayed when they asked for a room in which meetings and debates could be held. Svetionik may be fortunate enough to boast child and youth membership from all the communities, but it can hardly claim any credit for this half-hearted mixing, especially as it is plainly not so much sought by the young members as endured, the price of the activities provided.

But an initiative by a young Prijedor Bosniak, Anel Ališić, and one of his friends who is a Serbian Serb, Ljubiša, did lead in December 2003 to a first gathering of a small group of Bosniaks and Serbs from the town, along with some Macedonians and Serbian Serbs, to talk about the past and discuss reconciliation. A film about the Omarska camp was shown in Prijedor for the first time. One participant, a woman resident of Prijedor, chose to leave the auditorium, but in general the dialogue went well and the young people were able to converse together and compare their different ideas on reconciliation and the town's past. The meeting, made possible by a friendship cutting across the ethnic divide, showed that differences are not insurmountable and that an evocation of the past can be attempted.

Somewhat in the image of their elders, the young cohabit rather than sharing the same life. Their peaceful but numb coexistence completes the picture of a town that remains intrinsically divided between two parallel but disconnected worlds.

EIGHT

Survivors and Refugees Locked in Peaceful Struggle

'There's No Place for Us Any More'

Mention the monuments to Serb dead and Ibrahim Beglerbegović smiles in a tired way. He is a Muslim surgeon, born in Prijedor. His big surgeon's hands spread wide in a gesture of powerlessness and permanent incredulity. 'The way I see it, these monuments just for Serb victims and these altered street names and school names are to discourage us from returning to Prijedor. They want us to think there's no place for us any more.' Ibrahim is speaking in his apartment in Sanski Most. It is not far from Prijedor, only 30 kilometres away, but the two towns belong to different worlds.

Sanski Most is in the Federation. Prijedor is in Republika Srpska. The inhabitants of the two towns, although citizens of the same country, have different parliaments, different police forces and different alphabets (Roman in one case, Cyrillic in the other). Prijedor shelters some hundreds of Serbs who fled Sanski Most when the town was reconquered by the Bosnian army in September 1995.

Similarly, Sanski Most is still housing several thousand refugees from Prijedor, including many camp survivors who have returned after years of exile abroad. A lot of the refugees are hanging on there in the hope that one day they will be able to return to Prijedor. In the meantime they have the impression of being close to home: it is down there, just over the hills, past the signboard beside the road that marks the frontier with the words: Welcome to Republika Srpska.

Ibrahim could easily return to Prijedor to live. He still has a house there in a residential area. But the town's hospital, where he worked before the war, is not prepared to take him back. Bosnian Croats and Muslims were driven out during the conflict and are not always welcomed by the present-day staff. So this cheerful-looking fiftyish surgeon practises at the Sanski Most hospital. During the week he stays with his wife at his brother-in-law's flat. 'I can't help remembering that at the Prijedor hospital there's still a memorial to Milan Kovačević!' he says. Kovačević was the first to be indicted by the Hague tribunal for genocide committed in Prijedor and setting up the camps including Omarska. Ibrahim spent five days at Omarska before being discharged without explanation. Nine of his colleagues died there. 'Do you think I could walk past that every day? Anyway, they don't want me.'

In parallel with the welcoming official speeches, the monuments and street names of Prijedor address a silent message to any refugee who might think of returning. The message is that many people, especially those in senior posts, still feel no regret over the ethnic cleansing. And that alone is sufficient to dissuade some of the survivors from going back to live there.

'I don't want to live in Prijedor now. It's still all right in the daytime, but I'd find it impossible to spend the night there. It's too frightening,' confided Nusreta Sivac, a survivor of Omarska camp, in an interview in 2002. Before the war this elegant blonde woman with melancholy blue-grey eyes lived a carefree life in Prijedor, working as a judge in the town courthouse. She belonged to the élite of the city beside the Sana river. Of that life, there remain a few photographs and 8mm home movies, a handful of souvenirs ending abruptly at 9 June 1992. 'I went to work that day. The armed forces were there. There was a list of personalities who were to be arrested. I was on it and I was taken to Omarska. There were other judges there too. Not one of them survived.'

At first 'I didn't really understand what was going on. I was in a state of shock. I couldn't believe that sort of thing could happen again in this century, deporting people to camps. Until then I'd only ever seen it in films. It's hard to express how indoctrinated those people were. They all thought we were guilty. Sometimes I prayed to God to spare me a slow death, that I'd be killed by a bullet. But not many people were killed with bullets at Omarska. Most of them died from the effects of torture. I can still remember the screams of people being tortured. Even today I still can't watch films with violent screams in them.'[1] Like many of the women detained at Omarska, Nusreta was subjected to sexual abuse by her guards during her two-month detention.

Today, simply knowing that 'I can run into these people who did the torture at any time in the streets of Prijedor is immensely stressful,' she explains. Nusreta has already passed some of her persecutors, one of them Miroslav Kvočka,[2] an officer of the Omarska camp against whom she had given evidence at The Hague. 'I look them in the eye. I really want them to know that I've seen them and I'm looking them in the eye. But you know, it takes a lot of strength, that.'

This sort of thing keeps the past alive and omnipresent for the survivors of the camps. It resurfaces in a thousand ways, sometimes unexpected ones, in their daily life. Nusreta has panic attacks when she hears screams during a film. Ibrahim cannot stop himself from reliving the events of 1992 when he passes a hospital where he no longer has the right to practise. In other cases, the past helps people to justify their present living conditions: temporary lodgings, fragile health, unemployment despite good qualifications and the senior posts held before the war. A Bosniak refugee living in Britain refuses to give his name but babbles that he is unemployed in his country of refuge. Visibly humiliated by this precarious situation and crucial lack of money, he admits shakily that since his internment at Omarska, which lasted nearly three months, his life has been more or less on hold and he finds it difficult to concentrate on work.

For these people, it is impossible to think about the future without recalling the relatively happy pre-war period followed by the brutal rupture of the conflict. The evocation of this last, its months of dehumanization, enables the individual who wants to restore logic to his or her life to explain why exile in a foreign country, with the rootless sensation that accompanies it, can still be sweeter than return to the beloved homeland.

Displaced to Sanski Most, Nusreta Sivac at first did not want to go back to Prijedor, a town where she had constantly to deal with the denial of her sufferings. 'Every time I come to this town I feel ill at ease and nervous. I don't feel calm, because I was too exposed at The Hague when recounting what had happened in 1992,' she told us during an interview conducted in Prijedor in 2002. She chain-smoked during the interview, and from time to time peered anxiously into the street. Nusreta gave her evidence at The Hague under a pseudonym, but her real identity soon leaked out. In the summer of 2002, Nusreta finally recovered possession of her apartment in Prijedor. It had been occupied illegally since 1992 by one of her former work colleagues, a Serb woman who was a secretary and shorthand-writer at Prijedor courthouse. When vacating the flat, this woman had taken all Nusreta's things – crockery, furniture, linen, etc. – and destroyed all the photos that had been left there. Not long after returning to her home Nusreta had found the word 'Omarska' scrawled in large letters beside her door. She is standing firm, trying not to give way to the anxiety that sometimes grips her at night.

Nurka, on a holiday visit from the United States, seems to feel much the same. 'I couldn't live here any more, not after what happened,' she murmurs in an undertone. On the face of it there is something astonishing in this remark: she seems so relaxed, sitting in a café on the main street of Prijedor with her husband and son, watching the crowd of strollers enjoying the cool of the early evening after the savage afternoon heat. 'Look, he was a pupil, and there's our neighbours' daughter, I hardly recognized her.' Nurka looks about her, commenting and laughing. She is visiting Prijedor for the first time in ten years, rediscovering places once so familiar, now so remote: the restaurants where 'we used to go and eat until very late at night', the school at Hambarine, a small outlying village where she taught for several years, the houses of friends, rebuilt or still in ruins after the destruction of 1992 ... She jokes with the old peasant women in surrounding villages, stops to take snaps, tells in passing an amusing story about her life in the US. A small woman, five foot two, with unruly auburn curls and Mediterranean body language, Nurka seems to be at ease everywhere. She listens, soothes, jokes, appoints herself narrator of the past. Of 'a time when I didn't care whether someone was a Serb, a Muslim or a Croat', she says, elbows on the railing of the balcony outside her flat in the middle of Prijedor, which she has just repossessed. From here she can see the building of the Keraterm camp, just a few hundred metres away as the crow flies. Inside the flat, Serb decorators are busy repainting the walls. After years of bureaucratic effort, Nurka's family has recovered its dwelling. Serb officials have tried to delay the return of refugees by dragging their feet over such issues.

Nurka cannot help thinking about the events of 1992. 'I remember when we left... We were shut in our apartment. There were Serb soldiers on the roof who were drinking all night. You could hear shooting. No one came to protect us or offer help. Eventually I had to leave alone, with my two sons.' The authorities would not allow Muslim men of military age, like Nurka's husband, to leave. 'All we were allowed to take with us was the strict minimum. We took the bus to Banja Luka, then a plane. To be able to leave I had to pay them eight hundred marks, because on top of everything else they were making money out of driving us away.' Nurka had had to leave at home the new school things for her sons, who never did return to school at Prijedor. 'One of my sons, Anel, was crying because he wanted to take his new school satchel with him, but we couldn't. I told him we'd soon be coming back, although I didn't believe it.' Nurka's husband went underground. She did not see him until months later, in Croatia where they found refuge. He was one of the twelve survivors of the Mount Vlašić massacre on 21 August 1992. The Bosnian Serb policemen who murdered the prisoners in their charge had told them they were being taken to a safer area.

From Croatia Nurka and her family moved on to Switzerland, then to the United States where they settled. They started rebuilding their life. She and her husband secured teaching jobs helped by their good command of English. Anel and his brother did brilliantly at school. Life reverted to normal, with daily pleasures and joys, the happiness of being together and safe. So normal indeed that returning to Prijedor is no longer considered, except for holidays. Of course her Serb neighbours greeted her effusively, told her how good it was to see her after all these years. But when one of them invited her in for a coffee one day, Nurka recognized the sitting room table as her own. The neighbour did not offer to return it. 'They ask me if I'm coming back for good, and I tell them yes, I am, because I want to make them understand the apartment belongs to me and I'm taking back what's mine. But I know that really I won't come back. I think we're going to buy a house on the Croatian coast where the weather's better and life sweeter, and we'll come here for a few weeks each year to say hello to friends and family. But it's not quite time for that yet. I don't feel any hatred but I'll never be quite sure that what happened in 1992 might not happen again, all of a sudden, just like that.'

It is difficult to assess how many there are like Nurka, who do not want to live in Prijedor while the present conditions persist. There are no figures. Prijedor was purged of virtually its entire non-Serb population during the war, more than forty thousand Muslims and five thousand Croats. The numbers of those killed during the war or who died after it are not precisely known. In the trials concerned with the area, the International Criminal Tribunal for former Yugoslavia has established, after examining thousands of documents submitted by the prosecution and defence sides, that at least one thousand five hundred people were killed during the ethnic cleansing campaign mounted between 1992 and 1995. But this is a cautious, low-end figure. The prosecutor's office and other experts estimate the number of dead as 'several thousand'.

What *is* certain is that hundreds of people who lived in Prijedor before the war are still living abroad in Britain, Holland, France, the US, Sweden and elsewhere. They even have their own website[3] 'created by people who love their town and will always remember happy times in Prijedor, now gone for ever'. Nine thousand others have found refuge closer to home in Sanski Most.[4] Finally, against all expectation, several thousand others, mostly Muslims, have braved the many difficulties and come back, making Prijedor the municipality with the highest proportion of returnees in Republika Srpska.

An Astonishing Renaissance

The town is cited as an exemplary success in achieving the 'return of minorities' not just in Republika Srpska but in Bosnia-Herzegovina as a whole. The term is used for people returning to a zone where their ethnic group has always been, or has now become, a minority. The scale of this return, in one of the zones most scarred by the conflict, has astonished everyone, including officials representing the international community. The former British MP and Liberal Democrat leader Paddy Ashdown, the civilian High Representative of the international community in Bosnia-Herzegovina, points out that in Northern Ireland, Catholics whose houses had been burned had still not returned to them thirty-three years later, and the French Huguenots persecuted in the 17th century 'had not returned either'.

Just outside Prijedor city limits, where the road sets off across the plain towards Banja Luka, dozens of newly built houses appear on the left of the road, a scattering of raw, unrendered red brick, paintless wooden window frames and new tiles. A mosque with a fine new minaret rises from a hill. A signboard points towards the village of Kozarac. Concrete mixers grind and rumble incessantly in the sunshine. Tapping hammers and whining drills echo from end to end of the village and men in blue work clothes are busy finishing off the roofs: a real hive of activity. The cars parked outside the gardens in front of the small houses have registration numbers from France, Sweden, Germany, Holland… there are even a few from Bosnia. The picture is rather as one would have imagined the settlement of European immigrants in the US in earlier times, with the same energy brought to the construction of a complete village, from houses to school via place of worship and the inevitable corner café.

Then the name of Kozarac comes to mind. 'Kozarac is a ghost village, leveled, burned and empty. Scattered teapots and pans, lumps of melted glass, torn clothing, a dog carcass and charred bits of washing machines and stoves litter the streets and muddy lanes where 6,000 houses once stood,' wrote the Australian journalist Gordon Weiss in January 1997, just over a year after the end of the war.[5] Nils Groute of THW, a German organization that facilitates the return of refugees, fills out the picture: 'In November 1998, when we arrived, everything had to be reconstructed, electricity, police station, schools.' By 2002, ten years after the destruction of Kozarac, more than a hundred and fifty houses had been rebuilt, more than two thousand families had come back to live in the village,[6] the mosques had been rebuilt and the electricity supply restored.

Large numbers of Bosnian Muslims have resettled in Kozarac, and in other villages that surround Prijedor and depend on the municipality. In total, more than twelve thousand Bosnian Croats and Muslims have come back into the Prijedor municipality since the end of the war.[7] This figure represents about 20 per cent of the pre-war non-Serb population. Prijedor has thus achieved one of the best performances in the whole of Bosnia-Herzegovina. By way of comparison, barely 2,600 Muslims have returned to live in Srebrenica, despite the special efforts made by the international community in that region.[8]

Why Prijedor is Exemplary

'This is a story about an old man from the municipality of Prijedor, a Muslim driven out during the war. After the Dayton accords in December 1995, he found refuge with his wife at Sanski Most where the authorities gave him a nice little bungalow with a small garden. Then one day the bungalow was empty. I was worried, they were elderly people, I was afraid something might have happened to them. Eventually someone told me they had gone back to their village near Prijedor. I went there and found them living in a freight container on a small plot of land. I couldn't believe my eyes and asked the husband why they had left such a nice bungalow to live in an uncomfortable, windowless container. He told me the container was in the place where his house had been before it was destroyed and that his place was here, at home, on his land.' This story told by Gordon Bacon, head of the International Commission for Missing Persons (ICMP) at Sarajevo, illustrates one of the reasons why refugees and displaced persons want to come back: deep attachment to their land of origin.

Aware of the importance of the return of refugees, the international community has made it a central feature of its policy. A whole section of the Dayton accords is devoted to it.[9] Considerable financial, juridical and political effort has been devoted to ensuring that the Dayton commitments in this matter become reality. The High Representative's office, the UN and the Organization for Security and Cooperation in Europe (OSCE) have for the first time established specific rules intended to speed the process. Billions of dollars have been lavished on return aid by international organizations, governments and NGOs. Without the support of the international community, returns to Prijedor would not have advanced so far. But even these efforts are not enough, as can be seen from the dispiriting figures for returned refugees at Srebrenica, Zvornik or Stolac, near Mostar.

It would thus appear that Prijedor has some specific characteristics. One of them is its geographical location. The town is in the north-west of the country, further from Serbia than Srebrenica and other eastern towns. The result is that Prijedor, willy-nilly, is centred more on Bosnia than on the territory for which Milošević wanted to retain the name Federal Republic of Yugoslavia, but which has been known as Serbia-Montenegro since February 2003. This means that non-Serb refugees tend to feel somewhat more at ease there.

A second reason can be found in the demographic structure of Prijedor. The town is surrounded by numerous villages many of which were mono-ethnic even before the war. Omarska was always overwhelmingly Serb and Kozarac almost entirely Muslim. A family that had been forced to flee persecution would probably feel unsafe if it found itself alone in a mainly Serb village. To settle in a place that has been destroyed, but where there are no potentially hostile neighbours, would seem a lot more reassuring. And of course fears of insecurity remain one of the principal obstacles to returning. It is noticeable around Prijedor that refugees started returning to the ethnically mixed areas much later and in much smaller numbers. In the town itself, where the population used to be divided more or less equally between Serbs and Muslims, the flow is hardly more than a trickle. 'There's a lot more tension in town than in the villages,' confirms Milan Glusac, the local (Serb) leader of the hamlet of Donja Vola on the left bank of the Sana.

A third possible explanation, also linked to refugees' concerns about security, 'consists of linking returns to the arrest of individuals accused of war crimes', suggests Mark Wheeler, Sarajevo director of the political analysis body International Crisis Group. As ICTY deputy prosecutor Graham Blewitt underlines, the number of arrests in the Prijedor region, controlled by British troops, is fairly satisfactory and anyway superior to the level in other zones (especially French and American ones). The first individuals accused by the ICTY were arrested in Prijedor: British special forces captured Milan Kovačević on 10 July 1997 and the former wartime police chief, Simo Drljača, was killed during the operation. In 1998 Miroslav Kvočka and Milojica Kos, believed to have been senior officers at Omarska, were locked up, and three others followed in 1999. Some of those accused, who had been living openly in Prijedor, now went underground and left the area, like Milomir Stakić who was nevertheless arrested later in Belgrade. The imprisonment of leading faces from the ethnic cleansing campaign in Prijedor has made the refugees feel considerably safer than they did in the days when, as Human Rights Watch notes, Simo Drljača who had been one of the principal executives of the ethnic cleansing was still (until his death) personally obstructing the return of refugees and displaced persons, by giving weapons to the local population so that it could threaten anyone who came back.

A survivor from Srebrenica, Emir Suljagić, gives the clearest idea of why these arrests are so important to the refugees. 'In Prijedor, people are coming back and picking up their lives because they feel safer knowing that their torturers are no longer physically present near their homes. The situation in Srebrenica is in flagrant contrast. The survivors are refusing to come back because up to now only two of the people responsible have been tried. A lot of people directly involved in the massacres are living there today without being disturbed.'[10]

The arrival of a 'moderate' mayor, Nada Ševo, at the town hall did help encourage returns. 'She lends her weight to our efforts, she's known to turn up for the opening ceremonies of new quarters, unlike her predecessors,' confirmed Nils Groute of THW. Nada Ševo had the courage to throw in her lot with largely Muslim parties to make Prjedor the 'town of return' and spread the theme abroad. 'There aren't many towns in Republika Srpska where you find a mayor who doesn't belong to the SDS, it means something,' an anglophone diplomat commented.

To all of this must be added the incredible dynamism of two Bosniak leaders, Muharem Murselović and Sead Jakupović, who have made a crucial contribution to the return of such large numbers of refugees. As the UNHCR points out, the refugees' organizational capacity and the courage of their leaders are 'essential elements' in promoting their return to difficult zones.[11] There is not the shadow of a doubt that the strategic team formed by these two men, one the mainspring, the other the political arm, has been one of the key elements in the return of refugees to Prijedor.

A Pragmatist and a Politician in Charge

'My name is Jakupović. I was born on 9 September 1954 in Prijedor.' Sead changes into second. To tell his story and explain his struggle to encourage the return of refugees, this blue-eyed man might have chosen the comfort of his own sitting room or a restaurant. Instead he has insisted on his old white Golf, so that he can show off 'his' achievements: the rebuilt houses and new schools on the left bank of the Sana, in places where people were still living in tents two years ago. Here is a man capable of covering 1,000 kilometres of Bosnian mountain roads in a single day to supply a cooperative set up by refugees with enough seed for the next harvest.

In the two-man team he forms with the inflexible Muharem Murselović, he is the pragmatist, the mechanic who carries out projects, assembles the finance and proudly displays the concrete results to the donors. At first sight he gives the impression of being an overworked manager in a booming enterprise. Getting a meeting with him feels like a miracle: his diary is crammed for weeks ahead. If you want to telephone him it is important to have his mobile number, which he changes regularly to avoid being uselessly distracted all day.

Sead Jakupović's hyperactivity is not deployed in the service of some traditional business, however. He is not exploring new markets or hunting for new acquisitions. He is working to facilitate the return of refugees by finding sponsors to finance reconstruction of houses, schools and power lines. Of course he makes good use of his pre-war experience as a manager at the Celpak cellulose and paper factory, one of the success stories of the local economy. He admits that even in those days he often worked until midnight to get everything done. Workaholism apart, his life had followed an ordinary course, divided between his managerial job at Celpak, obtained after studies in chemistry at Banja Luka, a part-time public job as a fire and explosives inspector and family life with his wife and son.

In 1992 this 'quiet' life fell to pieces. In May, a month after the seizure of the town by Serb nationalists, Jakupović realized that it would be a good idea to send his wife and son to a safer place. With the help of a Serb friend he organized their departure abroad, but decided that he himself would stay in Prijedor.

At the end of June a policeman and some soldiers took him to Omarska. Sead is voluble on his plans and achievements, but when he talks about the camp has to squeeze the words out, as if they cost him dear. The description of what he lived through comes in chopped-off phrases, in an uneven voice. 'You really cannot imagine what it was like. While I was there I promised myself two things. One was that I should have another child, and if it was a son he'd be called Ilis, after my cousin who died there. Then I decided that if I got out, I was going to help people from Prijedor to come back. I have to fight, because I saw how brutal and violent they were at Omarska. Everything I'm doing today is because of that.' Sead was reprieved from hell on 5 August 1992 and was transferred to Manjača. In December 1992 he was freed and given refugee status in Britain. He went to London and kept his first promise: young Ilis is twelve.

Sead Jakupović did not forget his second resolution. 'In April 1996 I came back to Sanski Most.' At that time it was still suicidal for a Bosnian Muslim or Croat to show his face in Prijedor. 'I offered my help at the town hall. It wasn't all that easy because I hadn't been a soldier in the war. But they took me in the end because I spoke English. It was an advantage in dealing with NGOs and international organizations.' In that stamping ground of the

SDA, the Muslim nationalist party, Sead's presence at the head of the body charged with reconstruction set people's teeth on edge. He took no notice and steadily refused to join a party he thought excessively nationalist. So the town hall lumbered him with an SDA official director who in practice, however, remained a mere figurehead. Sead plunged into the reconstruction of Sanski Most. 'The organizations would turn up saying: "We don't have much money" or else "Where can we give most usefully?" I showed them what the needs were and took everything available.' Meanwhile Sead had not forgotten that his real goal was to return to Prijedor in the still-hostile Republika Srpska.

By now his duo with Muharem Murselović was taking shape as the two men set up an aid association for returnees, Fondacija 98. Sead and Muharem had both passed through Omarska and then Manjača, followed by exile abroad, one in Germany and the other in Britain. But the paths that took them back into Bosnia were different.

Muharem, 58, returned in 1995 to join the Bosnia-Herzegovina army and help reconquer the territories acquired by the forces of Karadžić and Mladić. As a result he has the credibility combatants enjoy among the refugees. Sead only came back when the war was over. He sometimes gives the impression of trying to compensate for this 'belated' return with an unlimited commitment to encouraging the return of others. But the difference between the two men was to make them a marvellous team. Muharem earned the respect of Bosnian Muslims by surviving Omarska, but also by his decision to return as a soldier on the side of those forced to stay behind. This credit enabled him to get elected as deputy mayor in the first municipal elections in 1997: refugees abroad and in other parts of Bosnia were permitted to vote in their own communes, a measure imposed by the international community to prevent the ethnic divisions created by the war from taking permanent root.

Muharem Murselović thus became the political arm of the duo. He went to great lengths to attend all the important town hall meetings, at a time when the SDS mayor would not even let him know when they were due to take place.[12] He spends long hours discussing projects in the municipal council meetings held two or even three times a week, rushes from inauguration to inauguration, attends refugees' meetings, gives interviews to journalists, a prudent, rigorous man who knows how to advance his cause by means of a finely-tuned public discourse. He insists that the Serbs have a moral obligation to help with the return of refugees.

Sead Jakupović by contrast benefits from the absence of this same combatant's history. In a town to which a lot of Serbs fled from Sanski Most as Bosnia-Herzegovina's troops closed in on that town, he has a profile that makes him look more amenable to consensus, enabling him to operate in disparate circles and areas. Curious about everything, eager for new ideas, Sead Jakupović flits from project to project assembling funds, tracking down seed or agricultural machinery, lending a hand to help build a school. Passionate and pragmatic, he knows how to convince the 'internationals' with his enthusiasm and organizational flair.

'I turn up with fully-planned schemes for the international community people: here you are, bang! It's concrete and it works,' he confides, a bit maliciously. Without entering into the moral case for the return of refugees, he grabs a grant here, some materials or equipment there, convinced that concretizing the return in bricks and mortar will have the same effect in the long run.

Despite the differences between them – among other things Muharem is a member of a Muslim-labelled party led by Haris Silajdžić, while Sead belongs to the multi-ethnic SDP – both men know that they share a common goal: to sweep away Radovan Karadžić's strategy by making the pre-war populations come back.

'By putting us in camps, the nationalist Serbs were telling us: "This is the last time we're going to see you here in Prijedor." So today I have to work against the ethnic cleansing and against the nationalists, for myself of course, but also for all the people who are against nationalism,' Muharem says. In 1998, their foundation began to register requests to return, then got the refugees to issue documents demanding the legal return of their properties or requesting aid for reconstruction. The reconquest was under way.

'We went and talked to Dorcas Aid, THW, Caritas and the Norwegian Refugee Council to see what they could do. Then, wham! the Prijedor town hall, still run by an SDS member, came up with a plan for the return of refugees with very little in it for Muslims,' Sead recounts. 'I said to myself, You've got to fight, go and see people, forge connections, talk to them and negotiate. I took them to see empty houses, waste land where it would be possible to build. I established some refugees in tents, then after that I showed everything to the NGOs.' In 1998 the first building was finished in Kozarac. Sead and Muharem wanted to prove that it was possible to live there permanently. 'We spent the first night there with Muharem Murselović and it was really dangerous. Actually I didn't sleep much, because there were a whole lot of Serbs from Bosanska and Croatia all around the building... Doing that, like putting up tents, was a way of putting pressure on the international community, because they were terribly slow. In fact they laughed at what we were doing and spent all their time making jokes.'

Muharem and Sead moved into another site, the left bank, a zone thought more dangerous because of the mixed nature of the pre-war population. 'We said to the refugees: "If you go and live over there we'll give you food, drink, necessities and fuel. It's your decision. We won't decide for you. But if you do it, we'll support you." That's what we told them, Muharem Murselović and I. They knew that at first they'd be living in collection centres until they could get their land back. They did it.'

By 6 June 1999 there were seven hundred people in the collection centres, the school was partially refurbished and tents were pitched on patches of waste land. Sead contacted the international organizations and offered to start the building work with the refugees to obtain a donation to pay for the next stage. Sead and Muharem beseiged the town hall to get help, harassed the American governmental organisation USAID to divert some of the food destined for Sanski Most to the refugees' collection centres. 'The sight of a truckload of food arriving was really important to those people. The UNHCR donated bedding and tents. We got a lot of help from international organizations, I'd like to mention them all because what they did added up to an enormous amount. Sometimes Serbs would drive by in cars and insult us, they called us ragheads and told us to go back where we'd come from.'

Large-scale reconstruction began in the spring of 2000. For the first time since 1992 Prijedor was being run by a mayor who was not an SDS member, Nada Ševo. Muharem Murselović was elected chairman of the municipal assembly, a body which is supposed to debate all decisions of the town hall. He became in effect the local second in command.

Fondacija 98 has become unavoidable on both political and communal levels. 'The refugees have to go through them,' says Andrew Gilbert, an anthropology student researching this subject in Prijedor. A full-scale lobby in the service of the return of refugees has established itself and controls this whole question in Prijedor. Any finance that the Fondacija 98 organization cannot wring out of the town hall can be found among the international organizations. 'In 2001, the municipality gave nearly 20,000 deutschmarks for electricity in Kozarac and Rakovčani. They didn't give it, we dragged it out of them. It was nothing, it's a small sum. The town hall gives virtually nothing for returning refugees. Just as well we've got good relations with the international community,' Sead says. He is enough of a diplomat to be aware of the jealousy this aid arouses among some Serbs. 'I notice it,' he observes soberly. 'So I arrange sometimes, when I've got some seed for example, to give some to the Serb farmers in the village too, it prevents friction.' Today some thousands of refugees have returned to Prijedor. In his native village of Ćela, renamed Petrovo by the Serbs, Sead gestures towards the new houses, close to the decapitated mosque whose minaret still lies in a nearby field.

A new challenge is looming: persuading these refugees to stay on when the public sector is reluctant to employ them and the scanty private sector is largely in the hands of the SDS. 'We're going to do everything to change things, find loans, start projects,' Sead promises.

By way of illustration he mentions the case of a Bosniak businessman established in Kozarac, a camp survivor who returned there in 1998. He now owns a service station and a building firm and employs sixty people. 'One day in 1997 he telephoned me from Switzerland. I said to him: "What do you think you're doing on your sofa in Switzerland, all cosy and quiet with your little family? You'd do better to come back here and invest." One has to try and make people stick. They need to know, the ones who come back, that they won't be alone in their struggle. That we'll be there beside them fighting for a new future. I believe in the future, I have hope.' Sead's optimism is far from universal in Prijedor where a lot of refugees still hesitate to contemplate a future in a town that is still divided and economically crippled. But it is real enough in his case. 'Prijedor is the breaking point of Republika Srpska's spinal column,' Jakupović says. 'They (the nationalists) still can't quite believe it. They're really surprised. But it's already too late, it's all over. It's happened over the last two years. No one would have believed that lights and people would ever return to the hills on the left bank – to Kozarac, to Ćela, to Trnopolje – in just two years.'

Sead stops for a moment. The car is parked on one of the hills on the left bank. Rebuilt houses, the school, the dispensary are all in view. 'When I see that I feel immense pride,' he says, his voice betraying heartfelt emotion. 'Sometimes in the evening, I go on the roof of my building in Prijedor. I can see from there the street lighting on the hills of the left bank. There wasn't any before the war. It's the same at Kozarac. It's a peaceful revenge.'

NINE

Expecting Words, Finding Bodies

'We Can Look at Ourselves in the Mirror'

Once back in Prijedor, survivors are confronted on a daily basis with the denial or belittlement of their sufferings. This only serves to intensify the duty to remember. How, they ask repeatedly, can a normal life be rebuilt on a lie; how can the denial of those sufferings and humiliations be tolerated? Some scenes of terror in the camps 'speak of madness', as Élie Wiesel points out.[1] 'The soldier assassins of Radovan Karadžić, their expressions gleeful and sneering, stop at nothing to dehumanize their prisoners,' he adds.

However, not all who escaped are prey to vengeful feelings. Ibrahim Kulielović, a former café owner who was interned at Trnopolje for eighty days and lost his brother during the war, explains why he has no wish to give his torturers a taste of their own medicine. 'Today I can tell myself that we, the non-Serbs of Prijedor, can look at ourselves in the mirror and declare that we stayed clean. I can tell myself that I committed no atrocities and at the very least I can say anywhere with pride that I'm a Bosniak,' he says, taking a rest from bricklaying as he rebuilds his house demolished during the war.

Brian Phillips, a Briton working for Amnesty International who helped the Omarska survivor Kemal Pervanić to write about his experience in the camps, has a similar story: 'One day as we worked together on the book, I asked Kemal what he would say today to some of those former schoolmates who had stood guard over him at Omarska were he to meet them face to face. With startling frankness, he told me that in his darkest moments – when he thinks of those who destroyed his home and his world and the lives of so many relatives and friends – he sometimes imagines what it would be like to murder them in turn. He told me, "I can actually see myself killing them – I watch myself doing it – and I feel nothing as I prepare to do it, or while I am doing it, or after the killing is done. But then… I realize that I do not *need* to do this – thet I do not *want* to do this – that in doing this, I would lose myself completely – lose everything that I am… And then, I just feel privileged".'[2]

This lack of desire for vengeance may seem surprising. But it demands respect.

Despite the divisive burden of the recent past Prijedor has been relatively untouched by the thrust of Bosnian Muslim nationalism. The SDA is almost non-existent except in Kozarac. The two leading figures of the Bosniak community, Muharem Murselović and Sead Jakupović, have remained moderate and convinced of the need to reconstruct a multi-ethnic society. Murselović often recalls that moderate Serbs were also victimized by the nationalists in 1992, and Sead is an active member of the multi-ethnic SDP. 'It's a bit of luck for Prijedor, not having nationalists leading the refugees,' observed Annalisa Tomasi, the Italian who headed the Agency for Local Democracy in Prijedor until the end of 2003.

But although they may not thirst for vengeance in the eye-for-eye and tooth-for-tooth sense, the survivors are quite keen to see their sufferings acknowledged, especially in Prijedor. They do not share the view that the easing of the economic situation can serve as the sole basis for living together in a satisfactory way. The dark chapter of the war and the camps ought not to be forgotten, they insist. 'That would hurt me too much. I can't imagine it,' Nusreta Sivac explains. Recognition of their sufferings would give the survivors some sense that justice was being done, a sort of dressing on wounds open for ever. It would represent the defeat of those counting on forgetfulness to mask their crimes. It would be a sign, too, that the Serb population is no longer willing to sink into that sort of collective insanity: one who recognizes the seriousness of a crime shows that he does not wish to see it repeated.

People have different ways of expressing this desire for acknowledgement. Some, like the Trnopolje survivor Nisad, would like a commemorative sign to identify the sites of the camps. 'I get upset when I see the monument to Serb war victims at Trnopolje. We ought to have one too,' he tells us in a café in Kozarac, a few steps from his just-rebuilt house. A former building technician aged forty-nine, the father of three daughters, he still lives at Nantes in France but would like to return to Prijedor soon. He tells us that his Serb neighbour cannot look him in the eye when they meet. 'During the war he was a bit extremist. It's up to him to talk about it, to recognize his errors and his crimes,' Nisad says. 'There are still too many taboos, people ought to know the truth.'

'A large number of Bosnian Serbs claim that nothing happened. There's a big propaganda effort. I'd very much like the Serbs of Prijedor to realize that crimes were committed on the local level,' Muharem Murselović says. 'No one, not a single one of my former Serb colleagues, has ever said they were sorry about what happened to me at Omarska. Oh, there are plenty of things they do want to talk about, but not that!' Nusreta says bitterly.

Sead Jakupović, too, notes that not a single Serb has ever said a straight 'sorry' to him for anything that happened, for the camps, for exile, for the war. 'That's why the Stakić trial is important, to remind people of all that. People are going to look at what happened, the story's going to be explained, the facts established,' he insists. 'Only then might it really be possible to envisage what comes next, and turn the page.'

The real hope of hundreds of survivors is that the truth be told so that real reconciliation becomes possible. Everyone has their own way of trying to bring this about. 'Just coming back is enough to confront your former neighbours with the past. You're there, so you can say what happened. It's no longer quite so easy to forget,' reasons Ibrahim Beglerbegović. Whether to talk openly or keep quiet to avoid putting themselves in danger is one dilemma that haunts many of the survivors of Omarska, Keraterm and Trnopolje. 'If I talk I'll be more exposed, more vulnerable,' explains the Bosniak lawyer Jadranka Cigelj, who was interned at Omarska and raped by the camp commandant, Željko Mejakić. But the imperative to remember tends to outweigh the fear. 'If the lion never tells his story, the world will believe the hunter's version,' runs an African proverb. If the survivors and refugees of Prijedor say nothing, the truth of the camps will be erased, the campaign of denial by the local authorities will replace the reality with a new version of the 1992 events.

Nusreta and the other women who survived Omarska decided, ten years after the war, to go back to the camp to commemorate the five who did not survive their detention. During a conference at Kozarac with representatives of foreign women's organizations, they asked the international police and the local authorities for permission to enter Omarska. The visit took place in May 2002. 'I was able to enter the room where I was detained at Omarska for the first time in ten years,' Nusreta confides. 'We stayed for nearly two hours. We left five roses for the five women who didn't survive. One of their mothers came with us, just to see the place where her daughter had died. In front of the White House, we laid wreaths of flowers. It was very painful, but in a sense I felt I was lucky, I felt happy to be able at last to go to that place after so long. We ought to have a memorial,' Nusreta adds. When we visited the place that September, one of the current Omarska security guards claimed never to have heard of any visit by survivors, but admitted later that there had been some sort of incident involving 'a few lost souls'.

Others, like Rezak Hukanović and Kemal Pervanić, decided to set their experiences down on paper. 'Kemal's aspiration in writing this book – in a language he scarcely knew six years ago – were never self-consciously literary, but moral. Like Primo Levi, he emerged from his imprisonment determined to tell the truth about what he had known in the grim, unsparing universe of the camps,' notes Brian Phillips in the foreword to Kemal Pervanić's book. Many others reserve their accounts for the family circle, telling their children what had happened to them. 'They ought to know so that they won't forget, but also to make sure that in twenty or thirty years' time people won't be able to manipulate the past to start another war like they started that one,' explains Ibrahim Kulielović.

And of course some survivors go to The Hague to give evidence before the ICTY. Nusreta's description to the court of her experiences at Omarska went on for three days. 'I was very ill afterwards, stress for sure. I was in hospital for several weeks. But if I'm called to give evidence again, I'll go.' Ibrahim Beglerbegović agrees emphatically: 'It's a moral duty to go to The Hague.' However disillusioned many of them may be, all are aware that the ICTY is their only platform, the one place where their word is not only listened to but used to administer justice. Without the ICTY Simo Drljača, Milomir Stakić and Duško Tadić would still be walking the streets of Prijedor. And justice, for the victims, is an essential precondition for a lasting peace, not just in the region but in their own hearts as well.

The Omnipresent Missing

Jasminka is one of those who cannot draw a line under the past and start looking to the future. Less perhaps than any other Prijedor refugee. Even with the best will in the world she could not turn the page and forget, this small blonde urchin-cropped woman. At the age of thirty-two Jasminka Kadirić is living with twenty-two ghosts, twenty-two registered missing: a brother, a husband, uncles, cousins of whom the best remaining trace is a single photo. And a fleeting entry in a white book with red edges. It contains the doleful register of all the individuals from the municipality of Prijedor of whom no trace could be found after the war. In it are listed the names of three thousand two hundred and twenty-seven individuals, their date of birth and the date when they were last seen, in some cases the place. Jasminka has this book with her at all times. She looks at it constantly, pausing on a face and falling into silent thought, but unable to lay the book aside.

Her husband vanished in 1992, at the beginning of the war. The Bosnian Serbs had just launched a brutal attack on the villages round Prijedor, killing several hundred civilians. Among their objectives was Rizvanovići, Jasminka's village, a peaceful little place among the hills. 'I saw my husband for the last time one Thursday. My son was sleeping. My husband didn't tell me anything but when he got to the door he said: "Take care of the baby." '³

She has not seen her husband since. There is no grave where she can mourn his death and she does not even know where his body is. For thirteen years now, all her attempts to discover the truth have failed. When she arrived in Germany as a refugee, after passing through Trnopolje and a long and meandering detour through Bosnia, Croatia and then Slovenia, Jasminka told herself that the war, still raging, would hamper any attempt to find anything out. Her son clung to a stubborn belief that his father was waiting for them back in Bosnia. But their return in 1998 was a disappointment. No father was there to meet them.

Jasminka and her sister did manage, on the other hand, to dig up from a patch of paddock below their house three bodies that were still recognizable: those of their father and two uncles, hastily buried in July 1992 just before the troops left the village. Further searches were carried out in the wild surrounding landscape. In the neighbouring villages, corpses were unearthed in the foundations of houses, lying in undergrowth, thrown down wells. Mass graves containing the remains of several hundred people were discovered nearby. The weeks passed, but there was no news for Jasminka and her son: not a single discovery or identification to enable them to start the work of mourning. 'When the exhumations began, my son told himself his father's body would be found. Later he believed I'd get all sorts of information from my meetings with other families of missing persons. All in vain,' she says.

'Of course the possibility exists that not all the bodies will be found.' Jasminka has reconciled herself to this persistent thought. But she still resists any idea of giving up. With her childhood friend Jasminka Dedić she has gathered the families of missing persons in the region together in an association called Bridges of Friendship.

The fact is that this question of missing persons is particularly pressing in Prijedor. Although, according to the local associations, 3227 people were registered as missing after the war, nine years after the end of the conflict the Federal Commission for missing persons states that 977 individuals are still registered as missing, 1990 bodies have been exhumed and of these, 419 have been identified through their DNA.

Most of the identifications were visual, based on recognition of a garment, identity document or other possession found on the body; a few were identified using DNA analysis. This technique which compares characteristics of tissue taken from a body or skeleton with a blood sample from a living presumed or possible relation produces results that are 'revolutionary and 99 per cent accurate' according to the International Commission for Missing Persons (ICMP) set up in 1996. It is most effective in preventing mistaken identifications, a possibility that haunts everyone concerned. And for very good reasons: the ICMP anthropologist Richard Harrington estimates that up to 50 per cent of the identifications made in the Balkans between 1995 and 2001 may be incorrect. This means that families may have buried strangers believing them to be one of their own members. 'The earlier identifications were made from a garment, a shoe or some other object,' Harrington explains. 'But we know that people used to exchange or sell their clothes, or take them from people who were already dead. When you see a family member setting off for work or school in the morning, you don't make a special effort to note what they're wearing on the assumption it's the last time you're seeing them. So ten years after the event, it's quite hard to remember a garment or other object.'

An ICTY investigator confirms this. 'On one of the bodies found in a mass grave near Prijedor, we found a wallet containing a miners' union membership card. The card had been issued to a male individual but when the autopsy was carried out the body turned out to be that of a woman. Fortunately, identification is not based solely on recovered identity documents but essentially on DNA analyses.' This is the reason why Richard Harrington has become an apostle for the method. However, it is time-consuming and requires political will, expert staff and enormous financial means, which the ICMP does not have. A bone fragment analysis alone costs about $300 (roughly equivalent to 300 Euros), and comparisons with other samples can take months or years before a positive identification is made. This helps to explain why some of the bodies found at Prijedor have not yet been identified.

Moreover, no trace has yet been found of 1,527 missing persons from the region.[4] 'You have to bear in mind that for every missing person, there's a wife or children or parents who are waiting and hoping every day for news, which makes the whole problem even more enormous for the whole of society,' says the head of the ICMP in Bosnia-Herzegovina, Gordon Bacon. Amor Masović, chairman of the Federal Commission for missing persons, makes a quick calculation that demonstrates the scale of the problem: 'I estimate that in the whole of Bosnia, nearly five hundred thousand living people are looking for at least one of their relations.' The ICMP estimates that in Bosnia-Herzegovina as a whole, the number of people of whom there has been no trace since the war of 1992-5 is about 25,000.

So some hundreds of thousands of others, like Jasminka, are waiting to find out what happened. Most believe that the man or woman of whom they can find no trace is dead, but they want to know for certain. They want to bury them honourably, with due ceremony. 'One day, I had to tell a mother that her son's body had just been identified. When she heard the news, she began to smile with relief. She told me she would at last be able to give him a decent burial and could stop thinking he was just in a hole somewhere. "I'll be able to do my mourning and start to live again," she said,' recounts Gordon Bacon.

All over the world, efforts to find missing persons come up against the reluctance of governments or local authorities to admit anything on the subject. For the discovery of a mass grave may well constitute proof that atrocities have been committed, something the leaderships in question often wish to deny. The problem certainly affects Bosnia-Herzegovina, and Prijedor in particular. The town hall has nothing to say on the subject of missing persons. It is relatively easy to maintain this silence as the local morgue is in Sanski Most, out of sight of the town's inhabitants.

The mayor, Nada Ševo, has not attended any of the ceremonies of remembrance organized by associations of missing persons' families. And in this matter the attitude of the local authorities, and of the government, can make a crucial difference, especially in persuading people who know where bodies are buried to give information. 'The main problem is knowing where to dig to find common graves, which are often hidden in out-of-the-way places that are hard to get to,' summarizes Jasmin Odobašić, deputy chairman of the Federal Commission for missing persons. In the case of Prijedor only the Serbs know where the graves are, and quite apart from their reluctance and fear, the importance of this matter is played down by local officials. 'People are afraid to give this information. You have to bear in mind that this sort of detail is only known to a limited number of people. If a mass grave is discovered, all eyes then turn to them,' explains an ICTY investigator.

So the information comes in a drop at a time. Some Serbs end by talking to ICTY investigators for fear of being accused. Others are not ashamed to demand money for telling what they know. One Serb even offered to identify the location of a mass grave near Prijedor if he was promised 100 deutschmarks for every body exhumed. 'Sometimes a Serb has an attack of conscience on his deathbed,' notes Jasmin Odobašić. 'Usually, though, we get information when people are drinking. That's when their tongues loosen. And at times like that there's always a witness who comes and tells us afterwards.'

Information of this sort has led to the discovery of several large mass graves in the Prijedor area. Indeed it is Prijedor's macabre privilege to be the site of one of the biggest to be found in Bosnia: three hundred and seventy-two bodies were uncovered at Jakarina Kos, near the Ljubija iron mine, in September 2001. 'I'd known there was a mass grave there since 1998. People who witnessed the bodies being covered up had shown it to me,' Odobašić recounts. 'But for security reasons I had to wait more than three years.'

In the past, the lack of security at some sites hampered searches and exhumations. Search teams were sometimes faced with the hostility of local inhabitants or certain nationalists, who would seek to prevent them from working. Today the situation has improved. SFOR[5] and the police are present in sufficient numbers to guard the locations and keep them secure. 'At one time we had the "protection" of the local police, one of whose officers had taken part in the exactions at Omarska,' recalls Jasmin Odobašić, who coordinated most of the searches in Prijedor. While trying to find a mass grave only vaguely located, one ICTY investigator discovered, by the simple expedient of getting his interpreter to listen to them, that the police supposed to be protecting the search knew that the site was really somewhere else but had, obviously, no intention of saying so.

The deputy chairman of the Commission for missing persons made a film on the exposure of the mass grave at Jakarina Kos, a titanic task that lasted thirty-two days. On an open hillside, in bucolic surroundings, a raw earth slope eighty-five metres high. 'The bodies were tipped down the slope, then a fire was made into which dynamite was thrown to destroy the bodies. Finally six metres of earth was put on top of the victims to hide them,' Jasmin Odobašić says. 'It shows how horrible the crimes were. The Serb forces didn't hesitate to blow up whole chunks of land to hide the bodies,' adds an ICTY investigator present during the exhumation.

In the light of this experience, Jasmin Odobašić has become aware of the lengthy task confronting his team and its successors. 'Near Mostar we found the bodies of fifty-six soldiers, German ones, there since the Second World War,' he says to give some idea of the scale of the problem. For the survivors, the wait promises to be a long one. The delays are causing growing resentment on all sides. In Prijedor, the families and friends of missing persons are becoming exhausted and angry, convinced that they are being sidelined. 'Every day that passes without one of their missing friends being found seems an intolerable delay,' Masović explains, before admitting tacitly that there are failings in the system. 'I often see families from Prijedor who tell me they're being forgotten. And it's true that by comparison with Srebrenica, Prijedor isn't well known. If you go to New York, Paris or anywhere and ask where Prijedor is, no one will be able to answer. It isn't like that with Srebrenica. There's a neglect of Prijedor and the local missing persons organizations on the part of the international community, that's certain. But all the same, we've exhumed nearly seventeen hundred bodies in the neighbourhood. There are a lot of towns in Bosnia where not a single body has yet been found.' A number of ICTY investigators admit privately that they understand the frustration felt by victims, who see it as unfair that some places are investigated while others seem to be abandoned or ignored.

For Jasminka, though, the exhumations have still brought no news, and the wait goes on. Little by little, as lines of inquiry are abandoned and promises not kept, she is falling prey to despair and bitterness. Arguments in favour of turning the page and no longer looking to the past strike her as insulting. She needs people to admit the past and reveal where the common graves and hastily buried bodies are, for the bodies of her husband and brother may be down one of those gullies or in one of those mass graves. She knows she will not be able to resume normal life until she has found them.

'Uncertainty over the fate of a loved individual is one of the major obstacles to the reconstruction of civil society and to reconciliation in Bosnia,' insist all those who specialize in this issue. The pain and suffering endured by the relations of missing persons resemble 'slow mental torture', states the UN Commission for Human Rights in a document on this question.[6] Amnesty International notes that more than thirty countries in the world are affected by the problem of disappearances. Argentinian families are still searching for members missing since the military dictatorship, Cypriot Greeks and Turks are unable to find the burial places of their relations and friends, the families of Spanish Republicans buried in mass graves during the 1930s are still seeking the bodies in vain: this is a problem that affects all cultures and all levels of society.

Jasminka's case shows that reconstructing the economy is not sufficient to heal the wounds of the missing persons' families. Having to earn her entire living – until an individual is officially pronounced dead, his relations have no right to any pension – she has set up a small agricultural cooperative with the aid of several NGOs. In their greenhouses the village women grow peppers, onions, tomatoes and other vegetables which they sell all year round.

The project has been a great success, but Jasminka insists that 'I'd still give every penny I have for just one thing: to know where my people are.'

That may take some time. After a number of threats and an assault on her son, Jasminka took him back to France early in 2004. They have become refugees again. They do not know how soon they will be returning to live in Prijedor.

PART FOUR

A Town's Past Faces Judgement

If we neither punish nor blame those who do evil we are protecting their barbaric age and shaking the foundations of justice for the generations to come.

Alexander Solzhenitsyn, *The Gulag Archipelago*

The Hague, Netherlands, 2 November 2001. Five men dressed in smart suits are waiting on the bench reserved for the accused in one of the ultra-modern hearing rooms of the Internationl Criminal Tribunal for former Yugoslavia, more than two thousand kilometres from Prijedor.

First in line, with brown hair untidily arranged in a vague pudding basin cut and a heavily-lined brow, is Miroslav Kvočka, forty-four, a former policeman from the village of Omarska. A good family man, his lawyers will insist, with two children and a Bosnian Muslim wife. Kvočka was deputy commandant of Omarska camp from 27 May to 30 June 1992. He is accused of crimes against humanity and war crimes, for having done nothing to prevent the torture and diverse persecutions inflicted on the prisoners although he had enough authority to stop them. While awaiting the verdict he fiddles nervously with his microphone lead and sometimes runs his hand over his forehead, then subsides into impassive calm.

Next to him sits a former colleague from Omarska police station, Mladen Radić: forty-nine years old, with grizzled hair, yellowish complexion and a morose scowl, Radic fixes the hearing room with an empty stare. With an incipient pot belly under his black suit, he looks the stereotype of a fussy communist petty official. Mladen Radić is being tried for having led the most violent team of guards at Omarska.

Next to him sits Zoran Žigić. Short jet-black hair, slim build accentuated by a well-cut black suit, rectangular face with dark eyes and finely-cut features, he is a man who cultivates a seducer's air. Forty-three years old and a former waiter, he appears here today accused of acts of torture, murder and inhuman treatment. He liked to drive over to Omarska, Keraterm or Trnopolje to torture his victims, his indictment specifies.

Another waiter, Milojica Kos, aged thirty-eight, appears in a light-coloured suit. Thin, with an aquiline nose and dishevelled brown hair, he seems more anxious than his companions. The last man on the accused bench, the oldest of the five, Dragoljub Prčac, waits impassively. A former technician working for the scientific police, now aged sixty-four, he had not resisted when asked to emerge from retirement to work at the camp.

All well-groomed and closely shaved; the accused sitting on their bench are five family men. They are not what one might imagine, these 'war criminals', they are not obvious bestial monsters of inhumanity. On the contrary, they had been normal people, long-time residents of Prijedor. 'I knew... Miroslav Kvočka, Mladen Radić and Željko Meakić, three policemen who worked at the police station which was on the other side of the road, a few metres below the school. I could never imagine that all these men would one day embody my worst fears,'[1] recalls Kemal Pervanić, one of the survivors of Omarska. The five men deny any part in the crimes and are pleading not guilty.

It is a little after three o'clock when a court official announces: 'All rise.' The three ICTY judges make their entrance in long red and black robes. They settle slowly behind their desks, on a podium that faces the public and closes the U shape formed by the benches for the accused and their lawyers on one side and the prosecutors on the other. With its spotless walls, cold, bright, white artificial lighting to compensate for the absence of windows and computer screens sprouting from every tabletop, the hearing room is resolutely and self-consciously modern. Behind the accused, a sheet of tinted plate glass covers the front of the interpreters' booths as the translators prepare to transmit the proceedings in the tribunal's three official languages, English, Serbo-Croat and French.

The public seats, separated from the courtroom proper by an armoured glass screen, are packed. The audience includes a lot of journalists and people working with the tribunal, but few victims and not many friends of the accused. In French tinged with a slight Portuguese accent, Judge Almiro Rodrigues starts to speak.

'Injustice anywhere is a threat to justice everywhere, in the fine expression coined by Martin Luther King. It is with that maxim in mind and in the hope of averting that threat that the chamber today passes judgement,' he says. The voice is quiet but firm. With his greying hair, bushy beard and thick spectacles the Portuguese judge resembles a village schoolmaster: he seems imbued with that desire to instruct. While some magistrates might be content to read out a dry, highly technical summary of their conclusions, Almiro Rodrigues tries to illuminate the universal aspect of the case, to reach the whole of the audience. He puts it back in context, recalls in passing the existence of a 'massive and systematic assault directed against the Muslim and Croat civilian population in the municipality of Prijedor' by Serb forces. The camps were one of the components of this attack. And firmly contradicting the reading of events now favoured by Serb leaderships, he affirms once again that he must 'refer not to interview or assembly centres but actual camps … the product of a deliberate policy aimed at imposing a system of discrimination on the non-Serb populations of Prijedor.'

At length and in detail, he describes the inhuman conditions, the ill-treatment, the rape of women prisoners, the dysentery, the torture, the bloodstained walls and the claimed ignorance of the accused. 'Men howl in agony. Not one of the accused hears their cries. Men are savagely beaten: when the women have to clean up, they see bloodstains or bits of human residue. The accused see nothing,' Judge Rodrigues says. He speaks the last sentence emphatically and looks fixedly at the men being tried.

The five men are listening, serious-faced. They are not laughing up their sleeves now, as they have in previous hearings. Almiro Rodrigues goes on to recall the exactions in the White House. 'The corpses brought out of it have open skull wounds, severed joints, cut throats. Some victims have been finished off with a bullet. The accused hear nothing, see nothing, do nothing.'

A silence has descended on the public benches. Some eyes have tears in them, and jaws are clamped tight shut. In the entrance hall of the Tribunal, where the hearings are transmitted live on closed circuit television, the usual buzz of conversation and the busy movement of staff and journalists have ceased. People are standing still, eyes fixed on the screens, hanging on the judge's words.

Now he is recalling that although the five men cannot be regarded as the originators of the system of persecution, they were one of its mechanisms. He asks the accused to stand, one at a time. 'Mr Kvočka, you are not a petty official at the very bottom of the scale who could not influence the course of events in any way. The evidence and proofs presented to the hearing show that you were the right arm of the camp commandant. You could intervene to stop the ill-treatment of a detainee but you took no meaningful action to that end. The chamber finds you guilty of the crime against humanity of persecutions and of the war crimes of murder and torture, and sentences you to seven years of prison.' Miroslav Kvočka remains stonily impassive.

Next to stand is his coaccused, Milojica Kos. 'You were no mere link in the chain, turning passively along with the wheel,' Judge Rodrigues states. 'You were a strong link and you did not hesitate when the occasion arose to contribute actively to the violence and terror in the camp. The chamber sentences you to six years of prison.'

Now it is Mladen Radić's turn. 'You had a reputation, as leader of the most violent team. Several detainees died from blows inflicted by guards in your team. And you did virtually nothing to prevent your guards from committing these acts of violence. Apart from that, you had a wholly inexcusable attitude to a number of women detained at Omarska. You subjected them to indecent assault. You raped… The chamber sentences you to twenty years of imprisonment.'

'Mr Žigić, you like using force, you like to inflict pain, you enjoyed driving detainees to the limit of their capacity to endure suffering. You enjoyed humiliating people too, forcing detainees to lap water from the ground like dogs or to drink their own blood. The chamber finds you guilty of the crime against humanity of persecutions and of the war crimes of murder, torture and cruel treatment, and sentences you to twenty-five years of imprisonment.' Dragoljub Prčac got five years.

The hearing was adjourned. Judgement had just been pronounced on one of the worst episodes of the war in Bosnia-Herzegovina. Journalists hurl themselves on their computers and telephones to announce the news. The verdicts on the Prijedor five go flashing across the entire world. From Tokyo to Quito via Paris and New York, the next day's press devotes many column-inches to this decision of international justice.

Just one town remains in ignorance: Prijedor, where the crimes were committed. The local radio and television are going to give the story a wide berth, and so is the local weekly. The Republika Srpska television station does not yet have its special programme on ICTY proceedings. The local leadership tiptoes away from a subject that would cast doubt on the truncated, inverted version of the history of the 1992 events that it chooses to maintain.

Nevertheless, the sentencing of the Omarska five has been one of the defining acts of a tribunal whose creation was originally greeted with scepticism and condescension.

TEN

The ICTY, a Birth Greeted with Indifference

When the United Nations Security Council adopted Resolution 808 creating the International Criminal Tribunal for former Yugoslavia on 22 February 1993, the impression given was that the new court represented a sort of *trompe-l'œil* justice, essentially intended to appease public opinion in Europe and the United States.

'No Address, No Offices and No Standing'

Although Western governments and the UN contrived to keep the disquieting reports they were getting on human rights abuses in Bosnia under wraps for several months, the images of skin-and-bone detainees at Omarska camp, broadcast worldwide on television in the summer of 1992, made the citizens of Europe and America sit up and take notice. Opinion was disturbed by the reappearance of detention camps in Europe and the brutal ethnic cleansing policy implemented by the Bosnian Serb leaders Radovan Karadžić and Ratko Mladić, with the support and inspiration of the man who was then still only president of Serbia, Slobodan Milošević.

The international press followed in close detail the barbaric siege of Sarajevo with its constant stream of dead civilians. Accounts of mass deportations of non-Serb populations were coming in increasing numbers from north-western and eastern parts of Bosnia. Faced with the sort of atrocities not seen in Europe since the end of the Second World War, western citizens could no longer understand why their governments were doing nothing to stop the barbarity.

Wedged in their tangles of internal contradictions and preoccupied with their electoral strategies, the American and European leaderships could find no adequate response. The UN did send some peacekeeping troops, but their mandate was so restricted that they could only respond if directly attacked, being otherwise held in a posture of paralysed neutrality. Just one example will illustrate the pathetic limitations of that peace mission: in Sarajevo, when the hospital ran out of blood to treat the dozens of people wounded by Serb shelling from the hills that surround the city, the UN troops were not authorized to give their own blood. That would have amounted to taking sides between the warring parties, the UN decided, forgetting that the victims were civilians and that Sarajevo, even during the siege, continued to be inhabited by Muslims, Serbs and Croats.

It was in this context of reawakening public opinion, with the ceasefires negotiated by international mediators being constantly violated, that the western governments opted for an International Criminal Tribunal. The French and the Americans even squabbled over who had thought of it first, both aware that this court could help get them off the hook with public opinion.

'In the mind of Roland Dumas (then French foreign minister), the proposed tribunal is seen both as a means of reducing anxiety for French public opinion and as political insurance against possible accusations of complicity after the war,'[1] writes the journalist Pierre Hazan. As if in illustration of the two-faced game being played by western governments and the UN, when the judges arrived at The Hague for the inaugural sitting on 17 November 1993 they noticed that no budget had been allocated for the ICTY, although it was supposed to 'provide justice for the victims of the conflicts in former Yugoslavia, prevent further violations of humanitarian law, work towards reconciliation and discourage any attempt at revisionism'.

'We had no address, no offices, no legal status, no logistics, not even a prosecutor,' recalls the French judge Claude Jorda. Then as at several crucial later junctures, the doggedness of some of its members was to save the ICTY. A brilliant jurist and fervent militant for human rights, the Italian magistrate Antonio Cassese, presided over the ICTY's destiny and was not going to give up easily. He gave western officials a taste of the lash by indicating that in the absence of supplementary means the judges would pack their bags, having no intention of serving as cover for the international community's political impotence.

Eighteen months after its creation, in July 1994, the ICTY was finally given a prosecutor in the person of Richard Goldstone. A judge by training from South Africa, he had worked alongside Archbishop Desmond Tutu in the Truth and Reconciliation Commission. In the meantime, the judges had written a code of procedure based broadly on the Anglo-Saxon model, but tinged with elements of (Latin) continental law. The tribunal had found premises in a V-shaped building west of The Hague. The first indictments were served.

The first individual charged by the ICTY, in November 1994, was Dragan Nikolić, a Bosnian Serb. He was accused of crimes against humanity for exactions committed at the Susica detention camp, in eastern Bosnia. Soon afterwards, on 13 February 1995, another Bosnian Serb, Duško Tadić from the village of Kozarac, was charged with crimes against humanity and war crimes for his role at Omarska.

In July 1995, the Srebrenica massacre cruelly exposed the limitations of the ICTY and the international community's fake commitments. Bosnian Serb forces took the enclave, officially under UN protection, on 11 July. In the days that followed, Ratko Mladić's forces separated the men from the women and children before the eyes of Dutch UN troops. These troops did not oppose the Serb forces and turned out to be unable to protect the refugees. More than seven thousand Muslims were killed over the next few days and buried in mass graves around Srebrenica. 'We failed to prevent a recurrence: Srebrenica happened two years after the creation of the Tribunal,' noted the former chairman of the ICTY, Claude Jorda,[2] rather bitterly. However, by assigning this task of dissuasion to the ICTY, the states concerned were divesting themselves cheaply of a job that was essentially a political responsibility, and not amenable to the decisions of a tribunal.

A few days later Richard Goldstone finally charged Radovan Karadžić and Ratko Mladić with genocide, crimes against humanity and war crimes for a campaign of persecution against Bosnia's Muslims and Croats. The indictment against the two men referred, notably, to the ethnic cleansing carried out at Prijedor. In November 1995, the Srebrenica massacres were incorporated with the other charges.

That December, the Dayton accords brought the war in Bosnia to an end. But while some of those held most responsible for the war were eventually indicted, no arrests followed. During 1996 sixty thousand NATO soldiers took up station in Bosnia, but the war criminals continued to strut about unmolested and known to all. The Dayton negotiators had refused to include the pursuit and arrest of war criminals in the NATO peace force's mandate. Alliance troops had to be content with stopping and questioning any suspects they happened to meet on their rounds.

Outcry Over an Indictment

'We realized that no one wanted the responsibility, but most of all that we couldn't count on cooperation from the member states in arresting people,' recounts the ICTY deputy prosecutor, Graham Blewitt. He describes the clamour that arose when the ICTY passed on an indictment to the command staff of NATO forces in Bosnia in 1997. The charges were laid against Simo Drljača, who had been the much-feared Prijedor police chief during the war. 'Even the local commander of NATO forces wanted to arrest him, but when we sent out the arrest warrant the NATO member states screamed the place down, saying it wasn't in their mandate. They refused to do it.' A few months later, however, British troops agreed to take the risk.

Aware of these stumbling blocks Louise Arbour, the Canadian woman magistrate who had succeeded Richard Goldstone in the prosecutor's job, thought up some new ways of putting pressure on the governments. To counter the complaint of NATO forces that it was dangerous to attempt the arrest of war criminals who were on their guard, she established a system of secret indictments to give the soldiers the advantage of surprise. This system, which started to come into effect in 1997, was to lead to a significant increase in the number of arrests.

Nor did Louise Arbour shrink from goading Paris by declaring that war criminals felt completely secure in the French sector which extends through the whole of south-eastern Bosnia. More arrests followed. Radislav Krstić, one of the most senior men responsible for the Srebrenica massacres, was pulled for questioning on 2 December 1998. By now the Tribunal had three ultra-modern hearing rooms and was running several trials simultaneously.

But the real turning point came on 27 May 1999. In front of a packed press conference, Louise Arbour announced the indictment for war crimes and crimes against humanity of Slobodan Milošević in connection with his role in Kosovo.[3] For the first time, international justice had indicted a head of state who was still in office.

Initially a paper tiger, the ICTY had become a model of international justice. Slobodan Milošević was transferred to The Hague on 30 June 2001. By the time his trial began on 12 February 2002 the Tribunal had a budget of nearly $100 million a year, and employed more than a thousand people. With the trial of Slobodan Milošević, it had become what Robert Badinter, president of the Constitutional Council, called 'the symbol of a functioning system of international justice'.[4]

A 'Biased and Anti-Serb' Tribunal

To many Serbs, in Bosnia as in Serbia-Montenegro, the ICTY nevertheless remains nothing but 'a biased machine' directed against their people. 'At The Hague, there's no one but Serbs being accused' is a remark heard over and over again in Prijedor, as throughout Republika Srpska. It is not accurate, however. A glance at the list of individuals indicted by the Tribunal shows that of nearly 130 indictments issued since the establishment of the ICTY, 77 are against Serbs (64 from Bosnia, five from Croatia and 18 from Serbia-Montenegro), 30 are against Croats (24 from Bosnia and six from Croatia), eight are against Bosnian Muslims and three against Kosovar Albanians.[5]

While top Serb leaders were indicted, including Slobodan Milošević, Radovan Karadžić and Ratko Mladić, the Tribunal had not hesitated to charge the chief of staff of the Croatian Army, General Janko Bobetko,[6] in connection with massacres of Serbs carried out in 1995. Two other Croatian generals regarded as national heroes, Rahim Ademi and Ante Gotovina, were also indicted for exactions committed against Serb civilians.

Similarly, Sefer Halilović, a Muslim former chief of staff of the Bosnian Army (AB-H), was charged with war crimes on 27 September 2001 for involvement in the massacres of Croat civilians in two villages in central Bosnia, Grabovica and Uzdol. The ICTY issued its indictment while he was still a serving minister in the Federation government. Three other senior Muslim generals were also indicted, along with Naser Orić, the Muslim former commander of the Bosnian Army at Srebrenica.[7] Apart from these ongoing prosecutions, two Bosniaks have already been sentenced for exactions committed against Bosnian Serbs in the Čelebići detention camp, near Konjic.[8]

'From the start of our mission in 1994, we were determined to investigate violations of humanitarian law committed by all parties to the conflict, and that's what we've done,' maintains deputy prosecutor Graham Blewitt.

It is certainly true that a large majority of those indicted are Serbs. But to insist on equal numbers of accusations for the three ethnic groups in Bosnia would be disproportionate and unjust. Without wishing to deny that Croats and Muslims had also been guilty of exactions and violations of humanitarian law in Bosnia-Herzegovina, it is important to emphasize that most of the crimes that occurred there were committed by Bosnian Serbs. As the former Serb nationalist leader Biljana Plavšić admitted in December 2002, these exactions resulted from a plan hatched by Serbs to reconstitute an ethnically homogeneous 'Greater Serbia'.

Other critics have suggested that the Tribunal imputes some sort of collective responsibility to the Serb population. In fact, the ICTY's raison d'être and the way it works show that this is the opposite of the truth, that on the contrary the Tribunal individualizes blame. It only prosecutes individuals for their personal acts and decisions; in a sense, it singles out scapegoats from the rest of the citizens, and thus avoids blaming them collectively. 'The Bosnian Serbs who finally answered our questions did so for the same reason the UN had created a war crimes tribunal,' wrote the journalist Elizabeth Neuffer. 'They wanted individual responsibility to replace collective guilt. They did not want every Serb to be blamed. "It is important for Serbs to know who is a war criminal and who is not," said one.' [9]

The only point on which the ICTY may be open to criticism on grounds of partiality concerns the NATO bombing in former Yugoslavia. In June 2000, Carla Del Ponte told the Security Council that she could see 'no grounds whatever' for opening an inquiry into the aerial campaign by the Atlantic alliance. After the outcry that followed this decision, in particular from a number of human-rights organizations including Amnesty International, the prosecutor decided to publish the contents of a report from a committee of jurists which had led to the decision. From the viewpoint of bodies like Amnesty or the International Committee of the Red Cross, the targeting of a civilian building – that of RTS, the Serbian radio and TV station in Belgrade –and the fact that NATO had continued to attack bridges after civilians had been noticed on or near them, could well constitute violations of the laws and customs of warfare.[10]

Instead of ending the argument, the report shown by Carla Del Ponte helped accentuate the impression of uneasy partiality. At several points, the jurists mandated by the prosecutor recognized that NATO had answered some of their questions only in the most general terms, while evading others altogether on grounds of military secrecy.[11] The unease stems from the fact that the prosecutor's team seems to accept this in justifying the decision not to open an inquiry: there are no complaints about the Alliance's manifest failure to cooperate, as there usually are when Serbia or Croatia is refusing to hand over requested documents. A jurist with the ICRC said regretfully: 'So all you need to evade international justice is to admit some errors, belong to a powerful military alliance and fail to answer the Tribunal's questions.'[12] Did the Western states threaten to withdraw their support from the ICTY if there were any prosecutions? Were they too afraid of the judges' independence? No one can say for sure, but the incident took some of the shine off the ICTY's image.

ELEVEN

In the Witness Box

In Nusreta Sivac's view, the ICTY from its very first appearance represented a ray of hope in a world still echoing with the clamour of war. The Tribunal may have seemed far away in that foggy, mysterious town The Hague, with its foreign babble. But it gave substance to the idea that justice could perhaps be done, the hope that one day her jailers would have to answer for their acts before a court, that they would be lined up on the bench of the accused and no longer parading about completely undisturbed in the streets of Prijedor, her home town, from which they had driven her.

Harvesting the Evidence

When the judges held their first plenary session at The Hague in November 1993 the ex-magistrate had been far away in Zagreb, just a Bosniak refugee among many others, trying to gather up the threads of a life turned upside down for ever. By the time she found her husband in Croatia after six months of separation, all Nusreta had to remind her of their past life together was a handful of family photos. When released from Trnopolje camp on 8 August 1992, she had been made to sign a declaration stipulating that she was relinquishing all her property to the self-proclaimed Serb republic of Krajina. Her flat was taken over by a Serb secretary working at the Prijedor courthouse. Before leaving she had tried to recover a few of her personal bits and pieces, but the new occupant had served her with coffee out of her own cups, as a way of pointing out that what had been Nusreta's now belonged to her.

As the war in Bosnia continued to rage, Nusreta understood that her life could never be the same again. Although in Zagreb she had found a refuge relatively untouched by the fighting, her nightmares and the physical aftermath of her stay in the camps had not gone away. With one of her former co-detainees, Jadranka Cigelj, she began to collect victims' accounts of their experiences and submit them to the Croatian information centre on war crimes. 'Recognition of our work will come when the people responsible for this war are appearing before a court. The ICTY could start to function one day,'[1] Jadranka explained at the time.

At The Hague, meanwhile, the prosecutor's office was trying to collect all the evidence and proofs it could find in order to put prosecutions together. The investigators could not enter Bosnia. So the testimony collected by a wide range of humanitarian organizations would be of crucial help, as the deputy prosecutor Graham Blewitt recognized. Although, while still in Omarska, women who had been raped said nothing about what had happened to them even to the other imprisoned women, Nusreta understood that she should now speak out and recount her experiences. 'That crime wasn't immortalized by the camera, just by the eyes of the victims,' her friend Jadranka noted perceptively.

On 11 February 1995 Nusreta was interviewed by two women investigators for the ICTY. The interview, duly registered and consigned among the other evidence against the people who had run the camps, lasted for two days. During her first contact with this international justice, a new phenomenon whose outlines were still very vague, Nusreta found herself talking to two women who were 'very relaxed and calm, quite normal in fact… No one forced me to talk about things I didn't want to talk about. I didn't feel under any pressure.'

Abroad, and in Bosnia after they had gained access to it, the ICTY investigators kept interviewing survivors and victims to bolster their future indictments. Under the ICTY's rules of procedure, an indictment had to be endorsed by a judge before becoming official. To give his consent, the magistrate had to consider that the act of indictment was based on sufficient evidence. To give an example, the indictment against Slobodan Milošević for his role in Kosovo was sent to Judge Hunt accompanied by more than three thousand pages of documents in support of the Tribunal's decision to prosecute.

Before the end of February 1995 the ICTY published its first indictment concerning Prijedor. In it fifteen Bosnian Serbs, including the presumed commandant of Omarska camp Željko Mejakić, were accused of crimes against humanity and war crimes. A second indictment accused a Serb from Kozarac, Duško Tadić.

Nevertheless the ICTY's record was still quite thin, with only three indictments after two years of existence. The judges were complaining that Richard Goldstone had not yet prosecuted any of the architects of the ethnic cleansing, people like Radovan Karadžić and Ratko Mladić. At the time Nusreta, too, thought it a pity that Karadžić did not figure on the list of criminals wanted by the ICTY, but she also felt strongly that the prosecution of fifteen guards and team leaders from Omarska represented a very satisfactory start. One of them, the former police officer Mladen Radić, had attempted to rape her at Omarska.

This illustrates the paradox built into the still-nascent system of international justice. On one side are the victims for whom the ICTY represents the only hope of justice, and who want it to prosecute 'small fry', the guards and petty officials they know to be directly responsible for crimes against humanity committed against them personally. On the other are the ICTY and its defenders, who know full well that the success of this very new international justice will be judged solely by the number of top leaders indicted, arrested and tried.

Indictments concerning the ethnic cleansing in Prijedor now began to appear in some numbers. On 21 July 1995 twelve individuals were indicted for crimes committed at Keraterm camp. Proceedings were subsequently dropped against six of these, considered to have played minor roles. On 13 March 1997, three members of the Prijedor Crisis Staff, the real organizers of the campaign of persecution against Croats and Muslims, were indicted by the Tribunal. They were Milan Kovačević, a doctor by training who had been deputy chairman of the Crisis Staff; another doctor, Milomir Stakić, who was chairman of the Staff from May 1992 onward; and the notorious Simo Drljača, Prijedor police chief from 1992.

In March 1999 it was the turn of the former leadership of the self-proclaimed Serb entity, the Autonomous Region of Krajina, to receive its summonses. Radoslav Brđanin, a civil engineer who had become president of Krajina, and Momir Talić, a Krajina corps commander during the war, were accused of genocide, crimes against humanity and war crimes.

But the prosecutor was aiming higher, at the people who had conceived and elaborated the persecution plan in which Prijedor had been a key theatre of operations. On 21 March 2000, Carla Del Ponte indicted Karadžić's right hand man Momčilo Krajišnik, the former president of the Assembly of Bosnian Serbs. The indictment was kept secret until his arrest a fortnight later, on 3 April 2000. Four days after that Biljana Plavšić, Karadžić's former wartime ally, was also indicted. And on 22 November 2001 there came at last the turn of Slobodan Milošević, described as the mastermind of the scheme to carve out a Greater Serbia and the attendant ethnic cleansing, to be charged with genocide and crimes against humanity in connection with the war in Bosnia.

Prijedor is named by the prosecution as one of the examples of the genocidal policy set up by Belgrade's former strong man. It can now also boast of a grim record: as the town with the largest number of citizens charged with war crimes, nineteen in all. And seven other individuals who are not native to the town have also been prosecuted for the ethnic cleansing in Prijedor.

Facing One's Torturers from the Witness Stand

In 1998, with the indictments flowing, Nusreta arrived in The Hague to give her evidence. Disappointingly, however, Milan Kovačević, the only political executive of the ethnic cleansing in Prijedor held by the ICTY, died of a heart attack in his cell on 1 August 1998, less than a month after the opening of his trial for genocide. This deprived Nusreta for the time being of the chance to describe what she had lived through. But the opportunity came at last two years later, at the trial of the former deputy commandant of Omarska, Miroslav Kvočka, and five of the camp guards. On 5 September 2000, she was called as a witness for the prosecution.

How does a woman cope with facing her torturers after eight years? This question and its cloud of attendant anxieties filled Nusreta's mind in the days before the trial. 'Anxiety reaches its peak just before going into the hearing room,' explains Wendy Lobwein, an Australian psychologist who monitors the witnesses when they are in The Hague. The fear is that they might not have the fortitude to endure hours of detailed and sometimes downright finicky questioning in the presence of people who have raped, tortured or beaten them.

The Anglo-Saxon legal process requires judges to base their decisions only on statements made in court, during the hearing. This means that witnesses have to go into the greatest detail on experiences like being beaten up, betrayed by a fellow prisoner or raped. Nusreta went through this, having to describe publicly and in meticulous detail the sexual brutalities and abuses to which she had been subjected. She also had to answer defence questions and hear her statements being belittled and contradicted, her very credibility cast into doubt. And quite apart from the substance of the proceedings, witnesses had to find their bearings in the alien, intimidatingly solemn ICTY environment. When Nusreta the Bosniak entered the hearing room on 5 September 2000 she found herself facing three foreign judges (an American woman and two men, one Portuguese and one Egyptian), an American prosecutor flanked by half a dozen black-robed assistants seated behind big computer screens, a dozen defence lawyers, three court clerks, a row of interpreters in glass cabins, and lastly, just thirty feet away from her across the courtroom, the five accused.

'The first sight of the accused is generally a moment filled with emotion,' Wendy Lobwein says. After working for years with victims of torture and ill-treatment, the psychologist knows that their reactions can vary considerably. 'Sometimes they see the accused as smaller than they remember him, or note with satisfaction that he can't do them any harm now.' But not everyone manages so well. 'One time, a witness came to see me in utter panic during the recess saying: "the accused can get me, he can strangle me." I went back in with her, pointing out that the accused was some distance away and that he was in the custody of two United Nations policemen.'

To support the people called to live through these delicate and painful moments, the ICTY has a special protection unit for witnesses and victims. The follow-up is personal, tailored to individual needs. 'We try to help them solve various problems before they leave. It may be a matter of finding someone to look after a herd of cattle during a few days' absence,' Wendy Lobwein explains. When they arrive in The Hague they are accommodated at addresses kept strictly secret. They are looked after day and night by a team of people who speak their language, who 'do everything they can to supply them with small familiar things, a cup of coffee, a brand of cigarettes, show them how to use a Dutch phonecard or take them to the seaside… The aim is to maintain the small things of everyday life so that the individual can manage when faced with the exceptional thing that giving evidence is.'

Witnesses make a preliminary visit to the hearing room to familiarize themelves with the positions of judges, prosecutors and accused. Then, when the day comes, they await their appearance in a specially appointed ICTY anteroom, with comfortable sofas, a coffee machine, games for children accompanying their parents, magazines, puzzles, all designed to provide a reassuring and welcoming environment. Wendy Lobwein finds puzzles useful. 'Some witnesses arrive here wanting to tell the world the whole story, and they're often disappointed when they find they're only being questioned about a part of what happened. So I explain to them that their story is like one piece of a puzzle, that other witnesses will supply other pieces so that in the end the judges can see the whole picture.'

The piece supplied by Nusreta in September 2000 helped the judges to grasp the true awfulness of the conditions in which thirty-six to thirty-eight women were held at Omarska. For three days, she replied calmly to questions from the prosecutor, the defence lawyers and the judges. 'I managed to refute eleven lawyers and all their documentation, by describing the facts as they occurred. It's a comforting feeling to have given evidence by telling the truth and saying what really happened,' Nusreta told us two years later when we interviewed her in Prijedor.

Enabling the victims to speak out in this way is surely one of the ICTY's great achievements. Thousands have been able, like Nusreta, to describe the sufferings and humiliations inflicted on them, to put the unspeakable into words. For, as Wendy Lobwein insists, most 'survivors and victims have an absolute need to tell the world what happened.'

Some perhaps, like Nusreta herself, may already have told their stories in a documentary[2] or at an international conference, but giving evidence at the ICTY – the first international criminal tribunal since Nuremberg and Tokyo – has the immense advantage of institutionalizing their narrative and placing it at the very heart of the process of justice. The ICTY was created by the UN to punish crimes injurious to everyone's humanity. Symbolically, a witness speaking before it is being heard by an internationl community that not so long ago was blind and apathetic when faced with the horrors of the war in Bosnia. Muharem Murselović recalls his 'fascination' on entering the courtroom for the first time. 'I'd never had anything to do with courts or tribunals before, let alone an international tribunal. When I had gone in, I said to myself that there was perhaps justice in this world after all.' Nusreta talks about an immense 'feeling of pride' that seized her on entering the courtroom, 'a pride that was as much internal as external'. For victims of crimes against humanity, who have been degraded and reviled in an attempt to exclude them from the human community, giving evidence in a trial can sometimes restore the person's sense of dignity. 'Victims who have been ignored, humiliated, expelled from the world, are once again entitled to speak… and to be listened to,'[3] explains the magistrate Antoine Garapon.

Their words are of crucial importance in that they help judges to assess the guilt or innocence of one or more accused. The victims can describe their sufferings but they can also name those responsible in a process of justice and establish what really occurred.

'I felt a personal satisfaction because I'd been able to help establish the truth, at least partially. You can never say too much about what really happened in Prijedor in 1992 given that you still see people today, in some circles, casting doubt on the camps and the events in Prijedor,' Muharem says when he thinks about what his two appearances before the ICTY have done for him. For Ibrahim Beglerbegović, the Bosniak doctor who used to work at the Prijedor hospital and who gave evidence against his former colleague Milomir Stakić, there is 'the satisfaction of having been able to play a full part in this process of justice'. Nusreta confides: 'I have the feeling that I've done something important.' The feeling has appeared gradually over time: immediately after giving her evidence, recalls this courageous and determined woman, her feeling was of severe 'psychological suffering'.

After Fiving Evidence: Trauma, Solitude, Sometimes Poverty

'After The Hague, the victims are proud of having given evidence but in many cases bad post-traumatic stress reappears, because they've been recalling very difficult events', comments Dubravka Dizdarević, a Sarajevo psychologist who studies torture victims who have testified before the ICTY. Thus, Nusreta Sivac was hospitalized for two whole months after her first testimony because of what she laconically describes as 'stress'. She is aware that the absence of professional psychological help following her return from The Hague had been 'very burdensome'. Psychosomatic and other stress-related problems are commonplace, according to the few psychologists who follow these victims in Bosnia. They are all the more glaring when the victims are left to their own devices on returning home. The close and high-quality support often provided before and during the witness's appearance before the tribunal makes the subsequent solitude all the harder to bear. And the solitude may be intentionally inflicted: witnesses who have testified against members of their own community can find themselves being ostracized on returning home. 'For some people in Prijedor, Serbs who cooperate with the ICTY are no better than traitors,' explained Miodrag Milanović, a psychiatrist at the town's hospital, during an ICTY seminar in The Hague where he had come to meet some of his colleagues.

Witnesses can also suffer quite severely from poverty. The prosecutor Mark Harmon, who has led the prosecutions in the case of the Srebrenica massacre, underlines the harsh lot of woman survivors who may have to return to refugee camps after giving their evidence. Justice, he points out, is more than just someone being tried and sentenced in court: it also means victims having access to the psychological and social support they need, psychological follow-up for traumatized children for example.

'Why should the victims who give evidence get more support than the others? It seems clear to me: going into the witness box lumbers them with an extra psychological and economic burden,' Wendy Lobwein explains. Of course it is not the ICTY's function to supervise social support, and it has no post-appearance follow-up system for witnesses, or indeed any compensation fund or system to make it possible for the tribunal itself to order improvements to the everyday lot of the victims.

Seeing this as a weakness the International Criminal Court, the first permanent tribunal for the repression of war crimes, has set up an aid fund for victims which is to be funded by donations but also, it is hoped, from the fines imposed on possible future war criminals.

Giving Evidence Can Also Turn Out not to be a Risk-free Act

Giving evidence can however turn out to be a high-risk act. Victims or former associates of an accused individual who agree to confirm the accusations against him may become the targets of reprisals, especially where the accused still has influential local connections.

A number of individuals responsible for crimes, still living at liberty in Prijedor, are unlikely to take a tolerant view of evidence damaging to a system they supported or helped to set up. To a Bosniak refugee returning to live in what is now a mainly Serb town, the local police cannot be seen as offering reliable protection. As the mayor of Prijedor Nada Ševo herself admitted, the forces of order are saturated with nationalists. 'Since the refugees have been returning to Prijedor it's become more difficult to obtain evidence from them. People are worried about their safety,' admits an ICTY investigator working on the region since 1999. 'In villages with big Muslim majorities it's still all right, but it's difficult in mixed areas. So you have to be really careful, you never visit people during the day but either at night or by meeting them in another town, not where they live.'

Wendy Lobwein says that since the Tribunal started work a large number of witnesses have been harassed, threatened and badgered with anonymous phone calls. 'For people already traumatized by the wars in the Balkans, this sort of menace is equivalent to being aimed at by a sniper,' she insists. Slobodan Milošević's trial illustrated the pressures brought to bear on witnesses. Just before it opened, the leadership of the former president's party (Socialist Party of Serbia, SPS) made a public declaration that anyone daring to give evidence against him would be considered a traitor to the Serbian fatherland and people. Potential witnesses could ignore the threat, but in a country where a lot of Slobodan Milošević's followers are still in key posts, the risk of losing their jobs or falling victim to trumped-up legal proceedings was a very real one. Not to mention threats of a more direct and physical nature. Through its links with local gangsters, the Milošević régime in the past had sometimes resorted to dealing with its opponents in direct physical fashion. According to Serbia's own justice system, the late Serbian prime minister Zoran Đinđić was assassinated in Belgrade on 12 March 2003 on the orders of Milorad Luković, a former protégé of the Yugoslav supremo, just as his government was preparing to surrender some new accused to the ICTY.

During the Croatia stage of the ex-president's trial, one prosecution witness was threatened, then physically attacked, before going to The Hague and within days of his identity being communicated to Slobodan Milošević and his legal advisers. Another received threats he took so seriously that he refused to open his mouth during the hearing.[4]

Well aware of the risks run by witnesses, the Tribunal established a special unit responsible for protecting them, as well as a set of operating rules to minimize the risk of their becoming the target of reprisals. 'Unlike Nuremberg where the trials were based mainly on written documents, the Nazis having kept a meticulous record of their crimes, the trials at The Hague are based mainly on spoken testimony,' says Diane Orentlicher, director of the War Crimes Research Office at the University of Washington. As a result, the Tribunal needs to be able to count on the participation of victims, survivors or former criminals who have 'repented' to prove the guilt of the accused. One example of the importance of this factor was the abandonment in 1995 of the rape charge against the Kozarac war criminal Duško Tadić, the principal witness, paralysed by fear, having decided on the eve of the trial not to appear.

To limit the number of such incidents the Tribunal provides two levels of protection. One operates during the witness's appearance at the hearing and in the period immediately before it, and the other is longer-term, covering the individual's life after giving evidence. The judges can order, at the request of either prosecution or defence, that the identity of the witness be kept secret; the witness then appears under a pseudonym, his or her face may be kept concealed and voice electronically distorted. They can also order a closed session to ensure a higher level of confidentiality.

However, the identities of witnesses are almost always disclosed to the accused and their lawyers. The accused have to be able to counter any declarations made against them to ensure a fair trial: a witness might after all be capable of making false allegations. If the defence does not even know the identity of the person making them, it becomes very difficult for the lawyers to make the investigations necessary to establish the truth.

When Nusreta stepped forward to give her evidence in September 2000, the protection unit had taken measures to conceal her identity from the public.

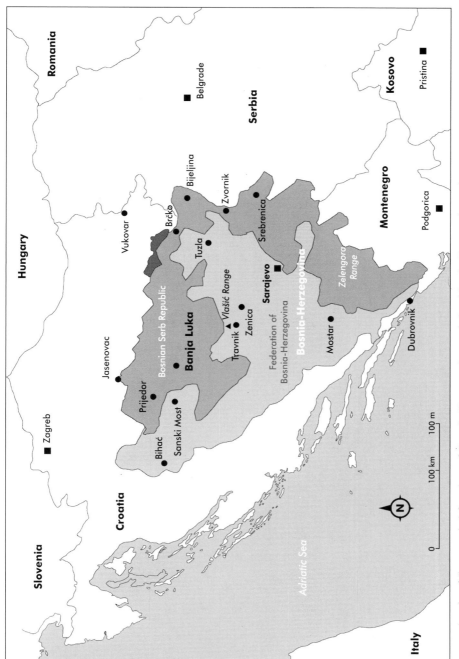

International and 'inter-entity' frontiers of Bosnia-Herzegovina as defined by the Dayton Accords in 1995.

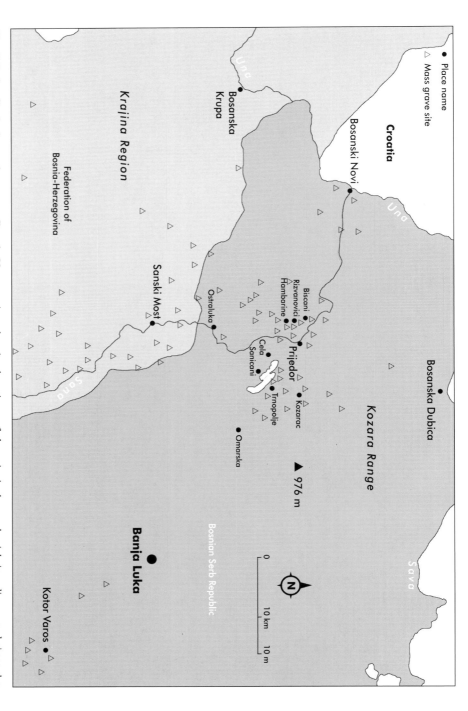

Croatia

Una

Bosanski Novi

Una

Bosanska
Krupa

Krajina Region

Federation of
Bosnia-Herzegovina

Sanski Most

Ostraluka

Biscani
Rizvanovići
Hambarine
Prijedor

Cela
Sanicani
Trnopolje
Kozarac

Omarska

▲ 976 m

Kozara Range

Bosanska Dubica

Bosnian Serb Republic

Sava

Sana

Banja Luka

Kotor Varos ●

0   10 km   10 m
N

The Prijedor district in north-western Bosnia-Herzegovina, showing locations of the principal mass burial sites discovered since the
end of the war (source: International Criminal Tribunal for former Yugoslavia).

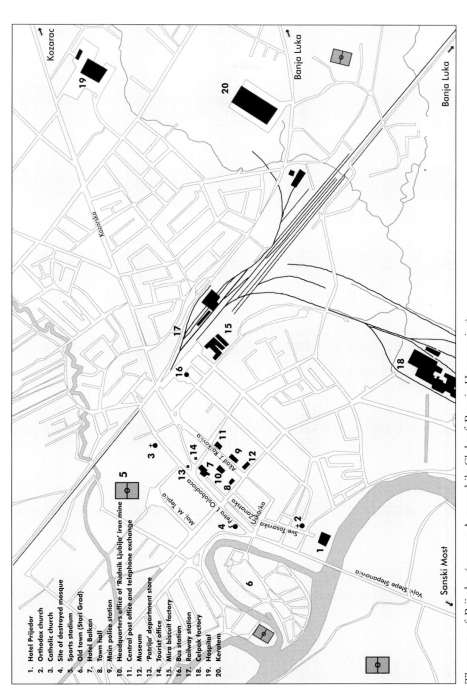

1. Hotel Prijedor
2. Orthodox church
3. Catholic church
4. Site of destroyed mosque
5. Sports stadium
6. Old town (Stari Grad)
7. Hotel Balkan
8. Town hall
9. Main police station
10. Headquarters office of 'Rudnik Ljubija' iron mine
11. Central post office and telephone exchange
12. Museum
13. 'Patrija' department store
14. Tourist office
15. Mira biscuit factory
16. Bus station
17. Railway station
18. Celpak factory
19. Hospital
20. Keraterm

The town of Prijedor (source: Automobile Club of Bosnia-Herzegovina).

Keraterm, the former tile and ceramics factory used as a detention camp between May and August 1992. Today the factory is idle. It is being privatized and parts of the building are rented out to local enterprises (photo: Vaulerin-Wesselingh).

A Muslim prisoner detained in the Trnopolje camp, photographed in August 1992. Several thousand people were imprisoned there between May and October of that year. Some wer tortured, raped or murdered (photo: David Cairns, AP/SIPA).

The Trnopolje detention centre today. The buildings were returned to their former use as a school in 1993. Not far from the entrance to the school yard, a monument to the memory of Serb war victims has been erected at the roadside (photo: Edin Ramulic).

Site of the ethnic cleansing camp at Omarska. On the left stands the White House, used as a torture chamber and killing room. The refectory is at the far end of the building on the right, with the *pista* – the tarmac area where prisoners were beaten – in the foreground, and the main hangar in the right foreground. In this building several thousand people were interned between May and August 1992 (photo: Vaulerin-Wesselingh).

The main entrance to the 'Rudnik Ljubija' mining complex, just outside the village of Omarska (photo: Vaulerin Wesselingh).

Exhumation in progress at the Jakarina Kos site, near the Ljubija iron mine, in September 2001. This is the biggest mass grave discovered in Bosnia to date: three hundred and seventy-two bodies were dug out of the hillside over a period of five weeks (photo: ICTY records).

Milan Kovačević at the ICTY in 1997. This former member of the Prijedor Crisis Staff, ex-director of the town's hospital, died of a heart attack at The Hague on 1 August 1998, a few days after the start of his trial in front of the international criminal tribunal (photo: Fred Ernst, Reuters).

Željko Mejakić during his first appearance before the ICTY, in 2003. The one-time commandant of the Omarska camp had surrendered to the tribunal in July 2003 after remaining hidden for eight years (photo: Dusan Branić, AFP).

Milomir Stakić, former Mayor of Prijedor, ex-chairman of the Crisis Staff and of the Serb Democratic Party (SDS), during his trial before the ICTY in 2002 (photo: Peter Dejong, Reuters).

Site of the main Prijedor mosque, burned and razed to the ground in 1992, beside the town's main shopping street, the (renamed) Peter I the Liberator Street. The graffito on the building to the left reads: 'Arkan, you are the greatest, we will always stay loyal to you. The Patriot Boys'. (photo: Edin Ramulic).

Monument dedicated to 'all war victims' in Prijedor. This allegedly oecumenical monument – in the form of an Orthodox cross – has been built immediately in front of the main entrance of the town hall, in the centre of town (photo: Edin Ramulić).

Orthodox church (on left) and (centre) the Hotel Prijedor, an architectural leftover from the Tito years, at the entrance to the town (photo: Vaulerin-Wesselingh).

Nusreta Sivac at the entrance to the municipal courthouse. The coat of arms is that of Republika Srpska. The former magistrate – one of the few women to have passed through Omarska and survived – has not so far been able to resume her profession (photo: Edin Ramulić).

Muharem Murselović (left), former chairman of the municipal assembly, and Sead Jakupović, chairman of the 'Fondacija 98' association. The two men, the main moving spirits behind the peaceful return of refugees to the Prijedor district, are both survivors of the Omarska camp (photo: Edin Ramulić).

Peter I the Liberator Street, named after Petar Karađorđević, king of Serbia 1903-18 and of the Kingdom of Serbs, Croats and Slovenes 1918-21. Until the war this main shopping street of Prijedor was called Marshal Tito Street (photo: Edin Ramulić).

But during cross-questioning later in the hearing one of the defence lawyers, apparently by accident, addressed her by her full name. 'As you know, this kind of situation is very difficult to put right,' judge Rodrigues told her. 'We're going to take every measure to erase the witness's name from the record but once it's been said, it's been said. We can't order members of the public present in the chamber to forget what they've just heard.'

Nusreta's name was removed from all the public transcripts and from the video footage of the trial, transmitted after the half-hour time-lapse provided to allow this kind of adjustment. To no avail: Nusreta was quickly identified in Prijedor as a witness in the trial. A few months later she gave us permission to use her name in coverage of her evidence.

Journalists have a duty to respect the measures taken to protect witnesses. Even when a name is uttered accidentally in court, the ethics of their profession should ensure that the journalists present do not cite it in their articles. To do so would be to compromise the safety of the witness. Unfortunately, however, this rule has not always been followed at the Tribunal. In the Milošević case Duško Jovanović, editor-in-chief of the Montenegrin daily *Dan*, admitted that he had endangered a protected witness by revealing his identity. The witness had subsequently received death threats.

For those witnesses whose appearance exposes them to extremely serious, life-threatening risk, the Tribunal has established programmes to resettle them in another country under a new identity. One beneficiary, along with his family, is Slobodan Lazarević, a former Yugoslav secret service officer who gave evidence against Milošević. In court, he had described the way the ex-president supervised the Serb leaders of the self-proclaimed republic of Croatia (RSK) during the war in the former Yugoslav republic, between 1991 and 1995. Sent by Belgrade to act as a liaison officer with the Croatian Serbs, he himself was originally a régime insider and fervent supporter of Slobodan Milošević's policies. Becoming disillusioned with the actions of the Serbian president, he made the decision to testify before the ICTY, giving a deposition essential to the prosecution case which sought to prove a direct link between Slobodan Milošević and the bosses of the RSK.

Despite the ordeal giving evidence represents, many victims have decided courageously to go to The Hague and testify. For some, including Nusreta, giving testimony had a 'partially cathartic' function although this could never completely heal the wounds left by the years of war. 'I live with that all the time,' she says. Would it have been better not to give evidence and try to forget everything, then? Nusreta thinks not: 'Not testifying would have been more difficult. In any case there's no point in trying to forget because it's impossible. I'd still be living with this weight for the rest of my days.' Nusreta,

Muharem and the many other war crime victims who testified at The Hague have the satisfaction of knowing that they have fulfilled 'a moral duty' to those other victims, the ones who did not survive.

TWELVE

The Hour of Judgement

The hour of justice started to strike for Nusreta on 2 November 2001. That afternoon, the magistrates before whom she had given her evidence handed down their verdicts on the Omarska five. All were found guilty. That was a first satisfaction from her point of view. Then came the sentences: seven years' imprisonment for Kvočka, six years for Kos, twenty years for her would-be rapist Radić, twenty-five years for Žigić and five years for Prčac. 'The deputy commandants of a camp where thousands of people were tortured or raped got away with a measly seven and five years,'[1] Nusreta commented indignantly. She remains bitter, believing that all her work in collecting evidence had been wasted effort. 'It's not worth going to the trouble of arresting war crime suspects if this is the way individuals responsible for torturing thousands of people are punished. I'm so disappointed, I wish I hadn't given evidence.'

Misunderstood Sentences and a Lack of Coherence

Like her, dozens of other victims of war crimes have greeted some of the sentences given by the International Criminal Tribunal with bitterness and disbelief. The women of Srebrenica have never been able to understand why Dražen Erdemović, a Bosnian Croat serving with the Serb forces, only got five years in prison for taking part in the execution of more than a hundred Bosnian Muslims at Pilica farm, just after the seizure of the enclave in July 1995. 'A mere eighteen days' jail per murder', they calculated indignantly.

The ICTY judges had considered a number of mitigating circumstances when sentencing Erdemović. In particular they noted that Dražen Erdemović, aged twenty-four at the time of the events, had been forced to take part in the execution of Bosnian Muslims at Pilica under threat of being killed himself. They emphasized that the accused had surrendered voluntarily to the ICTY, confessed to the killings of his own accord, admitted his guilt and expressed strong remorse. His cooperation with the prosecutor's office, especially in clarifying where responsibility lay for the Srebrenica massacres, had also weighed in the balance. 'The accused is young and has shown his honest character by never trying to avoid admitting his guilt and his remorse. He is married to a woman of a different ethnic group and can be reformed. The court is therefore of the opinion that he should be given a second chance to rebuild his life, and sentences him to five years' imprisonment,' the verdict reads.[2]

The judges explained the difficult balance that has to be struck in deciding sentences. On the one hand it is important to encourage and 'reward' those accused who admit the facts – a rare species in the ICTY's first years[3] – and who thus help to establish the historical truth which, according to the judges, 'washes away ethnic hatreds and enables the healing process to start'. On the other hand, the ICTY has to bear in mind 'that it is an agent through which the international community expresses its indignation over the atrocities committed in former Yugoslavia and should therefore not lose sight of the tragedy inflicted on the victims, or of the sufferings endured by their families.'[4]

In the Erdemović case, the families nevertheless felt slighted by the five-year sentence. And in fact even the very heaviest sentences have sometimes elicited disappointed reactions. Thus when General Radislav Krstić, one of the most senior men commanding the seizure of Srebrenica, got a forty-six-year prison sentence on 2 July 2001, some widows expressed a wish to see him condemned to death. This is a sentence regarded as unacceptable by the ICTY and by defenders of human rights. 'International justice marks the difference between itself and warfare by not attempting to annihilate its enemy: that's why it must reject the death sentence,'[5] Antoine Garapon explains.

But while it is true that the victims' sufferings sometimes induce them to demand more severe sentences than justice would normally impose, it is also the case that ICTY sentencing policy has been widely criticized and displays inconsistencies damaging to its credibility. The main problem is the absence of a sentencing code: the Tribunal's statutes, unlike those of national legal systems, contain no indications of the maximum sentences imposable for crimes against humanity or war crimes. The magistrates have to exercise their discretionary power to assess the individual case when the moment for sentencing arrives. It must be said that the sentences imposed so far give the impression of a lack of overall coherence.

The trials concerning Omarska and Keraterm illustrate these ambiguities. In the case of Omarska, Miroslav Kvočka was deputy commandant of the camp. He replaced his superior when the latter was absent, the judges concluded, and thus had a disciplinary power – which he failed to exercise – to prevent the ill-treatment and torture of detainees. Although he had not himself committed any murders or tortured anyone, he still occupied a hierarchical position that made him answerable for the actions of his subordinates, since he was the person in charge. Kvočka did not express the slightest remorse, and was sentenced initially to seven years in prison.

Duško Sikirica by contrast was head of security at Keraterm camp. As such, he had no power to sanction the guards or team leaders, the judges observed. So his command responsibility, unlike Kvočka's, was very limited. During his trial Sikirica had ended by admitting his guilt. He admitted the cold-blooded murder of a detainee, expressing remorse which the judges accepted as sincere. 'Paying dear for sincerity', noted the legal review *Diplomatie judiciaire* of the fifteen-year sentence he received, more than twice that imposed on Miroslav Kvočka.[6]

The same inconsistency can be found in the sentencing of two other accused, exactly similar in rank having been the leaders of teams of guards. Milojica Kos worked at Omarska. He was a 'strong link' in the chain of persecution and 'did not hesitate when the occasion arose to contribute actively to the increase of violence and terror inside the camp', the judges noted. But although Kos had not expressed the slightest remorse, he only got six years. By contrast the judges found that Damir Došen, a team leader at Keraterm, had sometimes used his powers to help the detainees. During his trial, he wept when hearing the accounts of some survivors. He expressed remorse for his actions and said he hoped that 'such horrors would never be able to occur again', but nevertheless got a five-year sentence, almost as long as Milojica Kos's.

But the feebleness of some of the sentences is hardly compatible with the idea of just punishment. Found guilty of crimes against humanity and war crimes, Milojica Kos was sentenced to a mere six years in prison. With remission, he was set free after four years and two months. 'In reality, all he got was preventive detention, which means he wasn't even in a real prison, he just stayed in a detention centre,' we were told by an ICTY staff member who did not want to be named.

The most flagrant case of this sort is that of Biljana Plavšić. A biologist by training, she was one of Radovan Karadžić's closest allies during the war. At that time, convinced that Serbs were genetically superior to Muslims, she even asserted that ethnic cleansing is 'a natural phenomenon and not a war crime'. After the Dayton peace accords, however, she took the pragmatic decision to cooperate with the international community, and distanced herself from Radovan Karadžić. Received in Paris by Jacques Chirac and welcomed in other European capitals, the new president of Republika Srpska projected the image of a moderate. On the terrain, however, neither her police nor her army lifted a finger to arrest any of the war criminals, still regarded as Serb heroes.

On 10 January 2001 Biljana Plavšić, who had turned seventy, decided to surrender voluntarily to the ICTY to answer the charges of genocide, crimes against humanity and war crimes that had been brought against her. Initially the ex-president, who had now given up politics, decided to plead not guilty. It seemed that the usual scenario was being played out once more: the accused denying any part in the crimes, even denying the crimes themselves, and thus reinforcing in Serb public opinion the idea that the ICTY is really just the instrument of an anti-Serb international plot.

However, in a dramatic development on 2 October 2002, Biljana Plavšić announced that she was changing her plea to guilty as charged of crimes against humanity. By uttering the word 'guilty', the former ally of Radovan Karadžić was admitting to having taken part in the persecution of Bosnian Muslims and Croats in thirty-seven municipalities, including Prijedor. She was recognizing the existence of the Keraterm, Trnopolje and Omarska camps, the forced movements of population, the expulsions and the murder and torture of civilians inflicted by Serb forces between 1992 and 1995.

'This is a central act and very important to former Yugoslavia,' said Florence Hartmann, Carla Del Ponte's spokeswoman. 'For the first time, an official of this rank is admitting the facts and expressing remorse to the victims.' Over and above her admission of guilt, this action by Biljana Plavšić constituted a substantial reverse for the revisionist camp. No one can doubt her involvement at the highest level, alongside Radovan Karadžić and Ratko Mladić. She knew of and admitted the crimes, while many of the inhabitants of Omarska went on blatantly denying the existence of a camp in their village.

Over the three days from 16 to 18 December, Biljana Plavšić appeared before the ICTY in hearings to determine her sentence. The fundamental importance of her new attitude now became even clearer. In a document that was made public, the former president confirmed that 'a number of individuals took part in conceptualizing and carrying out the objective of forced ethnic separation' in Bosnia. Among them she named Radovan Karadžić, his right-hand man Momčilo Krajišnik and Ratko Mladić; but also Slobodan Milošević: she revealed that Radovan Karadžić had frequently visited Belgrade to receive instructions. Biljana Plavšić emphasized that the Bosnian Serb leadership to which she belonged knew perfectly well that implementing this plan would involve 'a discriminatory campaign of persecution' directed against Bosnian Muslims and Croats.

This was a historic admission. For the first time, a Serb leader was recognizing the existence of a criminal ethnic cleansing scheme devised by the Serb leadership. It demolished at a stroke the line taken by some Prijedor officials to the effect that the Muslims had started the war; and it exposed the hollowness of the assertion by some Western diplomats that the conflict was just the latest manifestation of centuries of ancestral hatred and religious rivalry between the three peoples of Bosnia.[7]

However, the exemplary aspect of the Plavšić case is counterbalanced by what seems an inexplicably light sentence. On 27 February 2003 the ICTY judges sentenced the former president of the Bosnian Serbs to eleven years' imprisonment, citing a large number of mitigating circumstances. The prosecution, which had itself taken into account the age of the accused – seventy-two by the end of the trial – and her admission of guilt, had asked for a total sentence of fifteen to twenty-five years in view of the seriousness of the crime. But while emphasizing 'the horror of a campaign of ethnic separation that caused thousands of deaths and led to the expulsion of thousands of other people under conditions of extreme brutality', the judges found that Biljana Plavšić's actions in favour of the Dayton accords had been a major contribution to the achievement of peace and could therefore justify a reduction in her sentence. But the Serb iron lady's support for Dayton had been pragmatic, motivated essentially by a wish to obtain European and US financial support for Republika Srpska. The judges also mentioned the importance of her admission of guilt. It is nevertheless worth mentioning that Biljana Plavšić offered not a single word of apology to the victims and made it clear that she would not cooperate with the prosecutor in any other trials.

'The judges have to find a balance between the seriousness of the crime – and it shouldn't be forgotten that she admits to having played a key role in the ethnic cleansing campaign – and the importance of her confession which may help to bring about reconciliation. However, too light a sentence – and I take the view that juridically, a sentence of less than fifteen years is too light – can only have a negative effect on the reconciliation process; it's an insult to the victims,' commented Avril McDonald, a jurist specializing in international law at the T.M.C. Asser Institute in The Hague.

One of the survivors of Srebrenica who had been present at the trial was virtually incapable of speech after the sentence had been announced, so intense was his feeling of betrayal. 'Eleven years for all those lives, for all that suffering; we can't, I mean the survivors of the camps, we can't be satisfied with that,'[8] was Muharem Murselović's comment. A feeling shared by many victims. And there was some risk that such a light sentence might fail to promote the desired increase in awareness among the Bosnian Serb population: many would conclude from the eleven-year sentence that the crimes could not be as serious as all that. For Nusreta Sivac, though, the sentence imposed is only of secondary importance. 'The fact that she pleaded guilty, and above all that she called on others to do the same, is far more important than the sentence she was given,'[9] the camp survivor believes.

Explaining some sentences to the victims or their families can be pretty uphill work, admits Refik Hodžić, until 2003 director of the ICTY's Outreach communication programme in Bosnia. 'They do manage to understand and accept a conviction and sentence like the one in the Vasiljević case. A Bosnian Serb from Višegrad (eastern Bosnia), he was given twenty years in prison for the murder of five Muslims. The judges acquitted him in connection with another incident in which sixty-five people had been burned in a house, a courageous decision on their part. But they pointed out that the murder of five people was quite serious enough, still in the realm of crimes against humanity, people had been killed and others are still listed as missing. This isn't small-time stuff like stealing car radios or vandalizing bus shelters.'

Muharem Murselović takes the stern view that the tribunal 'hasn't fulfilled the expectations of the Prijedor victims. Some sentences seem more like rewards in view of the number of victims,' he said at the end of 2004. Nusreta too is strongly aware of the disappointment felt over some of the sentences, but she still feels that 'justice has been done in part, albeit a small part.' And despite the apparent inconsistency of sentencing policy and the disappointment and frustration caused by it, the victims continue to have some faith in the Tribunal. When we met Nusreta Sivac a few months after the conviction of the Omarska five, she had already regained her confidence in the ICTY. 'I was very disappointed by the sentences on Kvočka and the others, but I'm hoping for the best from the appeal hearing,' she told us. 'I'm not giving up. I'm ready to go and give evidence again in other trials on Prijedor. It's crucial to go to The Hague.'

Nusreta paused for a moment, her blue-grey gaze focused on infinity. She emanated dignity, wounded but intact. Disappointments notwithstanding, she was and is ready to go on investing in this international justice. Giving evidence will not have brought her any material benefits. The struggle to repossess her apartment will not have been made any easier, nor her life shuttling between Sanski Most and Prijedor. She is still suffering from kidney problems due, she explains, to the polluted water she had to drink at Omarska. Although on one level her testimony worked as a catharsis, it also reawakened traumas she had thought buried. Soon after her passage through The Hague she had been hospitalized for two months... stress, she told us laconically. But she is still ready and willing to give evidence again, partly on behalf of the ones who did not survive and in particular 'the five women who died at Omarska'.

Establishing the Facts

However imperfect it may be, however remote it may seem to the victims who do not give evidence, the ICTY has enabled some progress to be made along the road to justice. Without it, Slobodan Milošević would probably still be free to come and go in Serbia. Dragoljub Kunarac, Radomir Kovač and Zoran Vuković, three Bosnian Serb paramilitaries found guilty of using dozens of Muslim women and girls from Foča as sexual slaves, would still be living peaceful lives in that town in south-eastern Bosnia. And who can tell whether Biljana Plavšić would have admitted her guilt?

Even without that confession, the trials held in front of the Hague tribunal have established in unarguable fashion a great deal of what happened in Bosnia during almost four years of war. On the basis of thousands of documents and depositions submitted by prosecution and defence, expert testimony and jurisprudence as it applies to international law, the magistrates in The Hague have handed down rigorous decisions that will mark History. The conflict in Bosnia-Herzegovina was not a civil war between three ethnic groups torn apart by tribal violence, as maintained for many years by certain politicians, military and intellectuals.

In reality it was an international armed conflict between two states, Bosnia-Herzegovina and the Federal Republic of Yugoslavia in association with the Bosnian Serb nationalists. 'The armed forces of Republika Srpska were acting under the overall control and on behalf of the Federal Republic of Yugoslavia. Thus the conflict in Bosnia-Herzegovina between the Bosnian Serbs and the central authorities of Bosnia-Herzegovina may be considered to have been an international conflict throughout the period running from 1992 to 1995,' the judges specify in their verdict on appeal in the Tadić case.[10]

Srebrenica was the theatre of a genocide in July 1995. The word genocide, derived from the Greek noun *genos* (race) and the Latin verb *occidere*, (to cause to perish), was invented in 1944 by a Polish Jewish refugee in the United

States, Raphael Lemkin. It designates crimes committed 'with the intention of destroying, wholly or in part, a national, ethnic, racial or religious group'. Murders, serious assaults on the physical or mental integrity of members of the group (including rape) and the intentional subjection of the group to living conditions likely to bring about its destruction are all genocidal acts. 'The decision to kill all the Srebrenica males of military age was a decision to render the survival of the Bosnian Muslim population impossible in Srebrenica,' judge Rodrigues explained when giving his verdict on General Radislav Krstić.[11] The verdict was confirmed on appeal on 19 April 2004.

Showing their confidence in this ICTY function of establishing the true facts, Nusreta, Muharem, Sead, Nurka and her son Anel fixed their hopes on another case that opened in 2002, the trial of Milomir Stakić. It was of capital importance for them and for Prijedor. But it was prosecuted amid indifference.

THIRTEEN

Milomir Stakić or the Forgotten Trial

Doctor Milomir Stakić hoped to escape the attentions of the criminal tribunal in The Hague. In 1997, soon after his indictment for genocide, crimes against humanity and war crimes, the Prijedor notable had fled the town and taken refuge in Serbia. His name had never been mentioned publicly by the Tribunal, but the man who had been mayor of Prijedor during the war had sensed a change in the weather when his deputy, Milan Kovačević, was arrested by NATO forces.

For four years Milomir Stakić lived in Serbia without being molested, until 22 March 2001. The new Serbian authorities, under pressure to show tangible signs of cooperating with the ICTY, had decided to arrest a few of the people charged with war crimes living on their territory. Naturally Belgrade would hand over a Bosnian Serb in preference to one of its own citizens, and it fell to Milomir Stakić to inaugurate this new policy. On 22 March 2001 he was arrested without warning by a Serbian police unit, and he was in The Hague by the end of the next day. The former Yugoslav president, Vojislav Koštunica, was critical of the deportation which had been organized by his great rival, the late Serbian prime minister Zoran Đinđić. But Human Rights Watch praised the arrival in The Hague of a man 'accused of participating in and organizing the crimes committed in the municipality of Prijedor in the early 1990s'.

A Doctor Deeply Involved in Ethnic Cleansing

Milomir Stakić, his round face edged with a closely trimmed brown beard, appeared for the first time in front of his judges on 16 April 2002, three months after his fortieth birthday. After that this man, born in a country village near Prijedor called Marička, spent five days a week sitting in the blue chair provided for the accused in the Tribunal's hearing room no. 2. Only recently he had been a doctor at Prijedor hospital; now he was in the passive role of a patient whose past was under investigation. To help the judges with this task, two types of specialist faced each other across the hearing room. On one side was the prosecution led by an Irish barrister, Joanna Korner, and her substitute Nicholas Koumjian. They maintained that as chairman of the Prijedor Crisis Staff Milomir Stakić had been directly responsible for establishing the Omarska, Keraterm and Trnopolje detention camps and for the mass expulsion of Bosnian Croats and Muslims. 'The attacks on villages, the round-ups, the forced detention in camps, as well as the expulsions and forced movements of population, took place at the instigation and on the orders of the Prijedor Crisis Staff, with its support and assistance, and in the full knowledge of its members. Milomir Stakić played a central role in the events that occurred in the municipality of Prijedor and he knew that the Crisis Staff's decisions would result in murders and acts of persecution,' his indictment specifies.

On the other side of the chamber sat Branko Lukić and John Ostojić, two lawyers of Serb extraction who specialize in Prijedor cases. Unable to defend their client by denying the crimes committed in the municipality, they chose the strategy of trying to show that Milomir Stakić had not wielded any real authority in the town and the exactions had been committed by the army and the police. They were asking for an acquittal. Stakić himself paid close attention to the arguments that were going to determine his immediate future, back home to Prijedor or long years in jail. Always dressed in well-cut dark suits, he took occasional notes during the hearings, sometimes scratching his chin with a forefinger but showing few signs of emotion or nervousness except on one occasion, 26 June 2002, the day a Bosnian Muslim aged twenty-seven gave his evidence. Nermin Karagić had been seventeen in 1992 when he had been taken with his father and a hundred other men to the Ljubija stadium. Serb soldiers had executed dozens of the prisoners at random. Nermin had been made to load two bodies into a bus, one of them his father's. Later, the survivors were taken by bus to a wood where they had been executed in threes. Nermin by some miracle had escaped. Now he has multiple psychological problems, but he still found the courage to give evidence.

Milomir Stakić was moved by this tragic account, and ordered his lawyers not to cross-examine the witness in view of the dreadful experience he had lived through. 'It's the first time I've ever seen that in a trial,' remarked the Tribunal investigator who had arranged for Nermin Karagić to testify. What would Milomir Stakić have been feeling at such a moment? Did he realize, like his former deputy Milan Kovačević, that he had been swept away by 'collective insanity' during the events of 1992?[1] Was he sorry? No one could tell.

Other witnesses trooped through the chamber, many of them people who knew Stakić personally or professionally. Ibrahim Beglerbegović was one who came to testify against his former colleague. 'When I found myself facing him I was overcome with emotion,' he said later. 'He too was a doctor, he was the head of the Crisis Staff, and you know, nine of my colleagues died during the war, in those camps. It was really strange seeing him there in that tribunal.' Ibrahim Beglerbegović would have liked the doctor to be found guilty of genocide: 'that would confirm what we've been saying for the last ten years.'

But the judges on 31 July 2003 found Milomir Stakić not guilty of genocide. They considered that the intention of the Serb leadership in Prijedor was to displace the Bosniak and Croat population of the town, not to destroy it. However they did not rule out the possibility that other leaders, on a higher level, might have intended to annihilate the non-Serb communities in Prijedor. Then, underlining the seriousness of the crimes Stakić had committed – exterminations, persecutions, murders and forced expulsions – they ordered him to be imprisoned for life, the heaviest sentence so far imposed by the ICTY.

The proceedings however had taken place amid general indifference. While a vast scrum of more than five hundred journalists had rushed to the opening of Slobodan Milošević's trial on 12 February 2002, hardly a handful turned up a few months later for the first day of Milomir Stakić's. And after the first hearing, only one or two dogged souls stayed with the proceedings, relegated to the Tribunal's room number two which is very small and difficult to reach. To get there, visitors first have to find an available UN guard to escort them through aseptic corridors reserved for ICTY staff: unlike the other two hearing rooms, this one has no access from the public areas of the Tribunal. And when they get there, another big surprise: the public and journalists' area contains just five seats, in the UN colours, one already occupied by the security guard. Little better than a broom-cupboard really.

On the other side of the bulletproof glass separating the public from the courtroom, Milomir Stakić is astonishingly close owing to these exiguous dimensions. In January 2003 Nusreta's brother, Nusret Sivac, came to the court to testify that he had seen Dr Stakić making an official visit to Omarska camp in 1992, accompanied by other Bosnian Serb officials. Nusret, who had already given evidence in several other trials at The Hague, had not been able to help remarking to the judges: 'You know, your trial, I mean Mr Stakić's trial, no one mentions it.' As he spoke, the public seats held a total of two people.

Forgotten by the international media, this trial also passed totally unnoticed in Prijedor. *Kozarski Vjesnik* and RTV Prijedor had lost interest in the town's former mayor, whose most trivial declarations they had reported and broadcast exhaustively during the war in Bosnia. The Sarajevo daily *Oslobodjenje* did try to give it some coverage, but as its local correspondent Besima Kahrimanović points out, the paper only sells a handful of copies in Prijedor. Although some dozens of local inhabitants had given evidence either for or against Stakić, the Prijedor media did not think fit to publish any of their declarations, Muharem Murselović noted with a certain bitterness. There is something surreal about the way this trial seemed from Prijedor to be a sort of faint, distant mirage, and only assumed solid form at The Hague, two thousand kilometres from the place where the crimes at issue had been committed.

There is a strange sense of failure in recalling the declarations of judge Claude Jorda, then chairman of the ICTY: 'One of the Tribunal's missions is to prevent any attempt at revisionism by establishing the facts in clear fashion.' For this to succeed in the case of Prijedor, the town's Serb population would have to be given the facts established by the Tribunal as a counterweight to the siren voices falsifying History. A few visits to the region are enough to show that this has not happened.

In 1997, the verdict on Duško Tadić included a detailed description of the conditions endured by detainees in the Omarska camp to prevent Serb revisionists from denying its existence. Unfortunately no one in Prijedor read the verdict, nor did the local media cover the trial. Nor, alas, did anyone from the ICTY go there to explain a document several hundred pages long and only available in English or French (the Serbo-Croat translation did not appear for another two and a half years). Five years after the original trial verdict, a lot of Serbs in Prijedor and even Omarska were still denying the camp's existence, or at least its terrible reality.

Putting the Tribunal in Touch with the Scenes of Crime

By 1996, some members of the prosecutor's office were becoming aware of the need to 'put the Tribunal in touch' with the populations involved in and affected by the crimes. In national legal systems, trials are generally held in the region where the crime was committed. The victims and their families, the relations of the accused and other members of the population can easily attend the trials. Proceedings are reported in the local or national press depending on the importance of the case.

Established in The Hague for reasons of security – Bosnia still being in a state of war when it was first set up in 1993 – the ICTY is adversely affected by the resulting remoteness. The victims, apart from those called to give evidence, generally lack the means to attend hearings. The Serb population of Prijedor, subjected to years of relentless propaganda, is exposed only to the fragmentary, distorted accounts of the Tribunal's activities to be found in the local media – when, that is, they mention them at all – which do not convey the reality of the trials. But in the considered opinion of Branko Todorović, president of the Helsinki Committee, a human rights organization in Republika Srpska, being confronted with this information, traumatic though it often is, helps people to see and admit reality: 'I was in The Hague for some of the hearings in the trials of the Keraterm guards Sikirica, Došen and Kolundžija. It was very shocking. Most of all when the accused themselves, Bosnian Serbs, admitted to having killed or ill-treated prisoners. Unfortunately, there's very little press coverage of these trials here in Republika Srpska. As a result, people don't believe there were hundreds killed in the camps around Prijedor or more than seven thousand at Srebrenica. They think these are accusations made by those who are against them, by the international community or Muslims and Croats. They ought to be able to see the Bosnian Serb accused in the Keraterm trial admitting that they committed crimes and that the camps existed.'

The statements admitting guilt made by Dragan Kolundžija and Damir Došen went virtually unnoticed in Prijedor. Back in his home town after serving his sentence, Dragan Kolundžija keeps a low profile. 'I still haven't got a job, I'm still haunted by what I did, I'd really rather not talk about all that again, I don't feel strong enough,' he told us by telephone. He declined to meet for an interview.

Awareness of this damaging distance between the Tribunal and the affected populations led to the idea of holding some of the trials in Bosnia gaining ground among members of the prosecutor's office, including the deputy prosecutor Graham Blewitt who had held the post from the Tribunal's beginnings. Although moving the whole ICTY looked logistically complicated, holding some of the hearings in Sarajevo or Banja Luka seemed an interesting possibility.

In 1996, a plan to hold hearings in Tuzla (north-eastern Bosnia) was rejected by SFOR for security reasons. In 1998, NATO forces again refused to guarantee the security of a court of criminal appeal that wanted to hold hearings in the village of Ahmići in central Bosnia. The prosecutor at the time, Louise Arbour herself, did not seem all that keen either.[2]

Since the end of 1999, however, these security considerations have seemed less of an obstacle. 'Before that, we were confronted with questions of security. It's no longer the case now. It would be quite feasible to hold hearings in Sarajevo, even in Banja Luka,' Graham Blewitt told us during an interview at the ICTY headquarters in 1999.

Soon after taking up the post of prosecutor on 15 September 1999, Carla Del Ponte embraced the idea enthusiastically. At a press conference in Arusha, Tanzania (seat of the International Criminal Tribunal for Rwanda, of which she is also prosecutor) on 23 February 2000, she announced her intention to explore all possibilities for holding some of the hearings in Kigali, and also in former Yugoslavia, in order to strengthen awareness of the Tribunal among victims.[3] The proposal was soon forgotten, however, as the UN and the member-states were unwilling to find the money. As if making victims properly aware of the justice process were somehow an optional luxury.

The very limited awareness of the Tadić verdict in Bosnia caused the president of the ICTY, Gabrielle McDonald, to start questioning the Tribunal's credibility. 'She was not so naïve to have expected a revolution in thought, but she had hoped that the Bosnian Serbs, when confronted with firm evidence about the camp, would begin to change their minds,' observed the American journalist Elizabeth Neuffer.[4] Despite the complete indifference of the international community and sometimes even of her colleagues, Gabrielle McDonald then decided to establish a dedicated information service for the populations of former Yugoslavia, the Outreach programme. Its aim was to make sure that the activities of the Tribunal would be transparent, accessible and intelligible to the different communities in former Yugoslavia. 'Failing that, not only will groups hostile to the Tribunal be able to give a negative and distorted image of it, but the Tribunal will also be unable to fulfil one of its basic purposes: to help restore and maintain peace in the region,' Claude Jorda explained in his report to the United Nations.[5]

Since its inception in September 1994 the programme has opened offices throughout the Balkans, in Zagreb (Croatia), Sarajevo, Belgrade (Serbia-Montenegro) and Prishtina (Kosovo). The Tribunal has tried to speed up the production of Serbo-Croat translations of its verdicts and main decisions. The hearings can now be followed live on the internet in Serbo-Croat. The judges have been invited to former Yugoslavia to meet their local opposite numbers, but also to talk to victims' associations.

But the communication programme is somewhat weakened by the half-hearted support given by the international community. While the Tribunal, which has become a respected institution on the international stage, has an annual budget of more than $100 million, Outreach does not even have a fixed budgetary line from the UN. 'We're kept alive by donations alone,' explained Refik Hodžić, until 2003 its director in Bosnia. The UN member states have turned a deaf ear to repeated requests that they make provision for the communication programme in the Tribunal's overall budget.

Despite this shortage of allocated funds, Refik Hodžić and his assistant Ernesa brought earnest enthusiasm to the task of promoting the ICTY's achievements in Bosnia. In the minute ten-square-metre office they shared on the eighth floor of the UN building in the Sarajevo suburbs were piled copies of court proceedings in Serbo-Croat, with newspaper articles and posters in favour of justice covering the walls. 'Sometimes we have to wait months for copies of verdicts in Serbo-Croat,' Ernesa complained. For local journalists who cannot follow the trials in The Hague such a long delay is unacceptable, and it restricts the quality of the media coverage.

A former journalist partly schooled by the BBC, Refik Hodžić gave as many interviews and press releases as he could to explain the Tribunal's activities and counter false stories and rumours about them. While nearly all the inhabitants of former Yugoslavia have heard of the ICTY, 'most of them have a very bad image of it owing to the negative propaganda' in the media.[6] 'Biased and misleading coverage by the media in former Yugoslavia is not helping the tribunal to achieve its objectives,' Hodžić explains, giving the Milošević trial as an example. 'An Albanian witness from Kosovo is describing a massacre in his village. Let's say that at one point he says that the shutters of the house opposite him were blue. During cross-examination, Slobodan Milošević shows that the shutters of this house were green, but otherwise can't demonstrate any inconsistency in the testimony. Well, I can tell you that a lot of the media are going to headline the fact that the witness lied about the colour of the shutters but won't bother with his description of the massacre committed, in this case, by Serb forces in Kosovo.'

In Croatia, after the indictment of General Bobetko for crimes committed against Serb civilians in 1993, most of the mass media bombarded their audiences and readerships with declarations to the effect that the Hague tribunal had just cast doubt on Croatia's accession to independence. 'The crimes committed against the Serbs and General Bobetko's alleged role in them went virtually unmentioned,' Refik Hodžić adds acidly.

By speaking out whenever they can, the people running Outreach are trying to give the populations of former Yugoslavia accurate information stripped of all political distortion. They also maintain contact with the victims' associations and try to explain some of the Tribunal's decisions, in particular the prison sentences imposed or releases on bail. This task, not always easy in the first place, becomes more difficult still when the staff of the Hague tribunal seem to treat testifying survivors and 'ordinary victims' in an offhand manner. The verdict on Biljana Plavšić contains an example of this. Among their arguments, the magistrates said that the fact that Carl Bildt (former High Representative in Bosnia) and Madeleine Albright (former US Secretary of State), 'witnesses of international renown, should have come to give evidence to that effect (in favour of the accused) also argues somewhat in favour of a reduction of the sentence'. This appeared to make the evidence of the survivors, people who had lost everything, less important to Judges May, Robinson and Kwo than the opinions of a couple of international celebrities. Nevertheless it is the victims who enable the ICTY to function and bring the guilty to book: without their accounts, none of this would have been possible. And these simple Serb, Croat or Bosniak citizens had often had to brave bloodcurdling threats to give their testimony, while for someone like Carl Bildt it was a completely risk-free act. This makes the lack of regard shown for these witnesses, whether deliberate or not, seem particularly distasteful.

Another hard-to-explain aspect is the selective pattern of prosecutions. In order to expose the ethnic cleansing policy in depth, the prosecutors have concentrated on a number of municipalities one of which is Prijedor. Providing proof that ethnic cleansing took place in a limited number of localities is enough to demonstrate the existence of a criminal enterprise on a larger scale, and subsequently to prove the guilt of the prime movers, the thinkers behind this plan. But there are dozens of towns where horrible crimes were committed and no indictments have been issued, a number of people working for the ICTY have pointed out. The fact that the Tribunal cannot reasonably be expected to prosecute all the individuals who committed crimes during the war – there are ten to fifteen thousand of them according to some estimates – does not make this situation any easier for victims from these 'forgotten' municipalities to bear.

The ICTY's 'closure strategy', the way it means to terminate its activities, is also meeting with a measure of incomprehension. Various UN member states have been pressing for the the tribunal to be shut down as soon as possible, feeling that the 21st century would be dominated by the struggle against terrorism rather than the administration of international justice. In response the Tribunal has set itself the target of tying up all the investigations and indictments by the end of 2004, concentrating on the highest-placed individuals. But the choice of indictments is sometimes misunderstood, especially by victims. In February 2003 two Kosovo Albanians were charged with war crimes. They had been camp guards and were accused of causing the deaths of some twenty Serb and Albanian civilians and of inhuman treatment. Grave and reprehensible though these crimes were, a number of senior ICTY staff said repeatedly that the Tribunal ought to be aiming rather higher than the camp guards. Why charge these two individuals and leave Slobodan Kuruzović, the commandant of Trnopolje camp, at liberty? Was it to show that criminals from all the nationalities or populations were being indicted to silence the complaints of Serb nationalists? Was it felt that Prijedor had had its full ration of indictments? 'It would just be nice to be told frankly what criteria are used to justify an indictment. Either you admit clearly that the aim is to charge a certain number of people from all the nationalities in former Yugoslavia, in order to deflect any complaints of partiality made by the nationalists, or you stick to the issue of the individual's level of responsibility, but in the latter case the logic should be applied all the way. There are people in Bosnia, Croatia and Serbia who have the same sort of profile as those two Kosovo Albanians, but who haven't even been investigated as far as I know,' observes one Bosnian journalist who has been following the Tribunal's activities.

For Refik Hodžić these issues simply mean more work. 'We'd have to have ten people to do it properly,' he sighs. But the United Nations are unwilling to make the 'financial sacrifice'. As Pierre Hazan points out, the Tribunal has remained 'a peripheral element in the planning and execution of Bosnian reconstruction by the international community'.[7] With the consequent risk that the ICTY's assigned task of establishing the true facts may fail to counteract revisionism on the local level, as seems to be happening in Prijedor.

It may be thought that a Tribunal should pay no attention to public relations, that its job is to administer justice. That is true enough in the case of traditional legal systems. But the new international justice has the stated aim of working for reconciliation and preventing the falsification of History. It therefore needs to communicate its message to populations that lack the means to have instant access to its decisions. Only then can the victims have some feeling that justice is being done, and the burden of collective guilt that oppresses some peoples be lifted.

If the historical truth unearthed by the Tribunal becomes something no one can ignore, revisionism with its toxic spores of future conflict can be swept away. And to get there, the Tribunal does not just have to convince Americans, West Europeans and experts in international jurisprudence but also, and in the first place, the populations of former Yugoslavia. It needs to satisfy the victims in their quest for justice, while at the same time demonstrating the real scale of the crimes committed. To Refik Hodžić the challenge facing the ICTY is a stark one: 'If the communications programme succeeds in its work with the populations of former Yugoslavia, then the Tribunal will have fulfilled its mission. If it doesn't, it will have failed.'

PART FIVE

An International Community Trapped by its Own Incoherence

The Balkans are not the powder-keg of Europe, but the barometer of the Old Continent which, having turned its face to the future, is trying to rejuvenate itself. Europe exists to the extent that it is present in the Balkans. The inverse is equally true.

Vidoslav Stepanović, *Milošević, une épitaphe*

'Why should I comment a sentence by Claude Jorda! They say what they want in The Hague, but we are on the ground and we do not have to comment on what they say there in The Hague. They are there, we are here. And this is not our mandate.' Red-faced and glaring with indignation, Pearse McCorley makes it clear that he is heartily sick of the ICTY president and indeed the whole outfit. The spokesman for the Organization for Security and Cooperation in Europe (OSCE) in Republika Srpska seems not to have liked our question.

It is 25 June 2002, and we have just asked him whether, as representative of a body charged essentially with ensuring democratization and respect for human rights, he feels that the ICTY's activities in Prijedor are contributing to the struggle against revisionism and promoting reconciliation, two aims defended by Claude Jorda. This has made Pearse McCorley lose his temper, and his anger, sudden and unexplained, is slow to subside. From the start of the interview the spokesman has behaved restlessly, fidgeting in his seat, shuffling his feet on the carpet, making and receiving telephone calls, jumping up to consult advisers and generally destroying the calm of his quiet, neat office on the outskirts of Banja Luka.

We point out that whatever his feelings may be, these two aims – countering revisionism and fostering reconciliation – can hardly be matters of total indifference to the OSCE. 'Because you are insisting,' he snarls, 'I'm going to tell you what I think about the work of the ICTY. I think it's counter-productive! We are here on the ground and we have to work with the people here. And this woman, what's her name, this woman who came here last week …' (we remind him that her name is Carla Del Ponte and she is the ICTY prosecutor), '… yes, this Carla Del Ponte. She comes and tells us she is fed up that the local authorities don't cooperate with the ICTY ...' We interrupt to say that she is right, surely? 'Yes,' MacCorley says, 'but we're on the ground and she's annoying them and we have to work here on the ground. After all if she knows where Karadžić is she only has to say!'

During a visit to Banja Luka a few days earlier, Carla Del Ponte had complained once again about the absence of cooperation from the authorities of Republika Srpska in the search for Radovan Karadžić. For what it was worth, the prosecutor recalled that the RS was the only former Yugoslavian entity that had still not arrested a single war criminal wanted by the Hague tribunal.

Like the international community itself, the OSCE is uneasy about this, and so is Pearse McCorley. But the Organization's spokesman, who has insisted on talking to us himself in place of the man responsible for Prijedor, Jose-Luis Martinez Llopis, despite the latter's probable better command of the local situation, is calming down at last. Still irritably, but in a more measured tone, Pearse McCorley corrects himself on the subject of the international community's activity: it's true, he admits, that the authorities of the RS are very slow to collaborate and probably not much use when they do. But he cannot help adding that the international community ought not to involve itself in everything. He has not made himself entirely clear, but his Prijedor colleague touches up the analysis: 'The priorities in this region are access to employment and the resumption of economic activity,' says Jose-Luis Martinez Llopis, before admitting in an aside that these questions of justice, reconciliation and arresting war criminals seem to be of secondary importance. An odd way of defending work and actions which are supposed to promote human rights and reconciliation. This point of view is widespread, though, in the international bodies at Banja Luka as well as in Prijedor town hall.

FOURTEEN

The Tangle of Priorities

Appointed on 27 May 2002 as head of the most powerful administration in the country, if not in the Balkans, Paddy Ashdown,[1] High Representative of the international community in Bosnia, had listed his priorities clearly in his inaugural speech: first justice, then employment by way of reforms. In September, he had given us his point of view: 'This country cannot really build its future until there is closure on the war years. Act number one is to bring to justice war criminals, act number two is the completion of the return process and act number three, let me say something that might surprise you a bit, is the rebuilding of the Stari Most [Old Bridge] at Mostar.'

The line was positive, firm and appealing. In just a few months he had moved on to the second stage. The creation of a single economic space for the two entities of Bosnia-Herzegovina ought to be the first priority of the international community and of the authorities in Bosnia, Ashdown said at Mostar in August.[2] During the campaign preceding the legislative elections of 5 October 2002, he repeatedly urged voters to favour the moderate and reformist parties as being more likely to establish stability and create employment.[3] A few weeks later he was still more explicit, and perhaps a little hasty, when he asserted in effect that it is the economy that worries and divides populations, not security, and that 'people need jobs, not words'.[4]

A month earlier he had gone even further in projecting this new posture with a disdainful response to Carla Del Ponte's complaint that NATO was being slow and inefficient in arresting Radovan Karadžić. 'I am not going to comment on what Carla Del Ponte says … Have you been to the Zelengora, have you been to the mountains of the RS? Well then I suggest that those who sit aside and criticize NATO should go up to the Zelengora [a hundred kilometres south of Sarajevo, near the frontiers of Montenegro and Serbia] and spend a couple of days over there. It's very difficult to arrest Karadžić. Those who sit in the safety of their boardrooms or wherever ought to recognize how tough it is for the NATO soldiers,'[5] the former Marine had said forcefully.

But early the following year Ashdown performed an unexpected about-turn, quoted in an article in the British daily *The Independent*,[6] highlighting the limitations of NATO action and suggesting that its troops were being procrastinatory, if not downright passive, in the matter of arresting Karadžić. The piece caused an instant uproar. Spokespersons for the Office of the High Representative (OHR) scrabbled about desperately for several days trying to limit the damage caused by what they saw as a gaffe.

For a long time, the representatives of the international community seemed to be trying to bring the justice effort to heel, to make it show modesty, humility and discretion. As if it were thought improper to make waves; as if everyone knew that war criminals were still at large and it was therefore pointless to keep referring to the fact; as if pleading for justice were seen as an obstacle to the future. For a long time, the international community persisted in believing that repeated incantations on the primary importance of the economy would obtain rapid concrete results. It consistently avoided associating its approach with the need for justice, although without it neither stability nor investment were at all likely. Short of making justice its sole priority, the international community ought at least to have made it clear that achieving justice is indissociable from improving the economy.

International officials tend to see the declarations of Carla Del Ponte and others connected with the Tribunal in much the same light as rusty vans and old washing machines dumped on their lawn, where everything ought to go smoothly, where political effort should be focused on the future and the past forgotten as quickly as possible. Real support, not inspired by afterthought, is very rare. Pierre-Richard Prosper, the American itinerant ambassador for war crimes, has recalled certain truths on a number of occasions: 'There won't be any progress in Republika Srpska while Radovan Karadžić and Ratko Mladić are still at large. The Bosnian Serbs will continue to suffer as long as there is a lack of cooperation by the RS authorities with the ICTY.'

With these harsh words, the American diplomat voices some of the aims of the Bush administration, which wants to see the ICTY closed down as quickly as possible so that all efforts can be concentrated on the 'war against terror'. A European emissary who has worked in Bosnia for several years is more explicit: 'The arrest of war criminals is essential for the establishment of a state governed by the rule of law. So long as they remain at large, the law is just a joke that applies to some but not to others. It's only when the rule of law collapses, as it did in Bosnia, that we realize it's the mainstay of a civilized society.'

The impunity enjoyed by war criminals in the Serb entity of Bosnia weighs down on the future of the whole of Bosnia. In June 2004 Bosnia-Herzegovina failed to gain admission to NATO's Partnership for Peace, and its prospects for admission to the European Union were as remote as ever. After years of trying not to think about justice, the international community started thumping the table. In June 2004, Paddy Ashdown sacked more than sixty Bosnian Serb officials belonging to the nationalist SDS party, including the interior minister and the speaker of the RS assembly, accusing them of giving help and support to Ratko Mladić and Radovan Karadžić. In December 2004, the United States banned the leaders of the main parties in power in the RS from being granted US visas. Police chiefs were also sacked. Even more importantly, the High Representative pressured the Bosnian Serb authorities to work on a report on the Srebrenica massacre, whose scale they had previously attempted to minimize. After years of denials, the RS government in June 2004 admitted that its forces had carried out the massacre, then admitted the scale of the killing with over 7,000 Muslims murdered, revealed the sites of mass graves and offered its apologies. The military analyst Antonio Prlenda takes the view that 'the pressure should be maintained until the people charged with war crimes have been arrested'. According to EU military sources, Ratko Mladić had even spent six months of 2004 hidden in a bunker belonging to the Bosnian Serb army.

The editor in chief of the daily newspaper *Nevavisne Novine*, Željko Kopanja, believes that the continuing freedom of Karadžić has strengthened the country's organized crime networks and plunged Republika Srpska into decline.[7]

With every day that passes, the freedom of Radovan Karadžić and Ratko Mladić makes the establishment of a genuine rule of law in Bosnia more difficult, and delays the development of the country.

FIFTEEN

Five Million Dollars Reward

Halfway up a lamp post in Sarajevo, a black-and-white poster consisting almost entirely of a mugshot of Radovan Karadžić, ex-political leader of the Bosnian Serbs; a similar poster nearby carries the photo of his alter ego Ratko Mladić. Below each portrait, a line of text offers a reward for information leading to capture of five million dollars, and at the bottom there is a telephone number: 066 222 305. These posters have been displayed in Bosnia for several years, but essentially in the Federation. In the RS, although some courageous souls put them up here and there, they never stayed up for long, both men still being widely regarded as 'heroes of the Serb nation'. Mladić and Karadžić are nevertheless among the world's most wanted war criminals, having worked in concert throughout the war.

Ineffective Sweeps

Born in Montenegro on 19 June 1945, Radovan Karadžić was the leading ideologue of Serb nationalism in Bosnia. A psychiatrist by training and a rather poor poet in his spare time, he became president of the Bosnian Serbs' Republic on 17 December 1992. 'Between 1 July 1991 and 30 November 1995, he participated in crimes committed for the purpose of taking control of regions of Bosnia-Herzegovina that had been declared integral parts of the Serb Republic. To achieve this objective the Bosnian Serb leadership, including Radovan Karadžić, drew up and implemented a plan of action that aimed to create impossible living conditions, involving persecutions and terror tactics intended to drive non-Serbs out of these regions, by the expulsion of some of those who were reluctant to leave and the elimination of others.'[1] On this basis, he has been charged since 1995 with genocide, crimes against humanity, violation of the laws and customs of warfare and serious infractions of the 1949 Geneva conventions.

Aside from this last, the same charges were brought against Ratko Mladić. 'Born on 12 March 1942, he served as a career officer in the Yugoslav People's Army (JNA) before joining the army of the Serb republic of Bosnia-Herzegovina - Republika Srpska (VRS). On 10 May 1992 Ratko Mladić took control of the headquarters of the JNA's second military district. Two days later he was appointed chief of staff of the VRS, a post he held until at least 22 December 1996.'[2]

Justice has been on their heels for ten years and there have been numerous attempts to arrest them, particularly in 2002, but without success. In effect, ICTY pressure on Belgrade to cooperate in the arrest of General Mladić had been stepped up considerably. Carla Del Ponte claimed that the army was protecting him with the tacit backing of the Yugoslav authorities, and went on to say that he was living in the Serbian capital, that his addresses were known and that he had spent a short time in hospital in December 2002. These facts were broadly confirmed by Nenad Čanak, president of the provincial Assembly of Vojvodina in northern Serbia. 'He is here (in Serbia) and can be seen in nine different places,' this political leader declared, contradicting Belgrade's repeated assertions that Mladić was no longer in the country.

Most of the real muscle-flexing was over Karadžić. On 28 February 2002, SFOR NATO troops launched two large-scale operations in the Celebici region, in south-eastern Bosnia, where Karadžić had allegedly been spotted. On 2 July, this time in Pale, the soldiers burst into a house which he had once occupied, but which had been empty since 1997. A month later, SFOR combed Čelebići again for two whole days. With a force of 'several hundred soldiers, more than a hundred vehicles and a dozen helicopters,' trumpeted some NATO mouthpieces, the net was closing around the most wanted of all the war criminals. Reproaches quickly followed, with some of the diplomats working in the region leaking off-the-record doubts as to the effectiveness of such high-profile operations.

Carla Del Ponte, soon backed by Amnesty International, infuriated the military with her intemperate criticism of 'these public relations operations' in an interview given to AFP. 'SFOR should really do something about arresting Karadžić,' she declared angrily. 'I'm sick and tired of reading in the press that they're mounting operations to arrest him and then that he hasn't been apprehended.' She went on to advise the people running SFOR to say nothing until the day the former nationalist leader was caught. 'Otherwise they should keep quiet, it's better like that.' Carla Del Ponte remains convinced that SFOR has the means to arrest Karadžić. Asked what was preventing the arrest from being carried out, she said she knew what the reasons were. 'But I can't tell you,'[3] she added.

Some of Carla Del Ponte's own remarks have looked rather like public relations manoeuvres. One, the announcement in April 2002 that Karadžić would appear before the ICTY in October, was counterproductive in a way she understands only too well: if nothing comes of them, declarations of that sort generate rancour on all sides and feed the region's all-too-vigorous undercurrents of rumour. It seems more appropriate for her to use the media to bend the west's ear about the impunity still being enjoyed by these two war criminals. When she says that she has 'Karadžić and Mladić stuck in my throat' and that the International Criminal Tribunal for former Yugoslavia 'can't close its doors without having brought them to justice', she is inciting the international community to put pressure on Belgrade and really do something to have them arrested. It is a warning that daily underlines the failure, or perhaps the lack of will, of the Western powers.

For one crucial and very annoying question will not go away: why were these two criminals, indicted in 1995, able to come and go in the sight of all, including sixty thousand heavily armed NATO troops, until 1997 and beyond? Why are they still at large? There is a range of answers. Western spokesmen have mentioned the risk of reprisals against their troops in the event of an arrest, but one cannot help wondering how serious the threat is. After the recent, admittedly less important, arrests in Bosnia, local populations have not shown their displeasure in a violent way.

Paddy Ashdown still insists that 'Karadžić has the support of the local population' and indeed a whole support network in the Čelebići region. And in fact this is apparent throughout the RS, at Foča, at Bijeljina and in the Prijedor region: graffiti, posters, books, pirated CDs and calendars all 'honour the heroes of the Serbian people'. But ten years after the end of the war, nationalist fervour is no longer what it was. Unemployment, retirement benefits, salary scales, emigration and reconstruction are the themes that really mobilize public opinion now. It should also be noted that nearly twelve thousand well-equipped and well-trained men are still present in Bosnia. There may be some risk, but surely not enough to prevent action. Excuse after excuse has been refuted by the facts: climate, geography, the impossibility of finding him despite the presence of specialist investigators and clandestine, invisible local 'trackers' on the terrain.

The only thing really lacking to the military arm is political will. Without that, troops on the ground cannot achieve much. Paddy Ashdown said it straight to the Bosniak paper *Dveni Avaz* in January 2003: 'The West still hasn't taken a political decision on the arrest of Karadžić.' The High Representative's view is shared by a European diplomat: 'I'm sure the international community isn't really prepared for the capture of Karadžić or Mladić. Their capture is a national duty, if not an international responsibility. No nation is ready to risk the lives of its special forces to arrest an individual. It's the reign of deceit. Look at the amount of energy the US has put into capturing Osama Bin Laden who killed three thousand people in New York, while Mladić murdered seven thousand at Srebrenica. They didn't scruple to use their technology to intervene and strike in the Yemen. If the slightest will existed in Bosnia, I'm sure the same methods could be used against Mladić and Karadžić.' In June 2001 Jacques-Paul Klein, former UN representative in Bosnia, had given us his viewpoint and identified those responsible. 'Don't blame the soldiers. Soldiers need orders. To arrest Karadžić, the political will has to be there. The political leaders of the international community ought to give the order to arrest him. If they did, the operation could take place. We're in a situation with the Western world parading its powerlessness to deal with the demon. This situation is bad for our credibility in Bosnia-Herzegovina.'

One possible explanation for the foot-dragging could be that the Western countries are not all that keen to see Mladić and Karadžić taken to The Hague. The two myrmidons of Serbian nationalism could use the platform provided by the tribunal to disclose secret deals and dubious little arrangements operated during years of rather inglorious war during which the international community, led by the UN, had a singularly undistinguished record. 'It's a peacetime extension of what went on in the war,' a former Prijedor doctor comments bitterly.

On 7 March 2003, Paddy Ashdown finally launched a campaign of a new sort aimed at 'weakening Radovan Karadžić's support network'. By issuing a decree authorizing banks to block the accounts of individuals obstructing the Dayton peace accords, the High Representative hoped to shut off the sources of money that had enabled the former president of the Bosnian Serbs to stay hidden for eight years. Soon after the decision two of his close associates, Momčilo Mandić and Milovan Bjelica, saw their resources frozen and their transactions stopped. 'Mandić, a known war profiteer, served as Karadžić's financier, while Bjelica, who is implicated in weapons and contraband smuggling, was his link with the outside world,' explained the OHR in a communiqué. Banks that continued to deal with these two men or anyone else suspected of helping war criminals ran the risk of losing their operating licences. 'If we want to kill the poisonous plant that Karadžić is, its roots must be killed. These actions are aimed at making his escape more difficult,' Ashdown said.

In 2004, these measures were extended, with more assets frozen and the sacking of political leaders and police chiefs. The US and some European capitals lent explicit support to Ashdown's actions and sanctions. The US supported the policy of firm treatment by stopping aid credits to Serbia and freezing SDS and Serbian company assets held in the US, as well as refusing visas to SDS and PDP leaders. Perhaps a little indiscriminately. *'It would be quite useful if the US were better at distinguishing between the leaders who cooperate with the ICTY and the others,'* complained one French diplomat in January 2005. On the ground, however, according to an observer of several years' standing, it is felt that the international community *'has little choice, unfortunately, except to bang harder on the table. There are small signs of a beginning of political will, but it is absolutely not present so far in the population at large. The Bosnian Serbs thought for a long time that they would win this war of attrition, that the European capitals and Washington were going to get tired of the ICTY. They're only just beginning to understand that they're risking a great deal.'*

In 2005, the tenth anniversary of the Srebrenica massacre and the indictment of Mladić and Karadžić should lead to further intensification of this pressure on the local authorities, especially those of the Republika Srpska. Despite all this, however, the question still remains: why wait ten years before acting firmly?

Big Shots and Minnows

Behind these two high-ranking leaders, myriads of lesser war criminals are hiding all over Bosnia, indirectly 'protected' by the impunity enjoyed by their seniors. In the case of Prijedor, the ICTY sought Željko Mejakić for eight years. He is one of the 'big fish'. Known familiarly as 'Meagić', he was born on 2 August 1964 in Petrov Gaj, in the municipality of Prijedor. Pre-war, he had served as the officer in charge of the village police station at Omarska. From May to August 1992 he ran the Omarska concentration camp. In this post and with these responsibilities, he had exercised total authority over the heads of the guard teams, over the guards and all other individuals who worked in or regularly visited the camp[4]. He took part in crimes, gave orders for crimes to be committed and helped cover up, where he had not organized them, the atrocities committed during this period: he knew everything and he ran everything. Since 1995 he has been under indictment for crimes against humanity and violation of the laws or customs of warfare. After the camp closed, he seems to have resumed his post at Omarska police station until October 1996, when he disappeared and could not be found. Eventually, in July 2003, he gave himself up to the ICTY.

Until 2003 the ICTY was also looking for Goran Borovnica.[5] On or about 27 May 1992, while Serb forces were capturing most of the Croats and Muslims in the Kozarac district, he is alleged with Duško Tadić to have ordered four men out of the columns of prisoners and shot them dead. He was charged with crimes against humanity, violation of the laws or customs of warfare and serious breaches of the 1949 Geneva conventions. His case was dropped when enquiries showed that he had died some months earlier.

International justice is no longer looking for anyone named in the Prijedor file. The last secret indictment concerned Darko Mrđa, whose arrest in Prijedor by NATO troops on 13 June 2002 surprised the local authorities and population. This police reservist was taken to The Hague, charged with crimes against humanity and war crimes, and in March 2004 sentenced to seventeen years in prison for his participation the massacre of more than 200 non-Serbs from Prijedor on Mount Vlašić on 21 August 1992.[6] The arrest led to speculation that other captures might be imminent, especially as war criminals, and not minor ones – former political officials, military officers and other local bigwigs – are still circulating normally in Prijedor.

One of these is doing his best to lie low, living in quiet retirement. His house lies not far from the centre of town, fifty yards from the railway bridge on the Banja Luka road. Slobodan Kuruzović is not bothered by the past in any way. Kuruzović was head of the Prijedor territorial defence, a unit composed of one to two thousand Serb volunteers that was involved in the overthrow of the elected municipal authorities on 30 April 1992. In May this man, who in civilian life had been administrator of a Prijedor secondary school, was appointed commandant of the Trnopolje camp. He rejects the words commandant and camp, preferring to describe himself as 'coordinator' of a 'reception centre'. In May 1994 he became director of *Kozarski Vjesnik*.

Slobodan Kuruzović refuses to talk. He does not answer the telephone, all calls being filtered by his wife. She says that he 'isn't available, he doesn't want to talk to journalists, he's got nothing to say about the past and it isn't worth calling again.'

All the same, Slobodan Kuruzović was made to come and explain himself to the ICTY at The Hague on 26 and 27 March 2003, following a subpoena issued by the judges in the Stakić trial. A small man with brown eyes, thin lips and a cunning expression, he appeared in front of the judges wearing a navy blue suit and a somewhat bucolic nineteen-seventies tie. Throughout his examination he was unable to hide a certain unease: as Judge Schomburg reminded him, he was appearing as a witness but still had the status of a suspect.

So the fellow tried to wriggle out of all responsibility. 'People came of their own accord to shelter at Trnopolje. Kovačević and Drljača contacted me by telephone. They put pressure on me to get me to look after Trnopolje. At first I didn't want to, and then I saw the state of the people over there. I'm very sentimental and sensitive, and I told myself I ought to help them. Trnopolje wasn't a camp, people were well treated there. Babies were born over there.'[7] When Judge Schomburg reminded him that rapes had occurred, Slobodan Kuruzović claimed to have been unaware of them. He claimed ignorance, too, of the decisions by the Crisis Staff aimed at preventing people from fleeing the area. Kuruzović continued to claim that people had been free to come and go at will. The judge persisted: 'You were sent some prisoners from Omarska, why didn't you let them go as soon as they arrived at Trnopolje?' Slobodan Kuruzović stared down at his desk to avoid the judge's gaze. 'I never prevented them from leaving, I couldn't decide, but I know in the depths of my heart that Trnopolje wasn't a prison.'

When the Tribunal showed him the ITN footage of Fikret Alić's starved body, he made the unblushing claim: 'that man was skinny like that before the war'. He referred to the July 1992 massacre of more than a hundred men in room three at Keraterm as an 'incident'. The judge corrected him: 'You can hardly call an event of that sort an incident. It was a crime.'

Kuruzović admitted that in 1992 'a lot of people didn't agree with the SDS in Prijedor', contradicting the nationalists' line that they were defending the interests of the majority when they had seized power by force. But his attempts to minimize his own role in the events were hard to swallow in view of the interview he had given to Radio Prijedor, three years to the day after the seizure of power in Prijedor by force. In that interview, he described at length and in detail his role, both active and executive, in that operation whose progress he recalled hour by hour.[8]

The ICTY judges concluded that Slobodan Kuruzović had indeed been commandant of the Trnopolje camp. In the initial verdict in the prosecution of Milomir Stakić, they named him for the rape of a woman detained in the camp. Giving evidence under a pseudonym, this witness described being summoned for interrogation by Slobodan Kuruzović in August 1992, to a house he sometimes used near the camp. After beating her up, he raped her a number of times, on one occasion cutting her with a knife.

Kuruzović denied having anything to do with these rapes and asked the Chamber whether the witness 'was seeking to denigrate the Serbian people' with this story. He also told the judges he had no need to resort to such extreme measures being 'quite a handsome man'. 'After listening to Slobodan Kuruzović's denials and contradictions, the Chamber of the first instance was not convinced by his protestations of innocence,' the judges concluded.

Despite this discreditable past, Slobodan Kuruzović remained assistant headmaster of the Desanka Maksimović school in Prijedor until 2003, without being bothered.

Another figure who had been very active during the seizure of power in Prijedor is Simo Mišković. He too had made much of his important role in 1992 during the 1995 Radio Prijedor broadcast. He still lives in Prijedor today. Via his mother, then his son, this man proved to be reachable on his mobile telephone and available for interview. He turned up at the Bridge restaurant on 18 December 2002 in a frayed but clean suit, closely shaved. Simo Mišković has a direct gaze, a powerful handshake and a broken nose. He described himself as a 'legal adviser' following 'studies in law and criminology at Travnik'. But this fifty-seven-year-old retired police officer sometimes strays from the subject under discussion in ways that seem deliberately confusing, if not barking mad when, for example, he remarks that 'the Third World War started two or three years ago, it remains to be seen when it will end', or that 'there's a fine line between democracy and anarchy' since 'the people is a sheep'.

Once past the pose of false modesty, it does not take long to get him to talk about his former responsibilities. Better still, he takes his time, sets the scene and takes evident pleasure in telling his story. He insists that he was approached to become head of the Prijedor branch of SDS, the party for Serb nationalists founded by Karadžić, on three separate occasions. Naturally he had succumbed to these entreaties, made the sacrifice of closing his café and on 11 September 1991 (until 16 August 1993) taken the chairmanship of that party which he hoped to make an assembly of 'intellectuals'. He wanted to 'prevent the chaos and disorder that came to Prijedor from outside'.

A hand gesture hammers out each point, the grave voice seeks to explain, to 'tell the truth'. Simo Mišković becomes fussily learned. He is unstoppable on the difficulties faced by his people, on 'the natural tendency of Croats and Bosniaks to have it in for the Serbs... Look what's happening in Sarajevo today. People are always against us.' To show how wrong they are, he brings in his family: 'It's always been respected by all the nationalities. It's got a very good reputation, just ask around.' We did so, and discovered that Simo Mišković is feared in Prijedor, even by Serbs and members of the international community. One of his sons, presented by Mišković as violent and wayward but 'misunderstood', had been seen beating up a woman in the street. Simo Mišković brushes all that aside with an impatient gesture.

His name appears in at least two inquiry reports on war criminals. Even the Bosnian Serb defence minister, who can hardly be suspected of legalist proselytism, regards him as 'being able potentially to be prosecuted for war crimes'.[9] He denies it, and boasts of his good relations with a UN policeman from Marseilles who lived next door to him until December 2002. 'No, none of that's true, I'm leading a normal life,' he says in the tone of one stating an obvious truth. 'If I'm named, perhaps it's because I was chairman of the SDS, no more than that. People have tried to blame everything on the SDS, the nasty things that war throws up. Let everyone admit responsibility for their own acts!' And the camps around Prijedor? 'They were in fact search and interrogation centres. If something wasn't quite right, as people claim, they should have complained to the police [who ran the camps] and then it would have come to court. But there were no prosecutions in Prijedor. Perhaps the police weren't as professional as they should have been, since there isn't a single document.'

Once again Simo Mišković promises to say everything. 'Three times they've tried to kill me, twice they've tried to send me to The Hague,' he says, chin jutting in a habitual gesture. 'Soon I'm going to write a book with all the documents to affirm the truth, because everyone on both sides is too subjective.' But there is one unarguable truth on which he will not want to go into much detail. Of the ten members of the Prijedor Crisis Staff, two ended up in The Hague. One of them, Milan Kovačević, died of a ruptured aneurysm at the ICTY building on 1 August 1998 and the other, Milomir Stakić, was sentenced to life imprisonment on 31 July 2003. A third high-ranking Prijedor war-crime suspect, the former police chief Simo Drljača, had been killed resisting arrest in August 1997.

In her report, Hanne Sophie Greve also named Marko Pavić, today mayor of Prijedor, as one of the individuals who had played 'a pivotal role' in the seizure of power in 1992. Pavić had already been mayor of Prijedor in the past. He was also at one time director of posts and telegraph. However, the written ICTY verdicts, very detailed on the composition of the Crisis Staff and the principal actors of the ethnic cleansing, especially in the Stakić case, do not name him.

Other perpetrators of low deeds had befouled the town's atmosphere for some time before making themselves scarce. The case of Srđo Srdić, local boss of the 'Serb Red Cross', is fairly representative. A dentist by profession, said to be well known as an amateur actor, this character who would now be about seventy-seven years old was once a close associate of Radovan Karadžić, according to Hanne Sophie Greve. He has also been described as an SDS representative in the Bosnian parliament. International journalists, survivors of the events and UN representatives reported cases of abuse, robbery, trafficking, forced expulsion, etc., perpetrated by the local Red Cross during and after the war, when Srđo Srdić was supposed to be running it. No one knows where he is living today.

There are others. Human Rights Watch, the UN's commission of experts, and to a lesser extent the International Crisis Group have all devoted much time to retracing and examining, with due prudence and accuracy, the deeds and utterances of quite a few leading citizens.

SIXTEEN

Journalists on Parade

No survey of the 'fish' of various sizes who are of interest to the ICTY would be complete without some reference at least to the role of the media during the war, and to the continuing presence at their managerial levels of some thoroughly dubious characters. 'The media played a crucial role in the ethnic cleansing campaign in Prijedor. Radio Prijedor, directed by Mile Mutić, and *Kozarski Vjesnik*, bear a great deal of responsibility,' commented the ICTY chief investigator for the Krajina region.

Their Masters' Voice

Mile Mutić ran the local TV station RTV-Prijedor. His engagement on the side of the Serb forces is proven and unarguable. The Omarska survivor Rezak Hukanović wrote that 'Mutić had to be considered one of the founding fathers of the deformation of the history of this city and its people, the people of the Kozara Mountains.'[1] Of the many witnesses testifying to Mutić's activities, Muharem Nezirević stands out. Born in Prijedor and now resident in Sweden, Nezirević was editor in chief of Radio Prijedor and *Kozarski Vjesnik* until his resignation and internment at Omarska, then at Keraterm. On 22 May 1996, during the trial of Duško Tadić, he described the climate in the editorial offices during the war in Croatia and later during the seizure of Prijedor by force:[2]

Question from the judge: I would like to ask you a few questions about the way the war was covered by the local media. Was the coverage of the war by local media, Radio Prijedor, *Kozarski Vjesnik*, objective or not?

Answer: It was not objective. When I was editor at Radio Prijedor two journalists, Živko Ecim and Rade Mutić, without anyone's approval mine or I do not know who else could have done it, used to go to Pakrac or Lipik [in Croatia, about 150 kilometres north of Prijedor]. An armoured car used to come and fetch them. Sometimes they would turn up in uniforms and they brought reports from Pakrac or Lipik. Mile Mutić, Director of the *Kozarski Vjesnik*, also went to Pakrac or Lipik, but he went there, returned very quickly and said that he had been given a new mandate. In the beginning it was (...) photographs of the soldiers about their life or their statements, and then Mile Mutić came with the text about what the Ustashe were doing and what they had done to the Serb people in Croatia. There was an example in which they said they would make a wreath of children's fingers. (...)

Q: Let me just finish up quickly on the coverage of the war in Croatia. As time went on did it become more aggressive?

A: In the beginning it was not very aggressive. It had started after the takeover of power in Prijedor.

Q: As the coverage of the war became less objective, did you make an effort to remedy that situation?

A: I tried whatever I could do because at my news desk the people who worked there belonged almost to only one nationality. In the morning where I would come to work I would look around me, almost all Serbs were around. Four, five of them used to go to the front line in Pakrac and Lipik. Whatever I would tell them to do they would just lower their heads and continue, not taking notice. The only thing that I could do is not to give them as much time on the radio of their reports, just to shorten their reports to some 10 or 15 minutes. Sometimes I would take the text of Rade Mutić so it would not go on air, and the following day he would come up and threaten me. (...) So the Director, Mile Mutić, who would often come to the meetings of our news desk in uniform, who had a direct telephone line with the Defence, and he two or three months before the takeover brought the people from the Territorial Defence saying that 'there was a danger of somebody coming to burgle our radio', and two or three days (later) it came, it arrived, somebody burgled the place, and the people from the Territorial Defence came and they were armed and they were there sitting for two or three months before the takeover of the radio.

(...)

Q: Were you the only Muslim on the editorial board?

A: Yes.

Q: After the takeover did you resign from Radio Prijedor?

A: Yes, after a couple of days.

Q: You have mentioned the naturre of the coverage which followed the war in Croatia. What was the nature of the coverage of events from Radio Prijedor and *Kozarski Vjesnik* after the takeover?

A: For the first two weeks it was almost as normal, slightly attenuated. They were even, you could even hear Muslim songs up until 20th May, up until the incident at Hambarine on 22nd May 1992, and then after that everything became open, and then open propaganda started against everything Muslim and Croat.

Q: What kind of propaganda? Can you give us some examples?

A: Yes, I can. To me, as a person and as a journalist, it is inconceivable how much very respectable people in Prijedor, professional people like doctors... for example (...) it was said that Dr Mahmuljin wanted practically to kill his colleague, Dr Živko Dukić, because he was all the time after a heart attack of the other doctor, he was on purpose giving him the wrong type of drugs, and had it not been for a Serb lady doctor, Dr Živko Dukić would have died (...).

Q: In addition to these attacks on Muslims, were there other things which dominated the propaganda in the new *Kozarski Vjesnik*?

A: There were such topics, that the whole world was against the Serbs, that media the world over were writing only against the Serbs, that the Serbs were a celestial people, that they were a much-suffered people which was armed, and they knew how to defend themselves, they attacked numerous Western politicians and (displayed) a very low ethical level falling beneath both the human and journalistic code of conduct.

(...)

Q: Did you serve a useful purpose for the editorial board and the Serbian officials as a Muslim editor of *Kozarski Vjesnik*?

A: I believe so, yes, up until a certain moment when everything became open.

In her testimony during the trial of Miroslav Kvočka and others Nusreta

Sivac, too, said that Mile Mutić had been 'dressed in uniform, had a military rank and had a military telephone on his desk'. Even if some statements or articles had to be produced under armed threat, Radio Prijedor daily, and *Kozarski Vjesnik* (print run three thousand in 2003) each week, served as the mouthpieces of the Serb authorities.

Eleven years after the events Mile Mutić, not very surprisingly, denies everything from beginning to end. A fat, sixtyish nationalist hack, he sits comfortably in his gloomy office in a down-at-heel socialist-era apartment block. Reminded of his own declarations in the past, his membership of the Crisis Staff, his semi-permanence as a local media boss, he has a practised and winsome response. 'Look at my beard and white hair, my blue eyes: what do you see, a saint or a bloodthirsty ruffian? No, believe me, what's been written about me is full of lies and false stories. Everything that's said against me is propaganda by the nationalist parties,' he replies with an air of sugary bonhomie. So what about Muharem Nezirević's testimony to the ICTY? Mutić admits to knowing him. 'He's a Muslim who lives in Sweden [he went into exile there to escape the war and has stayed on]. But the truth of the matter is that when the war broke out Muharem Nezirević was on holiday in Sweden. I begged him on my knees to come back and stay at RTV Prijedor but he wouldn't. He preferred to stay over there on permanent vacation.'

Since the end of the war Mile Mutić has been promoted. He has become director general of a group comprising the three local media: Radio Prijedor, the weekly paper *Kozarski Vjesnik* where he doubles as editor in chief, and RTV Tele-Prijedor. For a while its broadcasting licence was in doubt, not for ethical or security reasons but financial ones; but the media baron eventually secured the coveted renewal.

From his throne, he exercises an influence on local life that is not inconsiderable, although happily less pervasive than it once was. To the international community he poses as an independent journalist confronting 'threats from the mafia, from the political forces and from extremists of every hue'.

Paddy Ashdown's Cock-up

It was the hand of this 'dependable and irreproachable' man that the High Representative of the international community, Paddy Ashdown, chose to clasp on 25 September 2002. Mile Mutić has been smirking about it ever since. Manna from heaven: the photo of the handshake appeared on the front page of *Kozarski Vjesnik* two days later. What should have been a news story illustrating Ashdown's support for the independent, courageous press emerged as a paparazzo-shot of a massive gaffe, sending a terribly negative signal to refugees and Serb moderates alike. The clip went to all the news agencies, infuriated the refugees and aroused a storm of incredulous complaint, even from inside the High Representative's office. 'It's *unbelievable* that given the number of advisers and experts covering the elections, human rights and God knows what else besides, who ought to have set him straight, he could still screw up like that,' muttered one appalled bureaucrat. Especially as genuinely independent media do exist in the region, whatever Paddy Ashdown's entourage may have implied after this incident in the hope of saving face. One of them is Radio Free, which the OSCE had rewarded in 1999 for the quality of its output. Paddy Ashdown cannot have heard its voice on that morning of 25 September 2002.

As the High Representative toured the officers' messes in Prijedor that day ('Well done! *Carry* on…'), Zoran Baroš was there too. He is not a journalist, anyway not officially these days: his primary job is communications officer of Prijedor town hall, but he files occasionally for the Serbian daily paper *Euroblic*. A quiet, discreet character in his forties, he was the director of Radio Prijedor during the war. In 1995, to celebrate the anniversary of the seizure of the town by force, he had conducted indulgent interviews with Simo Mišković and Slobodan Kuruzović, retracing the glorious hours of April 1992. But his personal career and history seem more sinuous and ambiguous than Mutić's. He appears to have been taken off the air for a while for allowing Bosniak families to make broadcast appeals for their missing relations. After clumsily rejecting all the responsibilities attributed to him by investigators ('the names of all the people who stayed during the war are on that list'), he ends with the plea: 'Show me a single journalist who would have said no to the political authorities.' Elsewhere, though, Zoran Baroš's discourse displays the same slightly distasteful tendencies as that of many present-day Serb officials, for example when Fikret Alić's name comes up. The photo of Alić's traumatized face and body reduced to skin and bone, behind the barbed wire at Trnopolje camp, was one of the most memorable images of the war, seen worldwide in 1992. In virtually the same words as Slobodan Kuruzović, Baroš claims that Alić was well known to be 'already skinny like that before the war'. An article published by *The Observer* in 2002 recalled, for those who needed it, that according to the Danish medics who treated him Fikret Alić had been in a pitiful state, having lost forty-two kilos of his body weight – six and a half stone – during his passage through the camps in 1992.[3] This revisionism, widespread among Serb officials, and this mixture of professional roles, do not prevent Baroš from sitting as a member of the very official Bosniak Press

Council which professes 'freedom of thought' and 'responsible use of words', and is always quick to deal with complaints alleging violation or infraction of press freedom.

Nusreta Sivac finds it regrettable that the ICTY should have chosen not to prosecute some of these media people. 'After Rwanda, some journalists were indicted by the ICTR [International Criminal Tribunal for Rwanda, based in Arusha, Tanzania] for their propaganda activities,' she points out.

In its November 2000 report on war criminals, the political analysis institute the International Crisis Group included a long list of recommendations for NATO, the ICTY, the OSCE, the OHR and the UN, but also for the central government of Bosnia. The measures suggested ranged from simple requests for information on the past actions of alleged war criminals, via the suspension of politicians, military officers and administrators to the arrest and trial of some of these. In the case of Prijedor these proposals have so far had little or no effect. The presence of these men may not cause immediate problems or rioting, but it does constitute a serious obstacle to reconciliation. And even worse, by agreeing to meet and work with them the international community becomes, willy-nilly, their passive accomplice. This encourages them in their false certitudes and at the same time inhibits the expression of moderate, independent or multi-ethnic opinion. The effect is utterly loathsome. Indirectly, the permanent presence of these 'small and big fish' – officially innocent, remember – helps maintain a persistent climate of unease and insecurity.

SEVENTEEN

Otherwise Everything's Fine

One or two of the international agencies have sometimes shown an inclination to rubbish the security record and insist that violations of human rights were continuing, or at least use isolated cases as evidence of a general tendency.[1] While there has been no surge in the number of incidents and attacks in the Prijedor area, there is a worryingly persistent feeling of instability which seemed to be worsening in the closing months of 2002.

Thus, the month of December maintained or improved the average, starting on the 4th with an attack on a building used by the Muslim community in Prijedor, the third in a year, occurring on the eve of Eid-el-Fitr (the festival marking the end of the month-long fast of Ramadan); continuing on the 13th, this time with an attack on a mosque at the edge of Prijedor that was undergoing reconstruction after being demolished during the war; the defilement and vandalism of two Muslim graves on the night of 22nd–23rd; a grenade attack later the same day on the Bridge restaurant (run by a Serb) in the centre of town; and so on.

Attacks had been less numerous in earlier months, but still far from negligible. A confidential UN report dated June 2002 listed, between January and May of that year, eighteen incidents linked to the return of refugees to the Prijedor area, comparable to the nineteen that occurred during the same period of the previous year (one of those involving the death of a refugee who had just recovered possession of his house, another the destruction of a journalist's car). Indeed there was an increased number of bombings during the spring, although some of these may have been linked to organized crime and gangsterism in the area. The UN commission established, without publicizing these sinister developments, that thirteen bombings and other incidents had taken place between 14 April and 31 July. In one of them, the son of a mediator had been severely beaten in a night club by two or more highly 'protected' thugs. The deterioration was taken sufficiently seriously for the police chief to deliver a public scolding about it on Radio Prijedor. But 2003 began in unchanged style with random shots fired, with an imam and Muslim pedestrians in the centre of town being insulted and threatened.

'Wogs Go Home!'

In September 2002, the climate of tension in Prijedor and the associated permanent risks were revealed in an emblematic incident. On the night of the 8th–9th, following the victory of FRY (Federal Republic of Yugoslavia) in the world basketball championship, a lot of youths in a convoy of a hundred or so cars celebrated the victory of their Serbian brothers by turning on the Muslims. Windows were broken, shots fired, threats and insults bawled: 'Turks and wogs go home!' From Omarska the basketball hooligans made their noisy way through Kozarac, a village with a large Muslim majority. The local police made practically no effort to intervene and the international police, taken by surprise, reacted incompetently. Only one policeman, a Serb, was injured. The violence took many people back to the worst moments of the war, exposing the weakness of the security apparatus and the poor cooperation between the local and international levels. All the refugees we spoke to said they had been frightened by these events.

And in any case, all these attacks could not have been more badly timed, coming as they did in the year the UN mission and its International Police Task Force (IPTF) were due to leave. This mission had been established in 1995 as part of the application of the Dayton peace accords, with the mission of 'policing the police'. The IPTF supervised, and when necessary corrected, the work of the local police forces in each of the Bosnian entities. The international policemen, from around forty countries of origin, were supposed to give concrete help with training a democratic and professional Bosnian police force working to international standards. In supervising the selection and training of future members of the forces of order, the IPTF sought to encourage the formation of a multi-ethnic body[2] and purge the ranks of political bigots and men with suspect war histories. Given the scale of police involvement during the 1992-1995 war, this was no small matter.

Of the seven hundred and fifty police officers checked in Prijedor district, seven hundred and twenty-three were allowed to continue serving, fifteen were suspended and twelve were reduced in rank and sacked, including the deputy chief of the public security centre and two station commanders, for their dubious activities in the past. Sixty IPTF officers and a number of administrative staff were made responsible for following up these operations.

Although the purge took rather a long time, no one can deny the IPTF's goodwill or hard work. All the same, one is entitled to wonder. The UN could really have done without the involvement of its people in prostitution all over the country and racketeering in Prijedor, scandals that obliged it to repatriate bent officers in several directions. And two other recent cases throw doubt on the effectiveness of the police reforms. After the basketball events of September 2002 in Kozarac when injuries were sustained by a Serb policeman in the village, some Muslim suspects had been arrested. When questioning them the local police asked about matters only very tenuously connected with the events of the night in question: 'Why are so many of you coming back? Are you getting ready for war? Where are you finding the money to rebuild such big houses?' It seemed the professional retraining still had some way to go. The other example seems more harmless than it really is: after an attack on a mosque in the Prijedor area, two Serb suspects were stopped for questioning. Asked why they had done what they did, they replied in effect that they felt they had to do something to respond to the removal of a Serbian flag from Mount Kozara, and were released forthwith.

These facts, passed on by a representative of the international community who is very well informed on the history of Prijedor, should not be taken as signs of an overall reality, but they do testify to a climate. They are of course grist to the mills of those who fear the consequences of the IPTF's departure from Prijedor. According to the international community's timetable, the UN mission in Bosnia should have ended on 31 December 2002, police matters passing into the supervision of the European Union on 1 January 2003. But the handover between the UN and the EU – more precisely between the IPTF and the EUPM (European Union Police Mission) – was to be accompanied by a drastic reduction in manpower, which in Prijedor's case would simply mean the closure of the international police offices, on the bank of the Sana at the edge of the town. For the EUPM seemed not to think it necessary, for the time being at least, to have any sort of presence in Prijedor, the second city of Republika Srpska and at one end of the territory, near an important frontier. In theory, a few European officers might be sent to Prijedor from Banja Luka, but only if necessary. It is hardly surprising that the changes worried the local population. 'Two polices were a lot better than one, especially here when one force, international and quite conscientious about the law, was supervising the other which was local and passably dodgy,' fretted one young Serb who lives in the town. Finally, after repeated calls from the mayor Nada Sevo for an international police presence in the town, and more particularly after a spate of new incidents, an EUPM office was opened. But only five officers were to be posted there permanently, senior men expected to work with their Bosnian counterparts.

Suspicion and Spying

This presence, largely symbolic though it is, will enable the somewhat cool and tentative cooperation between local and international forces to be pursued. During its training mission, the IPTF managed to establish links between the local police and NATO troops, although civilian and military activities are usually separate. 'It's a slow and complicated task,' said an IPTF spokeswoman before the end of the mission. 'SFOR of course has a very military approach, but the main thing is that it doesn't really trust the local police.' It is true enough that the latter, by failing to arrest a single war criminal since the end of hostilities, has done nothing to establish a climate of trust. And the continuing presence in its ranks of men who were officers or simple constables before and during the war is less than reassuring. The suspicion of SFOR's soldiers is not hard to understand.

Fifty kilometres from Prijedor, the SFOR base lies along the main road just outside Banja Luka. In his HQ surrounded by observation towers, sandbags and concrete barriers Major Alex Macintosh, commanding officer of the 2nd Company, 1st Battalion of the Welsh Guards (renowned for their work in Northern Ireland), dismisses the idea that there is any problem between his men and the local police. 'Relations are good and they're getting better,' he tells us. 'In our case, the events in Ireland taught us that we had to work with the local forces.' The remark is consciously upbeat and positive, but the reality is that Major Macintosh has little choice: the zone he covers is enormous, two thousand five hundred square kilometres, and the men under his command, although experienced, are not very many (167, around sixty of them in Prijedor) to monitor a population of half a million.

In practice, the official confidence is fairly relative, not least because from time to time it is severely shaken. Thus for example in May 2002, the troops discovered that two radar devices posted on high ground at Lisina, near Prijedor, were eavesdropping on SFOR communications.[3] In a raid on Republika Srpska's air force headquarters near Banja Luka, NATO seized documents and computers containing proof of the illegal listening. The affair preceded by several months the discovery that two Bosnian Serb firms had been selling weapons systems to Iraq under the very noses of Atlantic Alliance troops. The climate of insecurity and incipient threat in the Prijedor region did nothing to help calm SFOR's suspicions. In December 2002 it uncovered eight tons of weapons and ammunition in a private warehouse. The following month rockets and mines were found at a second location. These seizures were added to the results of Operation Harvest which NATO had been running since 1998.[4]

These misdeeds and the underlying chronic instability seem to require an international community that was initially ill-prepared, and whose trust has been abused, both to show more prudence and to consider a longer-term partnership with the local authorities. That will demand time and effort, but it is essential if the local system of justice, still lying fallow, is ever to be restored to some sort of normality.

EIGHTEEN

The ICTY School

The local legal system has become one of the international community's main priorities, being crucial to the country's future and its independence. It is a theme that comes up again and again whenever the questions of impunity, of arrests of war criminals, of security in general are raised. In February 1996, a few weeks after the Dayton treaty, a new agreement was concluded in Rome. Project 'Highway Code' was aimed at authorizing on local level, subject to ICTY approval, the trials of individuals other than those already indicted by the Tribunal. Before long the Prosecutor's office was inundated by some four hundred new cases.

The scheme did not swing smoothly into action. Just for a start, the long and costly effort involved would have to be paid for. But funds, alas, were limited and sporadic. A second and far from negligible problem was the risk of pressure being brought to bear on local courts. In 2001, for example, the UN mission discovered that the personality expected to run the canton of Mostar and its surroundings, Josip Mrdžo, had asked all civil servants to donate three per cent of their salaries to an organization known to support the families of Croatian war criminals, whether prosecuted by the International Criminal Tribunal at The Hague or by local courts in Bosnia. 'That led to a situation in which the judges and prosecutors of Mostar court were paying part of their salary to support the very people they were supposed to be judging and prosecuting, most notably in a case that involved Croatian war criminals... Incredible!' exclaimed a former UN spokesman, Stefo Lehman.[1]

Special Courts for Special Cases

Wolfgang Petritsch, who was Paddy Ashdown's predecessor as High Representative, decided to deal with these deviancies and eccentricities by correcting the internationals' aim. In the spring of 2002 he tried to recover the initiative by launching the idea of a supreme court. He envisaged it as a central institution that would establish a legal apparatus bestriding both the Bosnian entities, a step forward. A European diplomat who has served in Bosnia for nine years greeted the idea with approval. 'The existing local courts can't deal with war crimes and some of these monsters at large who terrorize prosecutors, judges, witnesses and also politicians, something they can't do at The Hague. I believe that for special cases you need special courts, like the ones they had for the IRA in Northern Ireland or the Mafia in Italy.'

The next stage began early in 2003. The ICTY, the Office of the High Representative and the central government met to define the outlines and mode of operation of a special chamber within the supreme court responsible for trying war crimes. 'This chamber ought to be capable of completing the ICTY's mission for a while, but it will also enable Bosnia-Herzegovina to acquire legal sovereignty,' the ICTY chairman Claude Jorda affirmed in January 2003. The institution, composed of Bosnian magistrates and prosecutors, sits in Sarajevo and practises the national legal code. The ICTY already means to pass some cases on to it, including the trial of the Omarska commandant Željko Mejakić.

This chamber has a fair amount on its plate. Of the five hundred crimes whose prosecution on local level has been authorized by the ICTY, only fifty had led to a trial by the beginning of 2003. A single example illustrates the difficulty of the exercise and underlines the need for support from the international community in these matters. In Mostar, ten accused (five Bosniaks and five Croats) had been acquitted in 2001. In the course of the trial all the witnesses had withdrawn their previous written statements. They had absolutely no faith in the court and not much more in the force of law. They were convinced that the accused would be freed and would then pursue them for the rest of their lives. Worse still, the former accused are free and cannot be prosecuted again. A stinging setback for the law and the witnesses, and a mockery of justice which the international community is still pondering.

The Serb authorities in Bosnia have so far shown very limited interest in prosecuting war criminals and have almost invariably refused to have anything to do with arresting them. Slow investigations, complicated by foot-dragging and obstruction, take place against a disorganized background inherited from the war and the communist system. Facts are difficult to establish, responsibility is diluted, pressures on individuals are persistent and sentences, when pronounced, are often inappropriate and arguable. 'It would be absurd and tragic if proceedings against policemen responsible for war crimes ended with simple suspensions from duty,' declared Refik Hodžić, the former ICTY spokesman in Bosnia. And just as sad if cases remained pending. At the end of 2002, sixty officers who had been suspended by the UN for alleged criminal activities had been waiting three months or more for their summonses.

Obrad Despotović regards himself as a victim of this system. His whole style is that of a hunted animal: furtive posture, few words, low voice, discreet meeting in the back room of a restaurant. An inquiry carried out by the IPTF revealed that he had taken part in interrogations at Omarska in 1992. He admits this but explains: 'I've studied law. I've always respected human rights. I questioned people at Omarska respecting those rights. I was obeying orders from my superiors. I didn't like what I was doing in that camp, but I didn't mistreat anyone. The worst things that happened at Omarska happened at night. But I only worked in the daytime, I never saw anything.' Downgraded and dismissed from the police at the end of 2001, Despotović has not been able to find work, his family is discriminated against and he has no recourse to local legal appeal, since this would contradict an international decision. 'It's a question of credibility,' a UN official explained. 'Omarska is an indelible stain. The mere fact of having worked there, even at the lowest level of responsibility, is enough to disqualify someone from the police.'

The UN authorized proceedings; the legal system did not follow up. No investigation opened, no trial scheduled: Obrad Despotović has not had a hearing, but he has been administratively sanctioned. Apart from having been an 'investigator' at Omarska – certainly something that requires looking into – he does not know what is alleged against him. Neither innocent nor guilty until his role in the detention camp has been elucidated, he remains in a sort of judicial limbo. And there is every probability that this will be a lasting condition, as it has been for others in the same position. The Despotović case exposes the disharmony between the international executive and the local judiciary. The lack of judicial tools, and in particular the general feebleness of political will, are also causing delays and inequalities which the future special chamber of the supreme court is going to have to deal with: to ensure justice not only for the expectant victims, but also for those who have been sanctioned without being tried.

This situation is today a rich source of misunderstandings and resentments in the local community, trapped by a policy decision that was certainly necessary but has not yet been followed by unarguable legal sanctions. 'The whole problem is there. Of course I'm bitter, it makes me angry to meet these people responsible for crimes, to be forced to see them, to know they've got the total support of the local authorities in Prijedor and the RS. But it's the way things are,' sighs the Omarska survivor Nusreta Sivac. 'The Hague can't prosecute everyone. We know they're only going to prosecute the top people. The ones at the middle and bottom of the scale will be left to local justice. But for the time being the conditions aren't right for these criminals to be tried locally,' the former magistrate says.

There is still a long way to go. The special Chamber for war crimes due to start functioning in January 2005 is only to try the most important cases. 'But there will still be hundreds of cases in Croatia and Bosnia that will need to be tried by ordinary local courts,' explained Richard Dicker, director of the International Justice Program at Human Rights Watch at the end of 2004. 'In local courts, we see bias against ethnic minorities, intimidation of witnesses and police stonewalling investigations.'[2]

NINETEEN

Internationals in the Dock

Ever since the start of its involvement in 1992 the international community has oscillated between indiscriminate interventionism and passive indifference, swerving unpredictably from one extreme to the other. This persistent ambiguity carries the risk that the initial plan – to turn Bosnia into a viable and peaceful state suitable for inclusion in the European Union – could lose support and even end by being abandoned.

The Limits of a State Within a State

There was no initial sign of such a development. From the beginning of the conflict, but especially after the peace accords, Bosnia quickly became a humanitarian and then military protectorate, governed by UN and then NATO troops on tactical level and by the High Representative's office (OHR) on the civil, political and sometimes legislative side, flanked by a whole swarm of international agencies and non-governmental organizations monitoring human rights, electoral procedures, the media, education, refugees and so on. A quick glance at the appendices to the Dayton accords[1] suffices to give some idea of the scale of the (often duplicated and contradictory) powers given to the bodies acting in the name of the international community, whose prime concern seems to be to proclaim grand principles – the multi-ethnic character of the state, its unity, its sovereignty, the right of return for refugees, the need for an independent judiciary and legal system, etc. – without always being able to guarantee their application in practice. In some cases, though, that of the OHR for example, prerogatives have actually been increased to enable it to attain its objectives, by the same token weakening the local authorities, marginalizing the central institutions and treating the country's sovereignty in a very offhand manner:[2] not so much a state *within* a state, rather a state placed *above* the Bosnian state and overruling it at will.

So the international community could soon face severe criticism if no progress is made on any of the problems that are looming. For, what with the economic slump and prevalent political bankruptcy, there is no shortage of grievances on either side of the frontier between Republika Srpska and the Federation. The Bosnian Serbs accuse the internationals of wanting the entities to dissolve and threatening the RS's long-term survival; at the same time they feel unfairly starved of humanitarian aid, too much of which they think goes to an outrageously favoured Federation. In the Federation no one can understand why Karadžić and Mladić are still at large despite the strong NATO presence; a very severe view is also taken of the ten-year record of the UN presence, which during the war failed to prevent the fall of Muslim enclaves – officially protected, but only on paper – or the Srebrenica massacre.

'You've seen the Dayton accords and the powers they give to the international community? And yet its representatives haven't arrested the war criminals at large and aren't helping refugees to go back home. Ever since 1992 there's been a flagrant lack of political will,' storms Mirsad Tokača, chairman of the state commission on war crimes, whose office is a stone's throw from the Bosnian presidency in Sarajevo. Schematic and impatient in his views, he dismisses the advances – real enough after all and fairly important – that *can* be credited to the international community: the ending of hostilities, the establishment of a single passport that does not carry ethnic identification and a single vehicle registration system that effectively abolishes the entities, the sacking of certain nationalists, sanctions against politicians resisting application of the Dayton accords, etc.

It has to be admitted however that what is missing from this list is the most essential thing: the vast and crucial enterprise of reconciling the communities. The internationals are staking a good part of their credibility on it, the country its shirt. Ibrahim, the former Prijedor hospital doctor who has given testimony and other help to the ICTY, explains that there are limits to what outsiders can achieve. 'We have to be grateful to the international community for stopping the war. But it still doesn't understand what's going on in Bosnia and Prijedor. The internationals work as if they were in a western country, but the situation's very different here. They should understand that the Bosnian Serbs are playing for time; they're dragging their feet in applying the international community's decisions, hoping that after a while it'll have had enough and leave things as they are, which is what the Serbs want. Just an example: Paddy Ashdown believes in the agreement signed in Sarajevo stabilizing the frontiers between Croatia, Bosnia-Herzegovina and Yugoslavia. Vojislav Koštunica (then president of what was still the FRY, now the prime minister of Serbia-Montenegro) ratified the text. But a few weeks later he went to Zvornik and declared that the RS is only temporarily cut off from the rest of the great Serb family. Koštunica signed the agreement to gain time, but in reality the ideas haven't changed and he's still propagating them.'

Lassitude and Incomprehension

It is everywhere perceptible that Bosnians are becoming increasingly disappointed with the international community. They feel that the internationals' meanderings and evasions (not to say indifference and aloofness) are persisting, that they are out of touch with reality. A mass of minor facts and details joins an already long list of criticisms and irritations. On all sides, for example, the idea is widely advanced that the humanitarian militants of the early days have been replaced by international civil servants, people who seem more interested in going by the book and advancing their careers than staking their all on a tumultuous cause. This perceived 'bureaucratization' causes bitterness and further alienation. 'Anyway, all these representatives are very well paid. If it's for doing nothing, they should go back home! They're living in excellent conditions. Weekends on the Croatian coast, sleeping through the winter in their nice warm offices. We expect concrete acts,' says Mirsad Tokača angrily. 'There's no point in all these blahblah conferences on human rights organized by the OSCE. And don't talk to me about peace. What peace do we have?' A European who works for an international organization is just as indignant. 'Some of the internationals here really don't give a damn about the local situation or what happened to these people during the war. There are incompetent ones too. I don't understand this lack of respect and concern for the country, and for the people we're working with.'

Thus, the representative of the Council of Europe, comfortably ensconced in the middle of Sarajevo, displayed remarkable ignorance and contempt for an important task. She was detailed to lead a British delegation to Prijedor and introduce it to the local authorities in October 2002. Perhaps this woman can be forgiven for not knowing the political party to which the mayor, Nada Ševo, belonged, but getting her surname wrong (Ševa instead of Ševo) was definitely a gaffe, while her total ignorance of the role or name of the president of the municipal assembly, Muharem Murselović, the only opposition politician of any weight in the town, was simply inexcusable. And adding insult to injury, she turned reality inside out by announcing that Sead Jakupović works closely and shares a good understanding with the mayor. In September 2002, quite astonishingly, the head of the OSCE office at Bihać (a hundred and twenty kilometres south-east of Prijedor) turned out not to know that thirty people had been working just outside Bihać for nearly a month in the rain and mud digging up more than sixty bodies from a mass grave. The exhumation had been reported at least twice on television and covered in the national press.

Prijedor is no exception to the rule. One simple fact says a good deal: in December 2001, following a drop in its budget, the High Representative's local office responsible for the reappropriation of properties and moving the inhabitants closed its doors, to concentrate its means and forces in Bihać from where it covers a large area of western Bosnia. In July 2002 the UNHCR closed its central office in Prijedor, its mission also being cut back because of diminished resources. Another reason for the reduction of High Commission activity in the area is the number and distribution of refugees deemed to have returned satisfactorily. But these figures should be taken with caution, and they exclude in any case the hundreds of Croatian Serb refugees still present in the town's environs, generally ignored by the international community. Nevertheless quite a few international officials explain this withdrawal by arguing that since the situation is so much more satisfactory in Prijedor than elsewhere, it would be better to concentrate effort on zones and populations that need it more. But 'satisfactory' does not necessarily mean good. This state of mind, often influenced by the discourse of municipal authorities who want their town to serve as a model, gives a leading role to information management and attaches exaggerated importance to visible results.

But the approach has the serious drawback of relinquishing too readily the pursuit of long-term concerted action by the agencies, local authorities and population. SFOR, the OHR, the HCR and other UN agencies, and to a lesser extent the OSCE, all approved more or less unequivocally, too quickly and too visibly the way Nada Ševo was running the town. While the eviction or relative marginalization of the Serb nationalists on Prijedor municipal council is to be welcomed, it hardly obliges people to give Mrs Ševo their unqualified support. Few voices have been raised to criticize economic choices that threatened the refugees, to question the mayor's silences on subjects like mass graves and racist vandalism or worse, to expose her lack of enthusiasm for real reconciliation.

The picture is the same with monitoring what appears in the local media, a domain where the OSCE and to a lesser extent the High Representative's office nevertheless have extensive powers. But the Prijedor official at the Organization for Security and Cooperation in Europe finally admitted that, despite his areas of responsibility, he 'wasn't monitoring their activities', or indeed paying much attention to the campaign for the 5 October 2002 general elections. Although these were the first elections being supervised unaided by the Bosnian state, it seems wholly extraordinary that the representative of an institution that had organized all the previous polls should seem so uninterested in these civic proceedings, fundamental as they were for the country and the balance of political forces in the region.

Fear of Showing Courage

This is less a problem of personnel than of the mission entrusted to the OSCE. What is the effective role of that international organization? The viewpoint of its representative in Banja Luka, Pearse MacCorley, and its limitations, were mentioned earlier. The head of the Prijedor office is a privileged and attentive observer of local life. But, the mandate perhaps being too vague or too broad, his work of observation and consultation is not followed up or listened to. What use is it, what can its destination be, in the absence of other international agencies? It could help to build bridges between communities, religious associations, generations. But that would take time; staff the OSCE does not have in Prijedor; and courage, not to mention luck.

It is difficult to assess how well-rooted the internationals are in Prijedor, where their field of action lies, what contacts they have with the local population and how they perceive it. There is one element, however, that must affect the way judgements are made: the fact that all the NGOs and major international agencies make extensive use of locally hired staff. In principle, through their knowledge of the terrain and the language, these individuals, 'the locals' – a term that can acquire a pejorative dimension on the lips of some internationals –, are an excellent source of information and analysis. But on closer examination, before the international agencies left Prijedor, it emerged that virtually all the local staff were Serbs, in apparent defiance of the principle of multi-ethnicity. Obviously the main reason for this was that Bosniaks, driven out during the war and in many cases still abroad, would have been less available because less numerous; there is nothing to suggest a plot or systematic pro-Serb bias. But their over-representation in the international bodies may well have had a subtle, pervasive influence on the point of view, the perceptive apparatus, of their foreign colleagues. One of these, working in Prijedor, confirmed (anonymously) that this was the case, that a particular point of view tended to come regularly to the fore. For example, during a meeting at the High Representative's branch office in Banja Luka, a Serb woman assistant with managerial responsibilities thought fit to explain the very good rate of return of refugees in these terms: 'The reason why so many of them are coming back is that what happened at Prijedor wasn't as terrible as all that. It wasn't as terrible as the media said it was.' The remark caused genuine embarrassment, but the international representatives present did not refute or even criticize it.

Whether from lassitude or a wish for moderation and even-handedness, it seems that the international community in Prijedor is sometimes afraid to show courage. Why the official resistance to a proposed peaceful multi-ethnic demonstration following the serious and violent events at Kozarac in September 2002? Why the veto on this proposal, made with the overt support of a local Serb community leader, on the ground that it was unimportant and did not represent the population? Why reject out of hand in advance any idea of public hearings for a truth and reconciliation commission? Why not encourage civil society to express its wishes, why not give more support to the moderate political leaders present – as we know – in Prijedor? These questions are all being asked by the population itself which is disappointed and dreams of moving away.

But for the time being the international community is unaware of these expectations. It has not yet absorbed their logic, or hardly. Its original action was 'parachuted' into Bosnia on a massive scale and marked by a desire for rapid, visible results. Today it needs to be recalibrated, adjusted and refocused. The spectacular should be abandoned for a 'long-term policy of small steps', to borrow Paul Garde's modest but penetrating analysis.[3] The international community is counting the cost and making out the report on its own lassitude. For fourteen years donors, NGOs and states have sat at the bedside of the former Yugoslav Republic. During that time other priorities – for example the war on terrorism – have appeared, marginalizing to some extent the aid available for Bosnia. In response, too many of the major international players have become impatient to end it altogether. They would be only too happy with the results achieved so far (establishment of democratic elections, progress with reconstruction, good food supply arrangements, successful return of some refugees) and the proclamation of grand principles. 'The western system of humanitarian aid would rather apply itself to the technical construction of institutions and the rhetorical promotion of human rights than to solving the country's real political problems,' writes Claudio Bazzocchi of the Italian Consortium of Solidarity.[4] Prijedor is no exception.

TWENTY

US Policy: Stick and Carrot

More through pragmatism than out of principle, the United States has often intervened in Bosnia using a well-tried method: fixing the objective to be achieved, imposing a timetable and, when necessary, applying sanctions. For giving its support to the political, military and judicial reforms and projects under way, notably in Prijedor, Washington has managed to profit from its intervention by extracting reciprocal concessions from the Bosnian authorities. Thus, after intense negotiations, Bosnia undertook to ratify the treaty of non-extradition of US citizens to the International Criminal Court established in July 2002. The commitment earned Sarajevo reproaches from the European Union, but it could hardly have defied the US which is the largest contributor of aid to Bosnia.

Washington Takes Prijedor off its Blacklist

On 15 May 2002 the US ambassador to Bosnia, Clifford Bond, announced during a visit to the second city of the RS that the American administration was lifting all sanctions against Prijedor. For the previous five years, along with Pale and 'Srbinje' (as the RS authorities renamed Foča), it had been on a US blacklist of places proscribed for their behaviour during the war. An American official in Bosnia explained the deal as follows: 'We had placed the town under embargo: no cooperation and no investment. Then after the arrests, the many trials concerning the area and in particular the arrival of Nada Ševo to head the municipality, we changed our attitude. So next we identified what the needs were and who to deal with: Nada Ševo on the Serb side, Muharem Murselović on the Muslim side. And we made them responsible.' The possibilities were then spelt out, the official explained. 'We told them: "We can unfreeze aid and facilitate business and investment if, but only if, you manage to reach an understanding. By 30 September 2002, you should have settled the problem of the old town market, and by 5 October, the mosque." ' The first of these issues concerned the illegal occupation of the historic quarter of Prijedor by a squatter-landlord, who was renting out to market traders thirty or so sites legally belonging to Bosniak families. It had been poisoning municipal life for years. The American arm-twisting got results. And despite some delay caused by the elections, the stick-and-carrot strategy seems to have worked in the matter of the mosque as well. After months of delays and some bitter polemic, it was agreed that the mosque would be rebuilt in its original place, on the waste site left on the main street of Prijedor by its demolition in May 1992. 'We pressed very hard and we also got angry,' admitted the US strategist, who has little time for inefficiency or evasive talk. This type of approach characterizes the whole thrust of US policy on Serbia. It should be remembered that the extradition of Slobodan Milošević to the ICTY in June 2001 followed threats of a trade embargo.

Pressure Over the Matanović Case

An identical method was used in the Matanović affair. The murder of Prijedor's Croat priest became an emblematic cause to the international community and, redundantly perhaps, demonstrated the resources available to it to apply the law and make its wishes felt, at the risk of offending those who had suffered from other criminal acts. On 24 August 1995, Tomislav Matanović and his parents were placed under house arrest, at home, by Prijedor police. For twenty-six days they were harrassed, robbed and threatened; then, on 19 September, they were taken away, never to be seen alive again. The three bodies were sought in vain for six years; eventually, in September 2001, they were found at the bottom of a well in the small village of Bišćani, outside Prijedor. All three had been shot.

An incredible legal marathon now began. The United States again, but also the Vatican, the European Union and their various representatives in Bosnia arrived in turn to harrass the authorities of the RS and in particular its then prime minister, Mladen Ivanić. The Matanović case was symbolic, high priority. And with this matter the Bosnian Serb authorities thought it possible to show goodwill to the international community, and to the ICTY

in particular, hoping of course to benefit from aid or credit in return.[1] Eight
months after the Matanović family's bodies had been found five policemen
were questioned, most unusually, by the local force. One of the best
investigators was put in charge of the case, and a fortnight later twenty-one
more policemen were arrested on suspicion of involvement in the priest's
murder. The RS authorities and the international community were now locked
into a game of poker, with the Bosnian Serbs hoping that all the arrests would
complicate enquiries and delay the start of a trial strongly disliked by the
population and the political class, and the foreigners thinking the RS had its
back to the wall.

In November 2002 the ICTY gave the go-ahead for local prosecutions
against eighteen of the suspects. No doubt the arrest of twenty-six policemen
for involvement in this crime had caused considerable shock. It seems highly
likely that those arrested who had not had anything to do with the priest's
murder would have done, and said, everything possible to avoid going down
with the real perpetrators. Another episode began on 9 December 2002 with
the opening in Banja Luka of a first trial of nine police officers, adjourned
more or less immediately because of a power cut. After a good deal of further
humming and hawing, the Republika Srpska justice department opened a
prosecution for the first time on 17 May 2004, this time not of nine but
eleven former policemen, accused of having illegally detained the Catholic
priest and his parents. If the eleven men, who were all on bail, were to be
found guilty, their sentences could be as long as forty years in prison.

It was difficult to tell whether Republika Srpska or the internationals
held the winning hand. Certainly the foreigners had spared no effort, either
to carry the matter through or to find those ultimately responsible on the
most senior level. But they ran the risk of projecting an image of two-speed
justice, suggesting the presence of a hierarchy of victims and giving the
impression that the priorities of international action are poorly ordered, or
anyway inscrutable. A good few survivors of the ethnic cleansing would like
to see representatives of the international community showing the same brisk
efficiency that they deployed in the Matanović case with the war criminals
who still circulate unmolested in Prijedor.

Italian Pacifist Activists

Perhaps the time has come to lend a hand, again slowly and modestly, with the
rebirth of civil society in Prijedor, in an associative rather than simply tutelary
and authoritarian manner. That is what the Agency for Local Democracy

(ADL) has been trying to do since it was set up in 2002, after groundwork by the Progetto Prijedor association launched in 1997. Although the name of this NGO elicits a wry smile from some Prijedor citizens – 'Never mind *local* democracy, how about *any* democracy?' is a remark often heard – it has become so deeply rooted in the municipality that, seven years after the first tentative efforts, the Agency is seen by many as a small institution that provides channels of communication between administrations, age groups, ethnic communities (not without difficulty) and associations.

Its creation happened by chance. In February 1996, a Prijedor Serb refugee living in Trento (northern Italy) made contact with some young Italian pacifists. Soon a first convoy of twenty trucks arrived in the town. Another followed six months later. A delegation met the then mayor, Milomir Stakić, and president of the local Red Cross, Srđo Srdić. Official relations between Prijedor and the Italian region of Trentino-Alto-Adige were formally established in December. 'We came to ask them for permission to develop projects for the local population,' recalls Annalisa Tomasi, the ADL director for Prijedor. 'After all that had happened in this town, the idea was to persuade the authorities to break the inhabitants' isolation. Our movement is basically pacifist. We wanted to prevent the people here, who had been abandoned in the most awful situation, from feeling like victims, which in a sense they were. At that time 98 per cent of humanitarian aid was going to the Federation and the rest to RS.'

Annalisa Tomasi is still surprised by the welcome given to the Agency's intervention, and by the relative ease of access to the populations, given the presence at that time of all the wartime police, political and economic bosses who were still established in the power structure. 'We told Stakić what we were doing. That we were there to create conditions for the return of refugees and displaced persons. That we were going to give resources to "positive" individuals. They believed in us.' Some of the war criminals have since been arrested and tried, others are still on the run. The Italian pacifists are still there.

The central principle of their action is local autonomy and development of local resources and powers. The approach is copied from the one used by the authorities of Trentino-Alto-Adige. This region in the north of Italy inherited, along with four others, a special status guaranteed under the 1948 Constitution. They all enjoy wide autonomy with strengthened local powers. It is therefore not surprising that the Italian missionaries should have arrived in Prijedor with similar ideas, or that they should have taken the trouble to gather information on the whole Krajina plain.

Concepts like 'local democracy', self-government and 'popular diplomacy' may seem vulnerable to irony. The ADL's projects, or rather its discourse, can similarly be taxed with other-worldliness or even naivety: there is slightly too much insistence on the equivalence and relatedness of victims in the name of equality, too much readiness to relegate the past to a closed chapter of terrible but unexplained misfortunes in justification of an obvious and rather facile pacifism. But there is an undeniable reality: ten years after the end of the war the volunteers are still there, with the support of the Trentino communes, the French department of Côte-d'Or and the Spanish province of Cordoba. Most notably of all, their work is done without ostentation. They differ from more than one NGO in that no refurbished or reconstructed building, no subsidized economic project, no managerial activity, mini-loan or other contribution to local life carries a prominent display of the ADL name.

The offices are in keeping with this approach. Headquarters are a modest two-room suite on the first floor of Hotel Balkan, in the centre of town near the administrative quarter. The discreet Annalisa Tomasi, the only 'foreigner' at the head of the organization for the past three years, has a penetrating awareness of the local situation. Patient and persistent, her work is complicated in a closed, divided town where representatives of the population and civil society are very thin on the ground: it is difficult to keep dialogue going, to get people to pool their experience and knowhow, to encourage private initiatives. But the first achievements were more than encouraging: courses in foreign languages and journalism, training for the local administrations, rebuilt dispensaries in Hambarine, establishment of a youth centre and senior citizens' centre at Ljubija, the provision of mini-loans for farmers, exchanges of artists and creative people between the two regions, long-range adoptions, the development of urban green spaces, support for agriculture (the region's main economic sector), etc.[2]

An excellent example of this work is the agricultural cooperative at Rizvanovići, which for five years now has produced organic fruit and vegetables, employing ten women whose prospects of finding work in the administrations or few functioning industries were poor at best, provides a living for dozens of other people and has revived a village shelled, emptied of inhabitants and 'cleansed' during the war. Dozens of rebuilt houses now surround four big greenhouses in the heart of the green landscape on the left bank. The well-tended fields of onions and peppers, the crates of vegetables on their way to market, the scent of cultivated earth irrigated in summer, say more than the longest speech about what can be undertaken or supported by the international community, which is still too easily satisfied with centralized action in collaboration with local powers claiming to be representative.

Annalisa Tomasi is nevertheless aware of the limitations of the exercise.

She may be the only representative of the international community to have detailed insight into the region's needs, to talk about popular and civic self-expression, to encourage debate, to support peaceful demonstrations, to grapple with the complexities of local management. But the young Italian has also noticed the wait-and-see passivity of the communities, their appetite for 'preconceived recipes' and 'parachuted interventions'. All parties, she explains, 'are struggling to identify the resources of the Prijedor territory ... We're still at the beginning of a journey that's going to take time and above all commitment from the younger generations.'[3]

Because although the international community can play a part in improving an everyday life that remains somewhat precarious, it cannot substitute itself for the population. The ADL wants to promote reconciliation. And that may well be the Achilles' heel of its effort, because for the time being it is an aspiration dependent on the mobilization of all parties. But perhaps this is where the international community's action was leading: the necessary examination of the past and of the truth, to which all the communities in Bosnia need to apply themselves.

PART SIX

The War of Memories

I read somewhere that after each genocide the historians explain that it will be the last one. Because no one will ever again be able to accept anything so infamous. What an extraordinary joke.

Innocent Rwililiza, talking to Jean Hatzfeld, *Dans le nu de la vie*

One freezing morning in 1996 Milan Kovačević felt a need to unburden himself. The director of Prijedor hospital talked to British journalist Ed Vulliamy of *The Guardian* at his house. Vulliamy was visiting the region again some four years after describing, in the hot summer of 1992, the horrors of Omarska and the ethnic cleansing being carried out by the Crisis Staff of which Kovačević was a member.[1] 'He remains a proud nationalist,' Ed Vulliamy wrote, 'but his certainties about the ends conceals doubt about the means.' After a couple of shots of homemade plum brandy, the former Prijedor strong man became talkative. '"The houses were burned at the beginning, when people were losing control. People weren't behaving normally. To be sure, it was a terrible mistake." A third glass', Vulliamy wrote, 'and suddenly: "We knew very well what happened at Auschwitz or Dachau, and we knew very well how it started and how it was done. What we did was not the same as Auschwitz or Dachau, but it was a mistake. It was planned to have a camp for people, but not a concentration camp … Omarska was planned as a reception centre But then it turned into something else. I cannot explain the loss of control. I don't think even the historians will find an explanation in the next fifty years. You could call it collective madness."'[2]

Milan Kovačević claimed to know all about concentration camps, 'having been born in one: Camp Jasenovac had been set up by the Croatian Nazi puppet regime' during the second world war. 'In Omarska, he claimed, "there were not more than 100 killed, whereas Jasenovac was a killing factory."' In an apparent wish to justify the happenings at Omarska, the hospital director swerved into a historical detour: "During the Second World War, the Muslims from Kozarac invaded Serb villages and burned everything. The Muslims and

the Ustashe [Croats] killed our people at Kozara [mountain near Prijedor]."'
The reality had been rather more complex. While some Muslims had fought
on the Nazi side, many others had joined the Partisans to fight the Ustashe
and the fascists.[3] Noel Malcolm notes in his history of Bosnia: 'Altogether
75,000 Bosnian Muslims are thought to have died in the war: at 8.1 per cent
of their total population, this was a higher proportion than that suffered
by the Serbs (7.3 per cent), or by any other people except the Jews and the
Gypsies.'

Milan Kovačević was not bothered about that. He is on record as saying
that 'history can only be set down fifty years after the events.' He mentioned
the post-war reconciliation between the Germans and the French, but did not
anticipate this outcome from the Bosnian communities, owing, he said, to
'the lack of culture of the people' in the region. Tito, he went on, 'said that
we're brothers. Perhaps his intentions were good, but how can we be brothers
knowing that the Turks were occupants here for five hundred years? We can't
be brothers given that throughout history Turks have always killed Serbs.' But
although 'we can't live together... we can cohabit as neighbours.'

At the time of his last interview with Ed Vulliamy he still believed that
'the facts showed it necessary to destroy Bosnia', but later the plum brandy
induced a reflective mood: 'Now my hair is white, I don't sleep so well... Of
course I think about my Muslim friends ... Are they all right? Are they alive?'
Milan Kovačević died of a ruptured aneurysm two and a half years later, on 1
August 1998, at The Hague, a few days into his trial before the International
Criminal Tribunal.[4]

TWENTY-ONE

Can a Commission Reconcile the Bosnias?

Contrary to every expectation, Milan Kovačević was one of the very first to open the way, to talk about an unbearable, omnipresent past that has never been digested: the war years of 1992-95, obscured and scribbled over like the years of the Second World War. Kovačević was the only official from Prijedor, indeed in the whole of Bosnia, to have attempted this sort of retrospective examination, of almost confessional analysis, as early as 1996. Historical obsessions apart, Kovačević's words prefigured the admissions of guilt made by the ex-president of the Bosnian Serbs, Biljana Plavšić, in October and then December 2002. Her declarations showed the same wish to be free of the past, the same feelings of incomprehension and powerlessness to explain those events or move beyond them. These words and new assessments of the 1992 war did not escape Jakob Finci, president of Bosnia's Truth and Reconciliation Commission, who welcomed Biljana Plavšić's testimony. 'She's the first leader of this country to have let it out, but she won't be the last,' he said in December 2002.

In fact these declarations by the ex-boss of Republika Srpska could not have come at a better time for the small, resolute, meticulous and optimistic Finci, now aged sixty-two. They were grist to his mill: he knew he would need a lot of other admissions to advance his project of establishing a Truth and Reconciliation Commission for the whole of Bosnia and gaining acceptance for an idea that still seemed ambitious and risky six years after its first beginnings.

The first meeting had been organized in 1997 by representatives of the Orthodox, Catholic and Muslim religions in Bosnia. The representative of the Jewish community joined his peers in signing a document calling for truth and justice. 'That was only about a year and a half after the end of the war,' he recalls. 'It was still too soon to use the word *reconciliation.*' The inter-religious council met again two years later, and this time the participants agreed to specify that 'the meaning and context of the words *justice, truth* and *reconciliation* differ according to our traditions and texts'. In any case, Jakob Finci recalls, they did not envisage the establishment of a commission as having a religious basis, but felt that it should 'emerge from society as a whole'. A conference held in February 2000 in the presence of NGOs, ambassadors and religious representatives gave birth to a citizens' association named Truth and Reconciliation.

The name has given rise to doubts and arguments. While some refer to the South African precedent between 1995 and 2000 set by the TRC or Truth and Reconciliation Commission, and the role played in it by its Chairman, Archbishop Desmond Tutu,[1] others point out that there are fundamental differences between former Yugoslavia and South Africa: that there should be no question of amnesty in Bosnia. This last was a point on which the ICTY dug its heels in. Under fire from the very beginning, somewhat marginalized and weakened by chaotic and inconsistent financing, the international criminal tribunal was less than enthusiastic in its support for a commission. 'Its officers told us the ICTY was establishing the truth and delivering justice,' Jakob Finci recalls. 'Then they added that with truth and justice established, reconciliation would follow.' More or less a thumbs-down.

The discussions were to last two years. Today Jakob Finci plays down the differences. 'We've had discussions with the ICT to make sure that we wouldn't be interfering in the tribunal's work or proceedings and that at the same time all our work would be accessible to them and there wouldn't be any mysteries.' The Truth and Reconciliation association is working a step at a time to formulate a law. The UN, the High Representative's office and the local and international NGOs gave their agreement to the drafting of this text at an international conference. The draft law, once submitted to the Human Rights ministry, was to be put before the Bosnian parliament.

Two and a Half Years of Openness

The plan was that after the law had been adopted, a transitional period of two and a half years would begin in Bosnia. After the first six months of groundwork and staff recruitment, the commission, consisting of seven individuals elected by Parliament, would start its real work. In each of thirteen

local offices distributed across the country – so that no one would have to travel
for more than an hour to testify – five staff members would be responsible
for collecting their statements which would be made in public hearings. The
Commission calculated that in eighteen months it would collect the testimony
of five to seven thousand people concerning the period between November
1990 – when the first free elections were held – and December 1995, when
signature of the Dayton accords brought the war to an end.

'Obviously the majority of witnesses will be victims from the three sides,'
Jakob Finci explained. 'I know perfectly well that numbers were very unequal
between the groups and that the Muslims paid most heavily, but a crime is a
crime, whether one person is killed or a thousand.' The second biggest category
was expected to consist of people who might themselves have committed
crimes,[2] in particular those who had been called up or drafted to fight in the
war. 'I don't think there will be very many. But I'm sure that some will want to
clarify their situation and explain their role, their commitment, say they saw
the look on the face of a child and the memory is giving them sleepless nights,
stuff like that. That's the sort of experience and testimony we're hoping for
but there's no guarantee of success.' The third type of testimony expected
was that of what nationalist terminology calls 'traitors', who in fact are 'the
real heroes of the war': people from all sides and every group who 'despite
serious risks, resisted ethnic cleansing and helped someone of different
ethnic origin', who saved, protected or defended an 'enemy' whose life was in
peril. In an interview with the *Osservatorio dei Balcani*, Jakob Finci said that the
Commission might also pay attention to 'the work of the media and the use
of language leading to crime'.[3] The idea is to *gather all the truths* to get an overall
view of the facts instead of three different 'stories'.

At the end of this year and a half of collecting, all the testimony will be
assembled into a broad database. The Commission will have six months to
write a report in which no names will appear, individuals being identified
by a code, the aim being to establish the facts on the roles played on the
terrain by political parties, international organizations, etc. 'Our Commission,
very differently from the one in South Africa, will make recommendations
which will comprise the most important part of the report. Then Parliament
will have to work out a way of putting them into effect.' With donations
and financial support from the Bosnian state, the Commission's budget was
estimated at between twelve and fifteen million euros to cover two and a half
years. The possibility that the hearings may need to be prolonged beyond this
period, as was the case in South Africa, has not been considered.

'This process should help us to understand finally what's really been
happening in this country over the last ten years. History changes every fifty

years in our country. We ought not to wait another fifty years before looking at records that might have been destroyed, when they haven't been rifled; quite a few people were afraid they could be used at The Hague,' Jakob Finci explains. 'The past should be clarified now. Our memory isn't perfect, or exact. Do you remember the place where you spent your holidays ten years ago, or the exact place where your tent was pitched?' And he insists on the need to talk, on the benefits of 'catharsis' for the witnesses and the value of the 'mass psychotherapy perfected by Freud a hundred years ago'.[4]

Isolated in his remote office in Bijeljina (eastern Bosnia), Branko Todorović, a member of the Truth and Reconciliation association and clear-sighted chairman of the Helsinki Committee for human rights in Republika Srpska, believes that testimony is of crucial importance. 'I remember a poem from school that says something like: the cock that crows always ends up on a plate. The idea in Bosnia is that if you say nothing you won't have any trouble, but we'll never be able to improve things if we sweep difficulties under the carpet. If we don't do this work of raising the level of awareness, the same evils will just reappear in twenty or thirty years.'

Pitfall and Hopes

What might induce leaders, or simple citizens either, to cross the threshold and admit the scale of the crimes committed? How – and why – should people step outside the vicious circle of suspicion, hatred and vengeance? A good deal is expected, in fact. The families of missing persons, for example, ought to find the Commission a body capable of fulfilling their need to be listened to, and to be given information. On another level, establishing the truth should also restore importance to facts hitherto deemed insignificant or simply ignored, especially since the Srebrenica massacre whose scale sometimes seems to have eclipsed or wiped from people's memories all the other crimes committed in the war.

To avoid disappointing these hopes, apart from the information campaigns already appearing in the media, the Commission needed to be and appear beyond criticism, its members accepted by all. Without meeting this first challenge the Commission would have been doomed at birth.

The members would all have to be citizens of Bosnia. They were to be representative of all the ethnic groups, and all people who had lived through the last war in Bosnia without holding senior political or military office. 'If we couldn't find seven individuals who were both worthy of trust and accepted by all parties, then I would really wonder whether we had a future in common,' Jakob Finci remarked.

Those who sat on the Truth and Reconciliation association were representative of this category. The notable members included Željko Kopanja, editor in chief of *Nezavisne Novine*, the biggest independent newspaper in Republika Srpska, seriously injured in an attempt on his life thought to have resulted from his exemplary work. Among the dozen or so other members were Branko Todorović, a freethinking personality known for his insight into the Serbian soul, and Srđan Dizdarević who ran the Bosnian branch of the Helsinki Committee for human rights in Sarajevo. It was not clear whether any of these reputable and honest personalities would want to be members of the Commission, or whether they would be elected.

The second challenge concerns the protection of witnesses. It was hoped that thousands of victims would come from all sides to recount the crimes committed against them during the war. These narratives would have a cathartic function, the Commission's promoters emphasized: as we have seen, a lot of victims of war crimes have an urgent need to talk about what happened to them. But talking about it in public may turn out to be risky, especially for refugees who have just returned to an area where their ethnic group is in a minority.

ICTY investigators emphasize that it is especially difficult to get Bosniaks who have returned to Prijedor to give testimony, as they are afraid that this may lead to acts of violence against them. Investigators often visit the individuals concerned secretly or discreetly, and testimony may later be given under a pseudonym or in closed session, to protect their anonymity. It hardly seems likely that someone who is afraid to give testimony at The Hague, despite the protection measures provided, will agree to tell his or her story in public to the Truth and Reconciliation Commission. Some of their jailers and torturers may still be in positions of influence in the town. Naming such people publicly, which seems appropriate when testifying before the Commission, might well expose the witness to reprisals of one sort or another, either acts of violence or something more insidious, for example discrimination in the employment market. While a substantial citizen like Muharem Murselović may be able to speak fearlessly about his experiences, our own observation is that many of the victims who have returned to the town remain too scared to talk about their experiences in a public place, even sometimes on their own doorstep. Jakob Finci has made it clear that the final report will mention no names, but the public hearings are sure to be widely covered by the media, particularly the local media. So the witnesses cannot expect anonymity.

A survey carried out in May 2002 for the Truth and Reconciliation association, questioning members of some fifty local NGOs, showed that most of the Bosnians questioned rated the area of fear and security as the major problem any Commission would have to face. So far nothing has been planned to ensure protection for witnesses. It should be noted that the problem does not just concern the victims of crimes, but also those who in one way or another opposed the ethnic cleansing. If all of these were to emerge from the shadows, it would become clear once again that the war was not the product of rivalries between Serbs, Croats and Muslims resulting from their race or religion, but was caused by a nationalist policy invented and inflated by some of the region's leaders. But it does not follow that these 'true heroes', as Jakob Finci calls them, feel safe enough to give evidence in public. We have seen that in Prijedor the nationalists still have considerable nuisance value. To give one example, a Serb in the municipality who did his best to protect the houses of Bosniaks driven out of his village during the war, then tried to help them return, has been threatened many times. We had to meet him at a location far from his house to make sure he would not be subjected to reprisals. How could such a man give evidence to the Commission without risk? For the process under consideration to bear proper fruit, with a serious and exhaustive collection of accounts, it seems obvious that a witness protection programme is essential.

A third challenge for any Truth and Reconciliation Commission would be the credibility of the accounts collected. The Bosnians interviewed in the May 2000 survey were emphatic that this was their second most serious concern after the security of those giving public testimony. It was felt that nationalist parties or organizations could be tempted to give privileged support to those witnesses whose stories tallied with their own positions, to the detriment of truth. The excesses of media propaganda during the war exposed the danger of secondhand, remotely-controlled accounts of atrocities allegedly committed by the 'other side'. To avoid having to deal with distorted or downright false stories of this type, the Bosnians questioned in the survey suggested that testimonies and accusations should be supported 'by proofs'. What might constitute a 'proof' remains to be decided. ICTY investigators believe that a detailed interrogation over several hours will usually enable the credibility of an individual's testimony to be accurately assessed. The task is to avoid treating the victim as a miscreant while patiently filtering out declarations that are untrue or simply erroneous.

Yet another problem concerns the origin and nature of testimony. Although, as Jakob Finci points out, 'the great majority of accounts heard will be those of the victims', it is still crucial that the Commission manages to persuade people who have committed crimes to speak about them. 'Such confessions or admissions have an important symbolic value and favour national reconciliation: they provide indubitable proof of the commission of

large-scale crimes and constitute in some sense a recognition of the victims'
suffering,' explains the former ICTY chairman Claude Jorda. In South Africa,
the victims of apartheid wanted to know what had really happened, and
therefore expected a lot from the testimony of those who had committed
crimes. Much the same is true in Bosnia. But while the amnesty granted in
South Africa to such guilty individuals in return for their telling the truth
persuaded some of them to give public testimony, the absence of an amnesty
arrangement could have the opposite effect in Bosnia-Herzegovina. What
criminal would be ready to admit anything in the knowledge that he might
later be prosecuted by his own country for war crimes? Claude Jorda believes
that there might be a way round the problem. 'To encourage subordinate
executants to participate in the process of national reconciliation, perhaps the
Commission could be authorized to make recommendations for the attention
of the local courts when these are prosecuting cases against people who have
admitted their crimes to the commission. These recommendations could be
taken into account as extenuating circumstances when sentences were being
decided.'

A realist nonetheless, Jakob Finci understands clearly that a Commission
will not be a miracle cure for all the evils of the post-war era. 'It might just be
able to improve inter-ethnic relations, though,' he says. Provided, that is, that
effective safeguards can be established and the minefield of common history
cleared and made safe.

TWENTY-TWO

A History Without Peace

Jasenovac, 'Grave of the Serbs'

Winter or summer, you can see the flower from miles away, solitary in the middle of a flat, grassy plain. A hundred feet high and thirty across, this concrete rose sprouts from the site of one of the worst Croatian concentration camps of the Second World War. Jasenovac, on the borders of Croatia in a no-man's-land between villages still bearing the scars of the recent conflict, marshlands, damaged bridges and the river Sava which marks the frontier with Bosnia-Herzegovina.

The camp was set up in 1941 by the fascist régime led by Ante Pavelić, allied with the Germans and Italians. Of the barrack-huts, prisons and crematoriums that once stood on five sites in this frontier region, scattered over a total area of two hundred and ten square kilometres, nothing, or almost nothing, remains: a rusting steam locomotive and a few railway trucks of the same vintage. Almost everything was destroyed by the Ustasha régime in April 1945; repeated floods and time have done the rest. The rose-shaped concrete monument, designed very much in the socialist-realist style by Bogdan Bogdanović, was put up in 1968 to prevent the site from being forgotten.

Jasenovac is one of the crucibles of Balkan regional memory. Sixty years after the end of the Second World War, this dreadful camp remains one of the main crossroads of the collective imagination, making it among other things the ostensible subject of a number of 'histories' combining every shade of revisionism, inaccuracy and fantasy. A place that still haunts conversations and personal destinies around Prijedor, hardly thirty-five miles away as the crow flies. We recall that one of the most important organizers of the ethnic cleansing in Prijedor, the ex-hospital director Milan Kovačević, passed through Jasenovac in infancy. Terrible coincidence, sinister sign of destiny or obvious consequence deeply satisfying to a moralist: former detainee becomes camp supervisor in his turn.

During the campaign for the October 2002 general elections, the boss of the powerful SDS in Prijedor region, Dušan Berić, brushed aside all accusations of genocide made against the Prijedor Crisis Staff. In our presence, however, he referred in some detail to the 'genocide carried out by Muslims and Croats on the Serbs during the Second World War'. He added as a final flourish: 'Don't forget that twelve thousand five hundred children died at Jasenovac.'

We have already seen how propaganda exploited this past and planted the seeds of 'martyrology'. Following Tito's death, as Yugoslavia was gradually dismantled, the nationalist leaders pounced greedily on a past that had remained frozen under the communist monolith. 'As communism crumbled in the late 1980s, Serbs, Croats and Slovenes began to dig up their dead and rebury them,' wrote the journalist Tim Judah.[1] By harping so resolutely on the past, these leaders were eclipsing the present with all its real and potential horrors. Even more disgustingly, the sufferings endured during the Second World War were used to justify the ones inflicted in the conflict of 1992-95.

Jasenovac was even coveted for a while, for its propaganda value, by the authoritarian nationalist president of the newly independent Croatia, Franjo Tuđman,[2] who thought he might be able to make use of the camp site. The Zagreb strong man, a former Partisan, wishing to reconcile all the Croats, sought to rearrange History by federating yesterday's fascists with the victims of today in the light of a pure and idealized new image of Croatia. In 1996 he was planning to transform Jasenovac into a 'common cemetery' for the victims of the Second World War and their persecutors, the Ustasha soldiers of the *Poglavnik* (Leader) Ante Pavelić. By these means he hoped surreptitiously to erase the traces of the 'Croatian Auschwitz'.

'We fought back and, with great difficulty, managed to get the politicians to leave this place alone. We try to avoid manipulations of memory,' says the deputy director of the Jasenovac memorial, Jelka Smreka. Thanks to the work of the team directed by Nataša Jovičić, support from the Holocaust Museum in Washington and the Croatian government under the presidency of Stipe Mesić, this terrible place is for the time being safe from controversy.

The site was captured by Serb separatists in 1991, then retaken by the Croatians in their 1995 counter-offensive. Since that time it has been cleared of land mines, restored and protected. In 1997, despite the loss of part of its records somewhere between Belgrade, Banja Luka and Washington, the memorial has resumed or supported the continuing rigorous scientific research on Jasenovac, and has tried to counter manipulations and inaccuracies. This is a long-term enterprise that has been going on for many years.

The worst of these polemics, grotesque by definition and still alive sixty years after the end of the Second World War, concerns the number of victims said to have died at Jasenovac. Crazily exaggerated figures have been widely circulated. 'On 15 November 1945 the Croatian National Commission, testifying before the international court at Nuremberg, estimated the number of deaths at Jasenovac at between five hundred thousand and six hundred thousand.'[3] Belgrade even raised the estimate to seven hundred thousand victims, then a million. In the immediate post-war period, such inflation would have been aimed at extracting the maximum in war reparations from Germany. But by the nineties, these escalations were being used to feed hatreds and fanaticisms, and encouraging the 'harmful use of rancours from the past', note the historians Mirko Grmek, Marc Gjidara and Neven Šimac.[4]

'The most recent independent studies on the subject have the merit of being in broad agreement on the order of magnitude, and so far have been little contested,' Jelka Smreka says. Vladimir Zerjavić, a Croat, puts the overall figure at about eighty-three thousand victims.[5] Bogoljub Kočović, a Serb, estimates the number of deaths at Jasenovac at seventy thousand. 'The precise figure will never be known for sure,' Jelka Smreka observes. 'We're going to publish a list of names in 2004. And we're trying to estimate the numbers of a category of victims which is poorly recorded and little-known: the Roma.' Work of this kind is effective in countering various received ideas, for example the one often heard in and around Prijedor to the effect that all those killed at Jasenovac had been Serbs and their killers had been Croats and Muslims. The reality is rather different.

Jasenovac is a lifeless, neglected place, virtually unsignposted, unlike other solemn, silent memorials of the same kind. As if the memory were too burdensome. No longer is it a compulsory destination for school and tourist parties; no longer is it the site of grandiloquent commemorations of the sort favoured by Titoist socialism. The rigorous, honest work of the site's curators is unpalatable to the nationalists of the region, to whom history is a myth cobbled up out of fantasies, lending itself to every form of manipulation.

The Battle of Kozara is Still Going on

While Jasenovac is presented as the 'tomb' of the Serb people, there is no doubt that Mount Kozara should be considered one of its 'family vaults'.

On the 2,500-foot mountain, twenty kilometres from Prijedor and about ten kilometres north of Kozarac, a Serb cross made of rough timber has been set up on the vehicle turnaround of this former tourist destination, once visited by school parties and families seeking fresh air. Higher up, on a hillside among pine trees and cool undergrowth, stands a massive tower of jagged concrete in the form of a wheatsheaf. 'Socialist realism' has not spared this place either. High walls and walkways in reinforced concrete lead to the memorial where the names of Second World War victims are listed on metal plaques.

Here, in July 1942, in one of the biggest battles that took place in the region, thousands of people were killed by Ustasha and Nazi troops, one of the latter an Austrian called Kurt Waldheim who later became secretary general of the United Nations (from 1972 to 1981). The victims, most of whom were mainly Serb Partisans – very active in this part of Krajina – but who also included Muslims and their families, were shelled, shot, mopped up and finished off. The operations went on for several weeks.

In 1970, the Titoist régime accordingly built a monument to their memory, intending once again to present History in such a way as to bring different elements of society together, to homogenize them. Today, though, the site has been appropriated. Orthodox emblems and Serbian flags are in evidence more or less everywhere in the neighbourhood. The museum which is supposed to recall the facts and the memory of the battle of Kozara is seldom open. Through the windows of the glass and concrete building can be seen the display panels of an improbable exhibition on 'genocides against the Serb people'. With a mass of photographs, drawings and a few objects, the organizers have tried to retrace and describe the horrors committed against their people. Visitors looking for truth and objectivity will go on their way unsatisfied. The museum is being used as a platform to project a running-together of places and dates, a conflation to go with the inflation of figures.

This appropriation of memory is worrying. Instead of being places where people learn and are told the truth, sites like the one on Mount Kozara become the stakes in a battle combining nationalism with propaganda. They crystallize passions, perpetuate divisions and help demarcate territory. As a result, to quote the very penetrating judgement of the researcher Xavier Bougarel, the 'memory of wars is also a war of memories'.[6]

Apartheid at School

The education sector is also a scene of these subdued struggles. Instead of helping to bring young Serbs, Croats and Bosniaks together, schooling is being run along the lines of an 'apartheid system.'[7] Primary and secondary schools in Bosnia follow three distinct syllabuses, set up in accordance with the nationalities (Serb, Croat, Bosniak), using three allegedly different languages and most of the time using textbooks filled with terms and interpretations that would inevitably offend pupils from another ethnic group, notes a survey by the International Crisis Group.[8]

By these means, the nationalists hope to perpetuate enmities and differences which they have often invented themselves, and establish permanent divisions between Bosnian Serbs, Croats and Bosniaks. 'Three educations, "three truths", are thus being dispensed, in a post-war context in which the possibility of establishing the facts and responsibilities for past events and formulating a viable future for Bosnia-Herzegovina will depend on the ability of its inhabitants to find a common language and common political standards', noted the journalist André Loersch after an investigation in the region.[9]

The breakup of the education system started immediately after the end of the war. Instead of establishing a centralized national system that might have encouraged a common outlook, the Dayton accords gave separate control of education to Republika Srpska and to each canton of the Federation. For the nationalists of every group, who retained power on local level, this decision came as a real blessing. Schools in Republika Srpska were then issued with textbooks used in Serbia-Montenegro, which informed pupils that their capital was not Sarajevo but Belgrade. In the same spirit, young Bosnian Croats were authoritatively informed that their capital was Zagreb. The school textbooks used by Bosnian Serbs and Croats constantly remind pupils that Bosnia does not exist as a nation and never has, although historically this is simply untrue. In the books intended for Bosniaks, references to Bosnian Serb and Croat authors are eliminated 'in favour of Bosniak writers whose literary quality remains somewhat arguable'.[10]

In the immediate post-war period, in fact, classes were split up against the wishes of the pupils themselves. Branko Babić, a Serb attending secondary school in Sarajevo at the time, recalled: 'I was sitting in my classroom the other day, and the teacher handed out a form where we had to write down whether we were Serb, Muslim or Croat. We were told that we would be segregated into different classrooms according to our ethnicity. It's not what any of us asked for.'[11]

Aware of the dangers posed by this fragmented education system, the office of the High Representative has tried to institute reforms. Schools situated in mixed areas are supposed to employ teachers from different ethnic backgrounds. Modules on civil rights and the cultures of other ethnic groups were introduced. Not long ago, Bosnian Croats and Serbs were given history textbooks of their own to replace the ones from Croatia and Serbia.

Despite these efforts, however, some of these books persisted in giving versions of the war in former Yugoslavia that are questionable to say the least. 'The Serbian government did everything possible to maintain the unity of Yugoslavia in order that the Serb people might continue to live in a single country,' asserts one school textbook published in Banja Luka and used in Prijedor.[12] A bit rich given the destructive role of Slobodan Milošević, who had been president of Serbia at the time. The text goes even further: 'The Slovenian, Croatian and Muslim nationalist parties, immediately after their creation and their victory in the 1990 elections, began the destruction of Yugoslavia.' The war in Bosnia-Herzegovina is described in half a page, and it is asserted that the Muslim and Croat deputies were taking decisions without consulting the Serbs, driving the latter to defend themselves by proclaiming their own republic. Very different words can sometimes be applied to the same thing. The RS history textbook describes the events of 1992-95 as a 'civil war', while the equivalent text in the Federation uses the term 'aggression by Serbia and Montenegro'.

Rather belatedly, the international community has charged the OSCE with organizing a reform of education, particularly in Prijedor. The programme started in 2002 but is regarded by most observers with some scepticism. The OSCE seems interested only in the modernization of teaching methods. While this may be necessary too, it is surely less important in this context than the content of these history courses, crucial to the future of Bosnia.

'The danger is that in the end pupils may conclude from all this that we are historical enemies. And if that's what we teach our children, that's the reality we'll create,' says Juraj Martinović, a specialist in Slav culture and member of Circle 99, an association set up in Sarajevo in 1992 to defend the multi-ethnic character of Bosnia.

TWENTY-THREE

Bosnia in the European Mirror

Bosnia has a sickness of the memory. That is what makes any serene analysis of its past so difficult, and hampers efforts at reconciliation between its three communities. It could be useful to withdraw from Bosnia for a while and see how other Europeans have managed in coping with the difficulties in their own past. Obviously every case is different and these comparisons go only so far. But there are three examples that do throw some light on the Bosnian experience, and may therefore repay study.

Franco's Mass Graves

General Franco's death after a long illness on 21 November 1975 brought to an end one of western Europe's longest dictatorships, originally imposed by an army coup d'état in July 1936 against the Popular Front republican government democratically elected a few weeks earlier.

Nearly forty years later, a parliamentary democracy and constitutional monarchy established themselves in Spain on the ruins of an exhausted régime that, in its heyday, had been responsible for the execution of several hundred thousand people. Priority was given to national reconciliation. Henceforward there would no longer be two countries, a Falangist one and a Republican one, but a single united Spain. By way of the *pacto del olvido*, the pact of forgetfulness, what the writer and former Spanish minister of Culture Jorge Semprun called 'voluntary collective amnesia'. 'When the democratic transition came [with the death of Franco], it was time to work for national reconciliation, it was best not to talk about it: there was a pact of silence,' in the words of José Luis Rodriguez Jimenez, historian and teacher at Juan Carlos I University in Madrid.[1] 'Once Franco was dead, the left renounced memory, refrained from requiring truth and justice,' recalls the journalist Guido Ramponi in an analytical and prophetic piece.[2] 'The socialists, in power from 1978 to 1996, thought it wise to neutralize the past.[3] Reviving dormant conflicts would have alarmed the middle class and set the Spanish Socialist Party at odds with the economic establishment inherited from Francoism as well as with the very influential Catholic Church.'

The same fear of reopening old wounds is omnipresent in Bosnia, among the international community and the great majority of Serbs. The discourse is very similar, emphasizing the need to look to the future and concentrate exclusively on the development of a viable and stable economic space. In Spain, the prospect of rapid integration into the European Economic Community – completed in 1986 – was presented as being of sufficiently fundamental importance to justify burying the divisions of the past.

Nevertheless, behind the appearance of a society reconciled with itself and at peace, Spain has been confronted anew with its embarrassing history. Yesterday's divisions have reappeared. In October 2000 the decomposed, intermingled remains of thirteen people were exhumed[4] from a common grave at Priaranza del Bierzo, in Navarra. A family had disinterred the bodies of civilians murdered by the henchmen of General Francisco Franco on 16 October 1936, a few weeks after the coup d'état. In March 2002, some sixty-three years after the end of the Spanish civil war, the University of Granada made the unusual decision to attempt DNA identification of four of the bodies. 'This was to be the first time,' wrote the journalist Martine Audeusseau, 'that non-combatants killed during the civil war would be identified scientifically.'[5]

There was nothing random or accidental about this discovery. It was part of a fundamental shift in Spanish society, which was now reclaiming the right to memory. Suddenly, after the turn of the new century, the phenomenon assumed a decisive scale without any specific event appearing to have had a key role in launching the national consciousness-raising. The Navarra exhumations ended twenty-seven years of *omertà*-style silence in Spain. After the exhumations, the Association for the Restoration of Historical Memory (ARMH), supported by a large number of families of missing persons, made contact with the United Nations' working group on forced disappearances.[6] The ARMH was demanding that 'the Spanish state order the exhumation of the bodies, their identification using DNA techniques and, if possible, the creation of collective cemeteries marked by a public monument'.[7] The Aznar government undertook to put any UN recommendations into practice. But the speeches were not followed by action. In November 2002 the deputies belonging to the Popular Party (centre right, majority) refused to pass a budget of 1 million euros to launch the work of exhumation.[8]

The same sort of thorny recent history weighs on Bosnia's future. So long as the great majority of bodies have not been found, let alone identified, any idea of a future, or of reconciliation, will be difficult to sustain. As in Spain, there is a real risk that the families of missing persons will say nothing until long after the war. In both countries the families of missing persons – oddly similar in number, at about thirty thousand in each case – have strong expectations. Sooner or later some response will have to be made. Bosnia, so far, seems lamentably indifferent.

But in the Iberian peninsula, the first tentative steps towards reconciliation have at last been taken. A motion was tabled by the Socialists and Communists, which the conservatives in power were unable to evade. The result was a historic step forward by all the main Spanish political forces, taken on 21 November 2002, the 27th anniversary of Franco's death: parliament adopted unanimously, and for the first time, a text condemning the Francoist régime and offering moral recognition to victims of the 1936-39 civil war and of the dictatorship that followed. After decades spent carefully ignoring each other, two Spains are at last face to face. After burying their divisions so calmly and for so long, they may now be within sight of reconciliation. It is still too early to be sure, although TV series, books and university courses are now being devoted to these issues.[9] The main work of explanation and teaching remains to be done, and a number of psychological and political obstructions remain tenaciously in place.

This admission of the facts by the whole political class in Spain, and this educational effort, are exactly what the Bosnian community lacks. Until recognition of past deeds and exactions, perhaps even a request for forgiveness and a response to it, have been formulated and addressed calmly by both sides, any reconciliation effort is likely to be vain. Such an approach, admittedly easier and more natural in a country with democratic and pluralist traditions than in a state emerging from a war, is essential for the establishment of a state ruled by law, able to resist the warlike temptations and autonomist tendencies liable to appear in Bosnia.

The Spanish example makes it fairly clear that there is little to be gained from requiring silence as the precondition for national reconciliation. Under these circumstances, without a sound foundation, reconciliation is just a façade, a backroom arrangement. Real reconciliation is a solid antidote to what Guido Rampoldi calls 'a thesis dear to others on the European right:

the equivalence of culpability between the two sides, and thus the innocence of a Spain that used to be moderately Francoist and is now moderately non-Francoist'. This tendency to homogenize wrongs and responsibilities is also present in Bosnia. As we know, it is accompanied by the misleading idea that in the final analysis there are only victims.

Two Sides and Thousands of Unwilling Conscripts

Alsace suffers from the evil of victimization, as elsewhere ancient and deeply rooted. It is worth risking the comparison and looking more closely at this region on the 'memory-frontier' (as the historian Jean-François Mayeur calls it).[10] Large numbers of people have been being victimized there since the Second World War at least. Given its particularisms – the coexistence of two languages, at least three religious communities,[11] the persistence of local law, etc. – the region is subject to its own internal tensions, but also to incomprehension on the part of the rest of France when what it really needs is special understanding.

Annexed in 1940 after the phoney war, Alsace was immediately Germanized and Nazified, and its population 'reeducated'. Soldiers or men of military age were drafted by force into the German army from August 1942 onward. Nearly a hundred and thirty thousand of these unwilling conscripts, from Lorraine as well as Alsace, fought in Hitler's wars, many on the eastern fronts from which more than a third did not return. 'These *malgré-nous* (against our will) encumber the national memory, which does not know what to do with them,' wrote Eric Conan in a long investigation.[12] 'Often treated shamefully as scapegoats in Alsatian villages after the Liberation, they ended by conquering local sympathy, but on the other side of the Vosges the reality of what happened to them is poorly understood, or travestied into the role of traitor.'

The journalist was recalling the trial in Bordeaux of thirteen of these *malgré-nous* (plus one willing volunteer) for having taken part on 10 June 1944 in the massacre at Oradour-sur-Glane. The trial and verdict, in 1953, had reawakened the pains of the war, but without facilitating a free and necessary examination of the past. 'Alsace has not done enough work on the history of the Second World War. It used to feel outlawed from the nation, it still does feel outlawed because its particular fate during the war remains misunderstood, because its singular destiny as a transitional region between two nations, entangled in the upheavals of two histories, two cultures, is not taken into account. Faced with that, Alsace has chosen to take refuge in myth rather than taking hold of the past and working out at last what to say to the coming generations,' says Alsatian sociologist Freddy Raphael.[13]

To the term 'take refuge' employed by the academic, one might have preferred something more like 'withdraw'. There are fairly strong communalist leanings within Alsatian society, which become manifest in the assertion of a very strong sense of regional identity. That in turn, rather unhappily, feeds a political extremism that tends to produce a high nationalist vote, favouring regionalist (mainly Alsatian) and nationalist (Front National) parties. The same characteristics can be found in Bosnia, most particularly in Republika Srpska, a region whose isolation is genuine, where there is a very strong feeling of being neglected, and where violently radical experimental politics are still current. The simplistic warmongering of the SDS still has support from a good third of the electorate, which stubbornly refuses to examine the reasons why the party launched and then supported warlike action.

Analysis of the ambiguities in the way Alsatian history is represented[14] has made Freddy Raphael something of a specialist in the reconstruction of memory. There is much to be done. The Alsace-Moselle memorial retraces the history of this region between 1870 (Franco-Prussian war) and the early 1950s, with particular reference to the events on both sides of the frontier during the Second World War. The building, designed to accommodate a hundred thousand visitors a year, is at Schirmeck (Bas-Rhin) on the site of the internment camp established for opponents of the Nazi régime on 2 July 1940. Officially, the memorial is meant to commemorate all aspects of the history of the region, exactions by the Nazis, unwilling conscripts, etc. But although the people behind the project emphasized the need to examine the past, some Alsatians saw the scheme essentially as an opportunity to rehabilitate the unwilling conscripts. 'If it's only a monument to their memory, it will be a failure,' Freddy Raphael warned.

And that apart, the memorial could suffer from competition with the European Centre for Nazi concentration camp deportees, only a few kilometres away, scheduled to open in 2005 to coincide with the sixtieth anniversary of the liberation of the camps. Conceived and financed by the state, this second project, being built near the site of the only French concentration camp, the Struthof (where twenty-two thousand people died, out of the forty-five thousand detained there), threatens to shuffle the cards of memory yet again. Presented as a 'well-deserved homage to the upright man, who refuses to be enslaved and is always in the right compared to the torturer who wants to break him', it seems to symbolize in an indirect sort of way what the other building ought to represent, but may not.[15] Instead of being complementary from the start, the two memorials could end by seeming more like the two poles of an unhealthy divided memory, endlessly seeking reunification.

The differences arising over these monuments reveal the existence of a persistent underlying malaise. The same kind of trap lies in wait for the Bosnians, equally tempted by revisionist tendencies and just as desirous of marking their territory with places of memory. In Prijedor this wish reached a pinnacle of idiocy with the erection of monuments specifically to Serbs, all victims of course. As a general approach it weighs heavily on the future and feeds frustration and bitterness. It amounts to a simple refusal to examine the past or recognize the sufferings of the other communities.

'Alsace ought to express its regret. The Alsatian memory should be brought out of its enclave and involved in the work being done in the rest of the country, not staying fixated on the past but envisaging the future. It's a matter of urgency to start really thinking about what induces people, just because they have a feeling of injustice, disappointment or disenchantment in their personal lives, to embrace a discourse and ideology that end with the eradication of the other,' Freddy Raphael concludes.

For nearly sixty years, Alsace has been struggling to turn the page. Lack of self-criticism, blood-is-thicker-than-water, political extremism, etc.: the evils are well known and named. All that remains is to find the collective will, or some sort of precipitating event, to turn away from the past. What has been repressed many times in Alsace, a region now part of the deep French countryside, needs to be launched on state level in Bosnia, if Bosnia really means to envisage the future.

The Education Effort in Post-war Germany

The war in Bosnia-Herzegovina confronted Europe once again with atrocities of a kind not seen since the Second World War. The execution by Serb forces of more than seven thousand Bosniak men and boys from Srebrenica in July 1995 led straight back to the Nazi precedent. It is interesting, therefore, to examine the way Germany and the Germans came to terms with their past and the crimes committed in their names. In the twelve years of its existence, Adolf Hitler's régime killed more than six million Jews in the execution of an organized plan whose objective was their total extermination. As the American historian Eric A. Johnson points out, 'millions of ordinary German citizens also bear part of the blame for the Nazis' crimes... Millions of Germans looked the other way when synagogues were burned, when Jewish shops were boycotted and when new laws, one after the other, were making life impossible for the Jews. Millions of ordinary Germans knew about the Holocaust and did nothing to oppose it.'[16] Nevertheless, in the immediate post-war period and well into the sixties, the Germans broadly regarded themselves as victims, a feeling reinforced by the terrible allied bombing of German towns like Dresden.

Today, part of the Serb population of Prijedor continues to pose as victimized in spite of all the crimes committed there by Serb nationalists. In Germany after the war, 'the official discourse, that of the people running the country, of the media or the cultural authorities, never really endorsed the exculpation of the German people and favoured an extensive education effort, particularly in the schools',[17] notes the historian Dimitri Nicolaïdis. Thus in 1952, barely seven years after the end of the war, the first president of the German Republic Theodor Heuss was already declaring: 'Germans should never forget what people of their nationality perpetrated during the shameful years.' In December 1970, the West German chancellor Willy Brandt knelt before the monument commemorating those killed during the uprising of the Warsaw ghetto in 1943. 'Ah! If only *we* had a Willy Brandt!' exclaimed the president of the Helsinki Committee for Republika Srpska, Branko Todorović, when we were interviewing him on recognition of their crimes by Bosnian Serbs.

Todorović, himself a Serb, was here underlining one of the main problems in Bosnia: the timidity of leaders who could in fact play a crucial role in the reconciliation process. Not a single Bosnian Serb leader, even the so-called moderate Mladen Ivanić (prime minister of Republika Srpska from 2000 to 2002), attended the commemoration of the Srebrenica massacre held every year on 11 July. 'They don't have the courage to do it,' Branko Todorović told us. 'They say the population wouldn't understand, when really it's up to them to show political courage.' An RS prime minister at last attended the event in 2003.

It seems that in a country like Bosnia the attitude of political bosses is a decisive factor. 'We haven't got a long-established culture of democracy. This territory was occupied for long years, and after that communism prevented the emergence of a class of genuinely active citizens. Fifty years of communism have created a certain mentality which, in a sense, could be compared with the effects of years of slavery. People continue to think that they're safer if they don't speak openly. And when the politicians shirk their responsibilities, there's no one among the people to press them about it,' adds the president of the Helsinki Committee in RS.

The determination of the highest-placed figures in the two countries was one of the key factors in Franco-German reconciliation. There was a fair amount to overcome, given that there had been three wars between the two countries in under eighty years. 'The courage of the politicians but also of the

Resistance leaders, the German Jews who had arrived in France as refugees and were saying to themselves: "Something has to be done to prevent this from happening again", was determining,' says Babette Nieder who runs the Office franco-allemand pour la jeunesse (OFAJ).

Of course this reconciliation was not achieved overnight with the wave of a magic wand. Indeed the historian Alfred Grosser points out that not long ago a French Euro-MP calmly asserted that Germany had always acted aggressively towards France, forgetting perhaps that in Napoleon's day, or Louis XIV's, France itself had indulged in a certain amount of neighbour-bashing.[18] Political will, associated with intellectual discussions, nevertheless made it possible to achieve genuine reconciliation. There hardly exists a French village today that is not twinned with somewhere in Germany. More than fourteen million young French and German people have availed themselves of OFAJ's exchange programmes. There can be no doubt that the clear and courageous admission of crimes committed and sufferings inflicted by the Germans has contributed substantially to this reconciliation. As has the (somewhat belated) recognition by the French of the Vichy régime's collusion with the Nazis in persecuting Jews.

The example of France and Germany helps encourage reconciliation in the Balkans today. OFAJ has launched a large number of programmes in Macedonia, Kosovo, Serbia and Bosnia-Herzegovina. 'Franco-German cooperation can give an example of hope and show that reconciliation is possible,' Babette Nieder says. 'Perhaps we'll be able to do the same one day, with the Serbs,' the Kosovar night porter of a Prishtina hotel had told her, on noticing a mixed group of French and Germans talking and joking far into the night.

And of course the German example gives an interesting angle on the role of international justice in the reconciliation process. At the end of the war, the top surviving Nazi leaders were tried at Nuremberg. 'At the time, the Nuremberg trials did not succeed as a lesson to the Germans, just as the trials at The Hague failed in the short and medium term to create awareness of the crimes in the Serb community,' notes the Danish journalist ChristianPalme.[19] The German historian Ingo Müller made the same point when he wrote that the Nuremberg trials were seen in the early nineteen-fifties as an expression of 'victor's justice' by German public opinion, at that time anxious to forget the past and to see all responsibility 'as being purged by the Nuremberg court.'[20]

Nevertheless, Nuremberg did enable the Germans to realize later the scale of the crimes that had been committed. 'There are not many countries that have made an effort of memory comparable to the one made by the Germans over the last twenty years,' commented Jorge Semprun, an impartial

European observer of these matters, in the course of a dialogue with Roman Polanski, director of *The Pianist*.[21] 'Every 27 January (date of the liberation of Auschwitz) for the last six years, Parliament has made a formal act in memory of the victims of Nazism. France has not done as much with the French state under Marshal Pétain, although of course the crimes of Vichy weren't comparable with those of Nazism, and neither has Spain with Francoism.'[22]

The evidence and facts established during the Nuremberg trials also enabled historians to start serious work on the Nazis and the Holocaust. 'These courts helped to establish historical facts that were important for the future. The deniers – and there are deniers in the case of former Yugoslavia as in the case of the Holocaust – would have a much easier life without this establishing of facts,' Christian Palme points out.

Although Adolf Hitler was not put on trial, Nuremberg made it possible to highlight, in unarguable fashion, the scale of the Nazi crimes. The ICTY could perhaps help establish once and for all the reality of the camps, the reality of rapes, murders and the expulsion of whole populations in Bosnia-Herzegovina.

These comparisons help to throw some light on the challenges facing the former Yugoslav Republic, and show in the process that some European countries are as much a warning to the Bosnians as they are an example. Like Spain which wanted to bury its civil war without talking about it, or the element in Alsace that persists in hiding behind a single discourse of 'we are all victims', Bosnia will not be able to do without a debate on its past along the lines of the one Germany was brave enough to attempt. If this is not started by the political leaders, sooner or later the population will deal with it, although it is impossible to predict the form the discussion will take: unlike its West European peers, Bosnia still lacks the democratic experience that would help protect it from drifting into violence. With this in mind, the Truth and Reconciliation Commission will be trying hard to prevent the falsification of memory. If it fails, the effects of the debate could be devastating for the victims and for the country: national reconciliation would be endangered and so, too, eventually, would be the unity of a state whose construction has barely started, ten years after the end of the war.

Select Chronology

1918

1 December: establishment of the 'Kingdom of Serbs, Croats and Slovenes'.

1919

Creation of Yugoslav Communist Party (later renamed League of Communists, LCY).

1929

6 January: King Alexander I Karađorđević ends democratic régime and proclaims royal dictatorship.

1941

25 March: Yugoslavia signs pact of alliance with Hitler.

27 March: coup d'état in Yugoslavia, Regent Paul overthrown.

6 April: Germany and Italy invade Yugoslavia, Belgrade bombed.

10 April: 'Independent State of Croatia' proclaimed by Ustasha leaders under Italian fascist patronage.

July: opening of concentration camp at Jasenovac

1942

July: battle on Mt Kozara between Partisans and Ustashe allied with Nazis.

1943

29 November: proclamation of the new federal Yugoslavia at Jajce (south of Banja Luka); establishment of a provisional government.

1945

April: closure of Jasenovac camp.

November: Communist victory in constituent elections throughout Yugoslavia.

1948

Break between Tito and Stalin.

1968

Inauguration of Jasenovac memorial.

1970

Inauguration of memorial to the battle of Mt Kozara.

1974

New Yugoslav Constitution giving more extensive powers to the republics and provinces.

1980

4 May: death of Marshal Tito, collective presidency takes over.

1986

Memorandum of the Serbian Academy of Sciences and Arts.

Slobodan Milošević becomes president of the Serbian League of Communists.

1989

March: 1974 Constitution revised to reduce the autonomy of Vojvodina and Kosovo.

28 June: speech by Milošević to an audience of a million Serbs, celebrating the 600th anniversary of the Battle of Kosovo near Prishtina.

9 November: Berlin Wall falls.

6 December: Milošević elected republican president by Serbian parliament.

1990

20–22 January: 14th Congress of LCY. Slovenian delegation walks out, followed by that of Croatia.

8 April: first free elections in Slovenia.

22 April–7 May: elections in Croatia.

August–September: first incidents in so-called 'autonomous regions' proclaimed in Croatia by Serb insurgents backed by Belgrade and Yugoslav People's Army (JNA).

Congress in Prijedor of the Reformist Party led by Ante Marković, last prime minister of Yugoslavia. Bosnian Serb electorate split between nationalists and reformists.

18 November–9 December: free elections in Bosnia-Herzegovina and victory of the nationalist parties SDA, HDZ and SDS; Alija Izetbegović appointed chairman of the collective presidency of Bosnia-Herzegovina.

November: victory of SDA in local elections in Prijedor, and agreement between the two nationalist parties representing the majority populations in that city: Muhamed Čehajić (SDA) becomes mayor, Milomir Stakić (SDS) his deputy; tension over the allocation of other senior posts.

1991

28 February: Serb 'autonomous regions' in Croatia proclaim their separation as the 'Republic of Serb Krajina'.

25 March: meeting between Slobodan Milošević and Franjo Tuđman at the Karađorđevo estate, a former residence of Marshal Tito: they reach a secret agreement to divide Bosnia-Herzegovina between Serbia and Croatia.

15 April: second secret meeting between Milošević and Tuđman to fine-tune the plan to dismember Bosnia.

25 June: Croatia and Slovenia proclaim their independence.

27 June–3 July: JNA intervenes in Slovenia, but is withdrawn by Belgrade after 6 days.

August: war breaks out in Croatia.

Summer: heavily armed brigade from Serbia arrives in Prijedor.

Autumn: military authorities at Banja Luka call on local population to mobilize and join the fighting in nearby Croatia – Bosnian Muslims and Croats refuse.

September-November: 'Serb autonomous regions' (SAO) set up in Bosnia-Herzegovina.

September: UN places an embargo on arms sales to any part of Yugoslavia.

Autumn: setting up of a parallel administration called the 'Serb municipality of Prijedor'.

15 October: Bosnian parliament proclaims sovereignty of the Republic of Bosnia-Herzegovina; Serb deputies belonging to SDS walk out.

10 November: plebiscite organized by SDS among Serbs of Bosnia-Herzegovina on whether to remain in Yugoslavia.

19 November: fall of Vukovar in Croatia.

1992

9 January: supporters of SDS leader Radovan Karadžić proclaim a 'Serb Republic of Bosnia-Herzegovina'.

15 January: European Economic Community (EEC) recognizes independence of Slovenia and Croatia.

February: establishment of Prijedor Crisis Staff.

29 February–1 March: nation-wide referendum on self-determination boycotted by most Serbs in Bosnia-Herzegovina (62 per cent turnout, 99 per cent of votes cast are 'yes' votes).

3 March: proclamation of independence of Republic of Bosnia-Herzegovina by Bosnian parliament.

21–28 March: Serbs seize control of television relay transmitter on Mt Kozara.

Spring: artillery unit of JNA stationed on Mt Kozara; transport equipment and trucks arrive in Prijedor by train; two hundred Serb soldiers move into Hotel Prijedor; insurgent Serbs set up nine police posts; JNA and SDS distribute weapons to Serb population.

5 April: first clashes in suburbs of Sarajevo.

6 April: EEC recognizes Bosnia-Herzegovina; peace demonstration in Sarajevo; siege of Sarajevo begins.

Mid-April: first roadblocks set up by insurgent Serbs around Prijedor.

28 April: debate on Radio Prijedor between the town's political leaders – Mišković (SDS) declares: 'We're going to carry on living together as we always have.' Some UN military observers leave the town, fearing for their safety.

29 April: a fax falsely claiming to be from the Sarajevo authorities, who deny having anything to do with it, orders Bosnian Territorial Defence units to attack troops and installations of the JNA.

30 April: at 2 a.m.police, army and civilians are ordered to get ready by the Prijedor Crisis Staff; at 4 a.m. seizure of the town begins – it is completed in twenty-five minutes; at 6 a.m. an insurgent Serb parallel administration takes up its functions.

2 May: curfew imposed on Prijedor and Ljubija.

10 May: Ratko Mladić named chief of staff of JNA's 2nd military district.

Mid-May: men belonging to Arkan's paramilitary group from Serbia move into the Hotel Prijedor.

22 May: exchange of fire at roadblock in Hambarine, near Prijedor; Serb insurgent forces give an ultimatum to the inhabitants to hand over a suspect.

23 May: shelling of Hambarine.

24 May: mainly Bosniak village of Kozarac attacked. Trnopolje camp opened.

25 May: Omarska camp opened in the Rudnik Ljubija iron mine complex. Keraterm camp opened.

30 May: around a hundred and fifty mainly non-Serb fighters try to re-establish Bosnian control over Prijedor; the Serb nationalists shell the historic heart of the town. First roundups, convoys and deportations.

29 June: François Mitterrand visits Sarajevo.

July–August: Serb nationalist offensive to join eastern Bosnia with west Bosnian Krajina region.

Mid-July: first attacks on villages on left bank of the river Sana.

25 July: killings at Keraterm.

2 August: *Newsday* publishes Roy Gutman's exposure of the camps in Bosnia.

Mid-August: Omarska and Keraterm camps closed down.

21 August 1992: massacre of two hundred and twenty-eight prisoners on Mt Vlašić, near Travnik.

Early October: Trnopolje camp closed down.

17 December: Radovan Karadžić becomes president of the Bosnian Serb parastate.

1993

22 February: UN Security Council adopts Resolution 808 setting up the International Criminal Tribunal for former Yugoslavia (ICTY).

16 June: Franjo Tuđman and Slobodan Milošević call for Bosnia to be divided into three ethnic zones, Croat, Serb and Muslim.

1994

5 February: Markale market in Sarajevo shelled, sixty-eight dead.

February: Washington Accords end hostilities between Croats and Bosniaks and set up a Croat-Bosniak (Muslim) federation.

1995

25 May: Serb nationalists shell Tuzla (eastern Bosnia), seventy dead.

May–June: NATO air strikes. Serb nationalist troops take UN peacekeepers hostage.

15 June: Rapid Reaction Force (RRF) formed.

7–11 July: enclave of Srebrenica taken by Serb nationalist forces. More than seven thousand Bosniaks are murdered in cold blood.

August: Croatian forces retake 'Krajina' and its capital Knin from the Serb insurgents.

28 August: Markale market in Sarajevo shelled, thirty-eight dead.

29 August: start of operation 'Deliberate Force' by NATO against the Bosnian Serb insurgents.

30 August: the Bosnian Serb 'national assembly' delegates its powers of negotiation to Slobodan Milošević.

9 September: start of Croatian-Bosnian offensive in western Bosnia.

September: the Catholic priest Tomislav Matanović and his parents are kidnapped, then murdered.

16–17 September: Bosnian Army retakes extensive territories in western Bosnia, including Ključ and Sanski Most.

12 October: general ceasefire comes into effect in Bosnia-Herzegovina.

16 November: Radovan Karadžić and Ratko Mladić charged with genocide by the ICTY.

12 December: deployment of IFOR troops begins in Bosnia-Herzegovina.

14 December: signature of the Dayton peace accords in Paris by Slobodan Milošević, Franjo Tuđman and Alija Izetbegović.

1996

January: Carl Bildt appointed High Representative of the international community in Bosnia-Herzegovina.

14 September: general elections in Bosnia-Herzegovina.

1997

Meeting in Sarajevo between Orthodox, Muslim, Catholic and Jewish religious dignitaries, who call for 'truth and justice'.

US government places Prijedor and its administration on a blacklist depriving them of all investment, aid and cooperation.

April: Milomir Stakić relinquishes his functions as mayor of Prijedor (he had resumed the post at the end of the war, replacing Dušan Kurnoga).

18 June: Carlos Westendorp replaces Carl Bildt in the post of High Representative.

10 July: arrest by NATO forces of Milan Kovačević, director of Prijedor hospital and member of the Crisis Staff. Former police chief Simo Drljača is killed resisting arrest in the same operation – his coffin is displayed in Prijedor town hall three days later, before a grandiose funeral.

13–14 October: municipal elections in Bosnia-Herzegovina.

Late October: Borislav Marić becomes mayor of Prijedor.

1998

1 August: Milan Kovačević dies in prison at The Hague.

12–13 September: general elections in Bosnia-Herzegovina.

1999

March-June: air offensive by NATO forces in Kosovo and Serbia.

16 August: Wolfgang Petritsch replaces Carlos Westendorp as the new High Representative in Bosnia.

10 December: death of Croatian president Franjo Tuđman.

2000

January: Duško Tadić sentenced to 20 years in prison.

5 October: Slobodan Milošević overthrown; next day the Serbian electoral commission announces the victory of Vojislav Koštunica in the presidential elections of 24 September.

February: inauguration of the Agency for Local Democracy. Nada Ševo elected mayor of Prijedor, replacing Borislav Marić.

2001

9 January: Biljana Plavšić surrenders voluntarily to the ICTY.

19 January: controversial visit to Bosnia by Vojislav Koštunica, president of FRY (Serbia and Montenegro).

22 March: Milomir Stakić is arrested in Belgrade (Serbia) and handed over to the ICTY.

7 May: serious rioting and large demonstrations in Banja Luka mark the laying of the foundation stone for a to-be-reconstructed Ferhadija mosque.

29 June: Slobodan Milošević transferred to The Hague.

2 July: Radislav Krstić, one of the senior military commanders in the seizure of Srebrenica, is sentenced to forty-six years in prison for genocide.

September: bodies of the murdered priest Matanović and his parents found in a well at Bišćani.

September-October: three hundred and seventy-two bodies found at Jakarina Kos, near the Ljubija iron mine.

2 November: five senior guards at Omarska and Keraterm sentenced in The Hague.

2002

12 February: trial of Slobodan Milošević by the ICTY opens in The Hague.

16 April: trial of Milomir Stakić on genocide charges opens.

May: for the first time, Omarska survivors gather at the site of the former camp to remember the victims.

15 May: Clifford Bond, US ambassador to Bosnia, announces that the US administration is to lift sanctions imposed on Prijedor in 1997.

27 May: Paddy Ashdown replaces Wolfgang Petritsch as High Representative of the international community in Bosnia.

13 June: Darko Mrđa, a wanted war criminal being secretly hunted, is arrested in Prijedor.

2 October: Biljana Plavšić, former president of the Bosnian Serbs, pleads guilty to crimes against humanity.

5 October: general elections in Bosnia, victory going to the nationalist parties.

9 December: trial opens in Banja Luka of the presumed murderers of the Catholic priest Tomislav Matanović.

31 December: end of UN mission in Bosnia.

2003

1 January: start of European Union police mission in Bosnia.

27 February: Biljana Plavšić, ex-president of the Bosnian Serbs, sentenced to eleven years in prison.

12 March: assassination in Belgrade of Serbian prime minister, Zoran Đinđić.

9 April: Muharem Murselović, a Prijedor Bosniak, resigns from the post of president of the municipal assembly in protest at the town's decision to choose a Serb nationalist symbol as the emblem of the municipality.

July: Željko Mejakić surrenders to the ICTY.

31 July: Milomir Stakić is sentenced to life imprisonment for crimes against humanity and war crimes.

2004

31 March: Darko Mrđa sentenced to seventeen years in prison for crimes against humanity.

19 April: the Bosnian Serb general Radislav Krstić has his sentence reduced on appeal to thirty-five years' imprisonment for complicity in genocide, war crimes and crimes against humanity in the Srebrenica massacre.

1 May: Slovenia joins European Union.

11 June: the Bosnian Serb Republic recognizes for the first time the massacre of several thousand Muslims at Srebrenica in July 1995.

16 June: the International Criminal Tribunal for former Yugoslavia decides to retain the charge of genocide among the charges against former president Slobodan Milošević.

31 August: opening of the case for the defence in the trial of Slobodan Milošević, thought likely to last until October 2005.

July-September: discovery of at least 150 bodies in Prijedor area, thought to be the remains of Bosniak prisoners murdered at the Omarska camp.

8 September: the ICTY prosecutor asks for the trial of four Bosnian Serbs – including the former commandant of the Omarska camp Željko Mejakić – to be carried out by the Bosnian courts.

14 October: for the first time since the end of the war in Bosnia, the Bosnian Serb authorities agree to accept the real scale of the Srebrenica massacre by mentioning the figure of 7,000 dead in a report.

Verdicts of the International Criminal Tribunal Concerning Events in Prijedor

Duško TADIĆ

Born 1 October 1955. Café owner and karate instructor, born in the village of Kozarac, Duško Tadić was sentenced on appeal to twenty years in prison on 26 January 2000, for crimes against humanity and war crimes. The judges found him guilty of acts of persecution, murder and inhuman treatment committed in 1992 against Bosniaks and Bosnian Croats in Kozarac and at Omarska. Duško Tadić had been arrested in Germany in 1994, then transferred to the ICTY in 1995. He is serving his sentence in Germany but has given notice of appeal for a review of his trial. He is the first individual to have been tried and sentenced by the ICTY.

Miroslav KVOČKA, Milojica KOS, Mlado RADIĆ, Zoran ŽIGIĆ and Dragoljub PRČAC

All from Prijedor, these men were tried together and sentenced in the first instance on 2 November 2001, for crimes mainly committed in Omarska camp.

Miroslav Kvočka
Born 1 January 1957. A former police station chief in the village of Omarska,

he was deputy commandant of the camp of that name. Sentenced in the first instance to seven years' prison for crimes against humanity and war crimes. He has given notice of appeal.

Milojica Kos

Born 1 April 1963. Former reserve policeman. Leader of a squad of guards in Omarska camp. Sentenced to six years in prison for crimes against humanity and war crimes. He was freed on 31 July 2002 after four years and two months of detention.

Mlado Radić

Born 15 May 1952. A former policeman in the village of Omarska, he led the most violent squad of guards in Omarska camp. Sentenced to twenty years' imprisonment for crimes against humanity and war crimes. Has given notice of appeal.

Zoran Žigić

Born 20 September 1958. A former waiter and taxi driver sentenced to twenty-five years' imprisonment for crimes against humanity and war crimes. Has given notice of appeal.

Dragoljub Prćac

Born 18 July 1937. Former police scientific technician who emerged from retirement to lead a squad of guards at Omarska. Sentenced to five years in prison for crimes against humanity and war crimes. Has given notice of appeal.

Duško SIKIRICA, Damir DOŠEN and Dragoljub KOLUNDŽIJA

These three men were tried together and sentenced on 13 November 2001 for criemes committed in the Keraterm camp.

Duško Sikirica

Born 23 March 1964. In charge of security at Keraterm. After initially pleading not guilty, he came in the course of the trial to recognize his guilt and was sentenced to fifteen years' imprisonment for persecutions amounting to a crime against humanity. He is serving his sentence in Austria.

Damir Došen

Born 7 April 1967. Led a squad of guards in the Keraterm camp. Agreed in the course of the trial to change his plea to guilty and was sentenced to five years in prison for persecutions amounting to a crime against humanity. He served his sentence in Austria and was released on schedule at the end of February 2003, after three years and four months of detention.

Dragoljub Kolundžija
Born 19 December 1959. Former long-distance truck driver, led one of the active guard squads at Keraterm. Sentenced to three years of prison for persecutions amounting to a crime against humanity after admitting his guilt. Freed on 6 December 2001 after serving two years and six months.

Biljana PLAVŠIĆ

Born 7 July 1930. This former biology teacher was one of the most senior Serb leaders in Bosnia during the war. After the Dayton accords, she became president of the Republika Srpska. On 27 February 2003, she was sentenced to eleven years in prison for crimes against humanity after admitting her guilt in a campaign of persecution against Bosniaks and Bosnian Croats.

Milomir STAKIĆ

Born 19 January 1962. Former head of the Crisis Staff and ex-mayor of Prijedor, he was arrested in Belgrade on 22 March 2001, then transferred to The Hague. His trial in the first instance began on 16 April 2002 and ended a year later, on 15 April 2003, with the prosecutor's closing address and the defence pleas. Charged with genocide, crimes against humanity and war crimes, he was not found guilty of genocide but was sentenced to life imprisonment on the other charges on 31 July 2003. This is the heaviest sentence so far handed down by the ICTY.

Also, *Milan Kovačević*, a doctor by training and former deputy head of the Crisis Staff, died of a heart attack in his cell in the ICTY building at The Hague not long after the start of his trial, on 1 August 1998. *Simo Drljača*, who had been Prijedor police chief during the war, was killed resisting arrest by NATO forces in Prijedor on 10 July 1997. Both were accused of genocide, crimes against humanity and war crimes by the ICTY.

Notes

To the Reader
1. Roy Gutman, *A Witness to Genocide*, Element Books, 1993.
2. The website www.prijedor-bosnia.com, created by the authors, contains their various published articles and interviews on the subject, along with information on the town of Prijedor and its environs.
3. Peter Maass, *Love Thy Neighbour, A Story of War*, Macmillan, 1996, p. 273.

At the Heart of the Ethnic Cleansing

1. For maps of the town, the region and the country, see section between pages 128 and 129.
2. Since the accords signed in Dayton, Ohio in December 1995, Bosnia-Herzegovina consists of two entities forming a single state: the Bosnian Serb Republic – Republika Srpska (RS) – whose institutions are based in Banja Luka, and the Federation whose capital is Sarajevo. A collective presidency (Bosniak, Serb and Croat) and a federal parliament govern the whole country, both based in Sarajevo which is the official capital of Bosnia-Herzegovina.
3. The region was the theatre of bitter fighting between 1941 and 1945 between Marshal Tito's Partisans on the one hand and on the other the Axis occupation forces and Ustasha militias deployed by Ante Pavelić's fascist puppet 'Independent State of Croatia', which also incorporated Bosnia.
4. Peter Karađorđević was king of Serbia between 1903 and 1918, and the first king of Yugoslavia from 1918 to 1921. The street was so renamed after the war of 1992, having previously been called Marshal Tito Street after Josip Broz Tito (1892–1980), founder of the Federal Republic of Yugoslavia.

Chapter One
1. Reconstruction of the mosque finally started in 2004.
2. 'Bosniak' is a term chosen by Bosnian Muslims to designate their own community.
3. The president of the municipal assembly represents the elected municipal councillors, while the mayor represents those administered – the population of the town.

4. The Democratic Action Party had been founded in May 1990 as the national party of all Muslims.
5. Ustasha means literally 'insurgent'. In this context it refers to the Croat militias formed by Ante Pavelić who, modelling themselves on the Nazis with whom Pavelić was allied, between 1941 and 1945 persecuted and exterminated tens of thousands of people, including Croatian and Bosnian Serbs, Jews and Gypsies.
6. The 'White House' and the 'Red House' were the two buildings at Omarska camp in which the worst atrocities were committed.
7. Omarska was a camp for men, but 36 to 38 women were held there too, in appalling conditions, mainly to act as maids, cook and clean.

Chapter Two
1. Public testimony deposed during the trial of Miroslav Kvočka, Milojica Kos, Mladen Radić, Zoran Žigić and Dragoljub Prčac by the ICTY. Quoted in the judgement first handed down on 2 November 2001.
2. Paul Garde, *Vie et mort de la Yougoslavie*, Fayard, 2000, p. 66.
3. *Vie et mort de la Yougoslavie*, p. 90.
4. Figures quoted in *Vie et mort de la Yugoslavie*, p. 116.
5. Written judgement against Duško Tadić. ICTY document of 7 May 1997, English version, p. 31.
6. Original document submitted to the ICTY during the trial of Duško Tadić and retained as an element of proof by the juges.
7. Opening address in the trial of Stanislav Galić, one of the generals in the Bosnian Serb army accused of being primarily responsible for the siege of Sarajevo. Delivered in December 2001.

Chapter Three
1. Figures supplied by the demographer Ewa Tabeau during the trial of Milomir Stakić by the ICTY in July 2002.
2. *The Prijedor report. Final report of the United Nations' Commission of Experts established pursuant to Security Council resolution 780*, 1992, Hanne Sophie Greve.
3. This is also the point of view defended by Tim Judah in *The Serbs, History, Myth and the Destruction of Yugoslavia*, Yale, 2000, second edition, pp. 199–200.
4. Verdict in the case of Duško Tadić, *op. cit.*, p. 32.
5. *Ibid.*
6. Verdict on Duško Tadić, *op. cit.*, pp. 48 and 49.
7. United Nations report by Hanne Sophie Greve, *op. cit.*, and Tadić verdict, *op. cit.*
8. Robert J. Donia, *Prijedor in the Bosnian Krajina: a background report*, Center for Russian and East European Studies of the University of Michigan.
9. UN report by Hanne Sophie Greve, *op. cit.*
10. Misha Glenny is the author of *The Fall of Yugoslavia*, Penguin Books, third edition, 1996.
11. Closing arguments by the prosecutor Nicholas Koumjian at the trial of Milomir Stakić before the Hague tribunal, 12 April 2003.
12. *Prijedor Report*, Human Rights Watch, 1997.
13. Rezak Hukanović, *The Tenth Circle of Hell*, Abacus, 1996.
14. Noel Malcolm, *Bosnia: a short history*, Macmillan, 2000, p. 252.
15. UN report by Hanne Sophie Greve, *op. cit.*
16. *Ibid.*

17. *The Tenth Circle of Hell, op. cit.*
18. Testimony given at the trial of 'Kvočka and others' before the ICTY, 8 May 2000.
19. Closing arguments in the trial of Milomir Stakić, 12 April 2003.
20. The ICTY's demographic expert Ewa Tabeau puts the number at a cautious two thousand five hundred. Local associations of the families of disappeared people have compiled a list of over three thousand missing persons. The International Commission for Missing Persons (ICMP), based in Sarajevo, gives no official figure but refers enquiries to the local associations.

The Prijedor Triangle

Chapter Four

1. *Bosnia: Witness to Genocide, op. cit.* by Roy Gutman first revealed the existence of these camps on 19 July but the news had passed unnoticed.
2. Extensive information on the Prijedor camps was collected by Amnesty International, Médecins sans frontières, the US government, the Conference on Security and Cooperation in Europe, etc.
3. Report on the ethnic cleansing process in the Prijedor region, 26 October 1992, prepared by Louis Joinet, of the UN Commission for Human Rights on arbitrary detention.
4. *War Crimes in Bosnia-Herzegovina*, volume 2, Helsinki Watch, p. 88.
5. Details of sentences, judicial proceedings in each case and a short biographical sketch of each of these cadres will be found in an appendix.
6. Interviewed by members of Helsinki Watch in Zagreb (Croatia) in December 1992.
7. Extract from the verdict of the first chamber of the ICTY in the Tadić case, 7 May 1997.
8. From Roy Gutman, *Bosnia: Witness to Genocide*, pp. 171–2.
9. See Ed Vulliamy, 'UK Magnate buys Death Camp', *The Guardian*, 2 December 2004.
10. 'No remains', letter from Nicola Davidson, LNM Group, *The Guardian*, 8 December 2004.

Chapter Five

1. *Le livre noir de l'ex-Yougoslavie, op. cit.*, p. 258.
2. Interviewed by Helsinki Watch in a refugee camp in Croatia, 16 January 1993.
3. *Le livre noir de l'ex-Yougoslavie, op. cit.*, pp. 439–44.

Chapter Six

1. See guilty verdict: Duško Sikirica, Damir Došen, Dragan Kolundžija, on website www.un.org/icty/sikirica/jugement/sik-011113.htm
2. *Idem.*
3. At the beginning of 2003 the Keraterm factory was privatized 70 per cent. The new capital came from pension funds, restitution funds and individual shareholders including some of the staff. 30 per cent of the equity remains state property.
4. Aryeh Neier, 'The Return of the Concentration Camp', in *War Crimes, Brutality, Genocide, Terror and the Struggle for Justice*, Random House, 1998, pp. 134–54.
5. *New York Times*, 25 April 1993.
6. AFP item, 17 December 2002.

7. Roy Gutman and David Rieff (eds), *War Crimes, what the public should know*, Norton, 1999. Chapter on 'Concentration camps', pp. 102–6.

8. For all discussion and criticism around this image of Fikret Alić, see Alice Krieg-Planque's very well documented book *Purification ethnique, une formule et son histoire*, CNRS Éditions, 2003, pp. 37–43. The author also gives a long analysis of the language used by the media in covering the camps, pp. 43–60.

9. Edited by Israel W. Charny, *Le Livre noir de l'humanité, encyclopédie mondiale des génocides*, éditions Privat, 2001, p. 171.

10. On this subject, see Jean-Michel Chaumont, *La Concurrence des victimes, génocide, identité, reconnaissance*, La Découverte, 1997.

11. *Libération*, 7 August 1992.

Two Parallel Worlds

1. Nada Ševo was mayor of Prijedor until October 2004. Following the municipal elections of 2 October 2004 she was replaced by Marko Pavić of the Democratic People's Alliance party (DNS).

Chapter Seven

1. Before the war Rudnik Ljubija employed five thousand five hundred people of whom 42 per cent were Serbs, 30 per cent Bosniaks, 20 per cent Croats and eight per cent other nationalities. Of the thirteen hundred workers employed today, only twenty are Croats and ten Bosniaks. At the Mira biscuit factory there used to be three hundred-odd Croats and Bosniaks out of a total of nine hundred. Today only twenty or thirty of the six hundred employees are Croats or Bosniaks.

2. According to Caritas representative Marijan Komljenović, Catholic Croats made up 6.3 per cent of the total population of Prijedor in 1991, numbering about six thousand three hundred people. Today there are fewer than fifteen hundred.

3. In the general elections on 5 October 2002, the SDS obtained twenty-nine of the eighty-three seats in the RS assembly at Banja Luka, as against thirty-one in the previous assembly. In Prijedor town hall the SDS group is eight strong, out of thirty-one altogether. The SDS candidate for mayor received fifteen votes, against the sixteen for Nada Ševo of the SNSD in April 2000.

4. Rezak Hukanović, *The Tenth Circle of Hell, a memoir of life in the death camps of Bosnia*, Abacus, 1998, and Kemal Pervanić, *The Killing Days*, Blake, 1999.

5. One could mention the case of Slobodan Kuruzović, former commandant of the Trnopolje camp and today a retired assistant headmaster living in Prijedor.

6. *Bosnia: a short history*, *op. cit.*, p. 252, and Keith Doubt, *Sociology after Bosnia and Kosovo*, Rowman and Littlefield, 2000, pp. 18–20.

7. Michael A. Sells, *The Bridge Betrayed*, University of California Press, 1998, pp. 72–3.

8. The 'four esses' are often interpreted as referring to the slogan 'Samo Sloga Srbina Spašava', meaning 'Only solidarity will save the Serbs', but in fact reproduce a Byzantine motif to be found in mediaeval Serbian iconography.

9. In 1998 the then mayor of Prijedor signed a contract with a local entrepreneur for the establishment of a free market in the Stari Grad (Old Town) quarter. Under the terms of this contract the owner could hire out plots to traders. Before the war this space was divided into forty-odd lots belonging to Bosniaks. Under American pressure, Prijedor

town hall rescinded the contract. Stari Grad is scheduled to be refurbished within the next few months.

10. Darko Mrđa was convicted in camera of war crimes by the ICTY, for having participated on 21 August 1992 in the execution on Mount Vlašić of two hundred and twenty-eight prisoners who were inhabitants of the Prijedor area.

11. Željko Kopanja was given the International Press Freedom Award on 21 November 2000.

Chapter Eight

1. Documentary *Calling the Ghosts*, made by Mandy Jacobson and Karmen Jelincic in 1996, and produced by the New York-based Women Make Movies.

2. Sentenced to seven years in prison by the ICTY, Kvočka was released on 29 March 2004 after serving two thirds of his sentence. An appeal is pending.

3. www.prijedor.ba

4. UNHCR figure, May 2002.

5. Gordon Weiss, *In the land of the war criminals*, 6 January 1997, see website www.salon.com

6. THW figures. Not all of the families counted live permanently in Kozarac.

7. Figure supplied by the UNHCR in 2004.

8. Figure supplied by the UNHCR in 2004. In 2002, with 10,000 Muslims and Croats already reinstalled in Prijedor, fewer than 600 Bosniaks had gone back to Srebrenica.

9. Chapter 7 of the Dayton accords, see website www.ohr.int

10. Emir Suljagić, 'The impact of the ICTY on the victims and perpetrators of the former Yugoslavia, and the importance of seeing justice being done', lecture delivered at The Hague in January 2003. Emir Suljagić is a journalist on the Bosnian weekly *Dani*.

11. UNHCR Prijedor report, May 2002.

12. 'Bosnian prisoners', radio feature by Lauren Comiteau for Voice of America, 9 October 1998.

Chapter Nine

1. Foreword to *The Tenth Circle of Hell, op. cit.*

2. Kemal Pervanić, *The killing days, my journey through the Bosnian war*, Blake Publishing, 1999.

3. *Voices of the missing*, photo booklet by Haris Memija, International Commission for Missing Persons, Sarajevo, 2000.

4. This figure is the one given by local associations.

5. NATO stabilization force in Bosnia, responsible for ensuring security during the application of the Dayton peace accords. It replaced IFOR which was itself the successor of UNPROFOR, the UN protection force. The European Union took over from SFOR at the end of 2004.

6. Fact sheet no. 6, *Enforced or involuntary disappearances*, Office of the High Commissioner for Human Rights at the United Nations.

A Town's Past Faces Judgement

1. *The Killing Days, op. cit.*

Chapter Ten

1. Pierre Hazan, *La Justice face à la guerre*, Stock, 2000, p. 39.
2. Appointed a judge at the ICTY in 1994, Claude Jorda became its chairman in 1999. He held that post until 11 March 2003, when he became a judge at the International Criminal Court.
3. Milošević was not indicted until later, in 2001, for his presumed responsibility in the wars in Bosnia and Croatia.
4. Interview with Robert Badinter, AFP bulletin, February 2002.
5. List of acts of indictment before the International Criminal Tribunal for former Yugoslavia as at 17 October 2004. Can be consulted on the website www.un.org/icty
6. General Bobetko died in Zagreb on 29 April 2003. Owing to his state of health, the Tribunal had suspended the arrest warrant against him in March 2003.
7. Enver Hadžihasanović, Mehmed Alagić and Amir Kubura were charged in July 2001 with war crimes in relation to attacks on Serb and Croat civilians in central Bosnia. Mehmet Alagić died on 7 March 2003, and the proceedings against him were accordingly adjourned.
8. The Bosnian Croat Zdravko Mučić along with the Bosniaks Hazim Delić and Esad Landžo were sentenced after appeal to nine, eighteen and fifteen years of prison respectively, on 8 April 2003.
9. Elizabeth Neuffer, *The Key to my Neighbour's House, seeking justice in Bosnia and Rwanda*, Picador, USA, 2002, p. 200.
10. *'Collateral Damage' or Unlawful Killings? Violations of the Laws of War by Nato during Operation Allied Force*, Amnesty International, 7 June 2000.
11. Final report to the Prosecutor by the Committee established to review Nato bombing campaign against the Federal Republic of Yugoslavia, June 2000.
12. *La justice face à la guerre, op. cit.*, p. 223.

Chapter Eleven

1. Documentary *Calling the Ghosts, op. cit.*
2. Nusreta Sivac has appeared in several documentaries including *Calling the ghosts, op. cit.*, and also *Viol, une arme de guerre*, by Sabina Subašić and Fabrice Gardel, 52 min., Dock en stock/Arte France, 2001.
3. Antoine Garapon, *Des crimes qu'on ne peut ni punir, ni pardonner: Pour une justice internationale*, Odile Jacob, November 2002, p. 165.
4. See article by Mirko Klarin, 'Protected witness endangered', in the IWPR's *Tribunal Update* no. 298, February 2003, which can be found on the website www.iwpr.net

Chapter Twelve

1. 'Bosnian rape victim protests lightness of war crime sentences', AFP bulletin, 3 November 2001.
2. Summary of the verdict on Dražen Erdemović, ICTY, 5 March 1998.
3. Fourteen individuals indicted by the ICTY had agreed to admit their guilt by January 2005. These guilty pleas became more numerous from 2003.
4. Summary of the verdict on Dražen Erdemović, ICTY, 5 March 1998.
5. *Des crimes qu'on ne peut ni punir, ni pardonner: Pour une justice internationale, op. cit.*, p. 187.
6. Article by Pierre Dalan, 'Le tarif de la peine', in *Diplomatie judiciaire*, 23 November 2001.
7. Noel Malcolm, in his book *Bosnia, a short history (op. cit.)*, points out that most international leaders saw the war in Bosnia as a 'civil war', justifying their refusal to intervene on the

ground that with three camps supposedly torn apart by ancestral hatreds confronting each other, it was not possible to determine who was the aggressor and who was being subjected to aggression. 'What was still not fully understood was that ethnic cleansing was not a by-product of the war. It was a central part of the entire political project which the war was intended to achieve, namely the creation of homogeneous Serb areas which could eventually be joined to other Serb areas, including Serbia itself, to create a greater Serbian state.'

8. Associated Press report, 27 February 2003.
9. AP report, 27 February 2003.
10. Appeal verdict against Duško Tadić, ICTY, 15 July 1999.
11. Verdict on Radislav Krstić, ICTY, 2 August 2001.

Chapter Thirteen

1. Interview with Milan Kovačević by Ed Vulliamy. Read out as part of Ed Vulliamy's testimony before the ICTY, 16 September 2002.
2. *La Justice face à la guerre, op. cit.*, pp. 257, 258.
3. AFP report.
4. *The Key to my Neighbour's House, seeking justice in Bosnia and Rwanda, op. cit.*, p. 335.
5. Annual report of Claude Jorda, president of the ICTY, to the United Nations Security Council in 2002.
6. Refik Hodžić, article written for the Institute of War and Peace Reporting and published in *Balkan Crisis Report* no. 390, 12 December 2002.
7. *La Justice face à la guerre, de Nuremberg à La Haye, op. cit.*, p. 262.

An International Community Trapped by its Own Incoherence

Chapter Fourteen

1. A former career military officer (Royal Marines, also served with the SAS Regiment) and former leader of the Liberal Democratic Party, Paddy Ashdown, a Briton, replaced the Austrian Wolfgang Petritsch in May 2002. His tenure was due to end in the spring of 2004, but was extended until November 2005.
2. HINA news agency bulletin, 9 August 2002.
3. Interview on RTV-Prijedor, 25 September 2002.
4. Interview with the independent daily *Nezavisne Novine*, 12 November 2002.
5. Interview in *La Croix*, 4 October 2002.
6. Stephen Castle, 'Ashdown attacks Nato's half-hearted efforts to bring Karadžić to justice', *The Independent*, 1 February 2003.
7. Documentary *The Fugitives*, made by the Sense agency, 2004.

Chapter Fifteen

1. Extracts from the act of indictment issued by the ICTY.
2. *Ibid.*
3. Agence France-Presse, 23 August 2002.
4. Consolidated writ of indictment dated November 2002. Can be consulted on website www.un.org/icty/indictment/enlish/mea-ci020705e.htm
5. Amended writ of indictment dated 14 December 1995. Can be consulted on website www.un.org/icty/indictment/english/tad-2ai951214e.htm

6. He pleaded guilty in July 2003. Writ of indictment dated 16 April 2002 on the website www.un.org/icty/indictment/english/mrd-ii020416.h

7. Slobodan Kuruzović, testimony before the ICTY in March 2000.

8. Interview seized from the files of Radio Prijedor in 1997 by ICTY investigators and NATO troops, and submitted as evidence on 9 July 1992 at the trial of Milomir Stakić. Can be consulted on website www.un.org/icty/ind-e.htm, under the heading Stakić, then transcript, 9 July 1992.

9. *War criminals in Bosnia's Republika Srpska, who are the people in your neighbourhood?*, ICG Balkans Report, No. 103, pp. 38–41.

Chapter Sixteen

1. *The Tenth Circle of Hell, op. cit.*, Abacus, p. 8.

2. Can be consulted on the ICTY website www.un.org/icty/ind-e.htm, heading Tadić, under transcripts, 22 May 1996.

3. Feature by Kate Connolly, 'He was the face of Bosnia's civil war – what happened next?', in *The Observer*, 4 August 2002. Can be consulted on website www.observer. co.uk/Print/0,3858,4475422,00.html

Chapter Seventeen

1. This is one of the theses developed in David Chandler's *Bosnia, faking democracy after Dayton*, Pluto Press, 2000, pp. 96–97.

2. In 2002 there were forty-three Bosniaks, six Croats and three members of other minorities serving in the Prijedor police, a force totalling seven hundred and twenty-three members.

3. Article by Senad Slatina, 'Bosnia claims in Nato surveillance scandal', in the IWPR's *Balkan Crisis Report* no. 344.

4. Between 1998 and the end of 2002 nearly 110,000 grenades, 27,000 small arms and 24,000 explosive devices were collected in house-to-house searches in Bosnia. In the year 2002 alone the material seized and destroyed included 8,000 small arms; 2.26 million rounds of ammunition; 35,385 grenades; 4,120 mines; and 47,492 other items including mortars and rocket-propelled missiles.

Chapter Eighteen

1. Quoted in *La Croix*, 3 July 2001.

2. Human Rights Watch report on local courts in the Balkans, October 2004.

Chapter Nineteen

1. For the Dayton accords see OHR website www.ohr.int.default.asp?content-id=380

2. See David Chandler's harsh and detailed analysis *Bosnia, faking democracy after Dayton*, Pluto Press, *op. cit.*

3. In *Libération*, 2 March 2002.

4. 'Nuove guerre politiche sociali nei Balcani', ICS, Roma, June 2002. May be consulted on website www.unimondo.org/balcani/approfondimenti/biblio.pdf

Chapter Twenty

1. See Gordana Katana, 'Serbs delay war crimes case', published in *Tribunal Update* no. 269, IWPR.

2. See *La comunità maladetta. Viaggio nella coscienza di luogo*, by the Italian land development specialist Aldo Bonomi, Edizioni di comunità, 2002.

3. Interview in *l'Osservatorio sui Balcani*. Annalisa Tomasi left this post at the end of 2003.

The War of Memories

1. See Ed Vulliamy's astonishing piece 'Horror hidden beneath ice and lies' in *The Guardian*, 19 February 1996.
2. See also Ed Vulliamy's testimony, in the form of notes submitted to the ICTY, to the Hague tribunal on 16 September 2002, on website www.un.org/icty (transcript).
3. See Noel Malcolm's analysis of this period in his book *Bosnia, a short history, op. cit.*, pp. 174–92.
4. On the Milan Kovačević case see Tina Rosenberg, 'Defending the Indefensible', *New York Times Magazine*, 19 April 1998, can be consulted on website http://anthonydamato. law.northwestern.edu/Adobefiles/R1998pix.pdf

Chapter Twenty-one
1. See Sandrine Leblanc, *Politiques du Pardon*, PUF, 2002, pp. 51–73, and (Ed.) Louis Joinet, *Lutter contre l'impunité, dix questions pour comprendre et agir,* La Découverte, 2002, pp. 63–5. See also condensed accounts of the work of the TRC by Maria Mallagardis in *Libération*, 31 July 1998, and Frédéric Chambon in *Le Monde*, 31 October 1998.
2. On the basis of ICTY estimates, Jakob Finci gives the number of war criminals in Bosnia as approximately seven thousand six hundred individuals.
3. See website http://auth.unimondo.org/cfdocs/obportal/index.cfm?fuseaction=news. view2&NewsID=1669
4. In South Africa, Archbishop Desmond Tutu spoke of 'a gigantic national psychoanalysis that made it possible to express our collective pain'. Interview with Maria Mallagardis published in *Libération*, 4 June 1998.

Chapter Twenty-two
1. Tim Judah, *The Serbs, history, myth and the destruction of Yugoslavia*, second edition, Yale, 2000, p. 133.
2. Thomas Hofnung, *Désespoirs de paix, l'ex-Yougoslavie de Dayton à la chute de Milosevic*, Atlantica, 2001, pp. 241–6.
3. Jean-Arnaud Dérens et Catherine Samary, *Les Conflits yougoslaves de A à Z*, Les éditions de l'Atelier, 2000, pp. 158–9.
4. For a decoding of discourses and figures, see *Le Nettoyage ethnique, documents historiques sur une idéologie serbe*, collected, translated and with commentary by Mirko Grmek, Marc Gjidara and Neven Šimac, Points histoire/Le Seuil, 2002, p. 291.
5. This total, accepted by the Jasenovac memorial, breaks down into between 45,000 and 52,000 Serbs, 12,000 Croats and Muslims, 13,000 Jews and 10,000 Roma or 'Gypsies'.
6. See Xavier Bougarel's article 'Guerre et mémoire de la guerre dans l'espace yougoslave', in *Le Retour des Balkans, 1991–2001*, ed. Stéphane Yerasimos, Autrement, 2002, pp. 44–59.
7. *The continuing challenge of refugee return in Bosnia and Herzegovina*, International Crisis Group, 13 December 2002, p. 19.
8. *Ibid.*
9. André Loersch, 'Territoires morcelés, pensée éclatée', in *Le Monde Diplomatique*, June 1999. See also the long survey by Christian Lecomte, 'Bosnie, les écoles de la ségrégation', in *Le Monde*, 14 February 1998.

10. Nermina Durmić-Kahrović, 'Bosnian education struggle', in *Balkan Crisis Report* no. 159, IWPR, 25 July 2000.

11. Chris Hedges, 'Bosnia Journal: Ethnic diversity distorts history, art, language', feature in *The New York Times*, 25 November 1997.

12. Ranko Pejić, *Istorija za osmi razred osnovne škole, Zavod za udžbenike i nastavna sredstva*, Republike Srpske, Srpsko, 2002.

Chapter Twenty-three
1. AFP news item, 20 November 2002.

2. 'Torna il fantasma di Franco e risveglia la Spagna del sonno,' *La Repubblica*, 25 November 2002.

3. Especially after the attempted coup d'état that shook the young democracy on 23 February 1981.

4. Martine Audeusseau, 'Des Espagnols cherchent les disparus de la guerre civile', *La Croix*, 12 and 13 October 2002.

5. *Ibid.*

6. ARMH website www.memoriahistorica.org

7. José Maldavsky, 'Les charniers de Franco', *Le Monde Diplomatique*, January 2003.

8. *El Pais*, 7 November 2002.

9. On the exhumation of the years of dictatorship, see François Musseau's piece 'L'Espagne y va Franco', *Libération*, 25 February 2003.

10. Jean-François Mayeur, 'Une mémoire-frontière: l'Alsace', in *Les Lieux de mémoire*, vol. I, ed. Pierre Nora, Quarto Gallimard, 1997, pp. 1147–68.

11. Note that Bosnia has two alphabets and three major religious communities, not counting the small Jewish community.

12. 'L'Alsace, éternelle incomprise', *L'Express*, 9 January 2003.

13. Interview in *Libération*, 15 and 16 February 2003.

14. See article by Matthieu Gorisse, 'Se souvenir malgré l'oubli', consultable on website http://mcsinfo.u-strasbg.fr/article.php?cPath=3&article-id=1795, and article by Nicole Gauthier, 'La mémoire écartelée des Alsaciens', *Libération*, 28 December 1999.

15. *L'Express*, 9 January 2003.

16. Eric A. Johnson, *Nazi terror, the Gestapo, the Jews and ordinary Germans*, Basic Books, 1999, p. 484.

17. Dimitri Nicolaïdis, 'La nation, les crimes et la mémoire', in the book *Oublier nos crimes, l'amnésie nationale: une spécificité française*, ed. Dimitri Nicolaïdis, Autrement, 2002, p. 9.

18. Alfred Grosser, 'Relations franco-allemandes, deux siècles de haine et de passions', *L'Express*, 14 February 2003.

19. 'Public perception and accounting process', paper delivered by Christian Palme during the Forum for reconciliation held in Stockholm in 2002.

20. This is the view put forward by Ingo Müller in the article 'Comment les Allemands ont-ils jugés les crimes du nazisme?', in *Barbie, Touvier, Papon, des procès pour la mémoire*, ed. Jean-Paul Jean and Denis Salas, Autrement, 2002, pp. 78–87.

21. *El Pais semanal*, 1 December 2002.

22. We would recommend on this subject the book edited by Dimitri Nicolaïdis, *Oublier nos criomes, l'amnésie nationale: une spécificité française*, Autrement, 2002. Algeria, the colonies, the French camps, revolutionary violence, etc., are all issues that tend to be swept under the carpet since they trouble the French republican identity.

Bibliography

General works

Jean-Pierre Bacot and Christian Coq (ed.), *Travail de mémoire,1914-1998, une nécessité dans un siècle de violence*, Autrement, 1999.

Aldo Bonomi, *La comunità maledetta. Viaggio nella coscienza di luogo*, Edizioni di comunità, 2002.

Xavier Bougarel, *Bosnie, anatomie d'un conflit*, La Découverte, 1996.

David Chandler, *Bosnia, faking democracy after Dayton*, Pluto Press, 2000 (second edition).

Israël W. Charny (ed.), *Le Livre noir de l'humanité, encyclopédie mondiale des génocides*, Éditions Privat, 2001.

Jean-Michel Chaumont, *La Concurrence des victimes, génocide, identité, reconnaissance*, La Découverte, 1997.

Jean-Arnault Derens and Catherine Samary, *Les Conflits yougoslaves de A à Z*, L'Atelier, 2000.

Jovan Divjak (interviewed by Florence La Bruyère), *Sarajevo, mon amour*, Buchet Chastel, 2004.

Keith Doubt, *Sociology after Bosnia and Kosovo, recovering justice*, Rowman & Littlefield, 2000.

Antoine Garapon, *Des crimes qu'on ne peut ni punir, ni pardonner. Pour une justice internationale*, Odile Jacob, 2002.

Paul Garde, *Vie et mort de la Yougoslavie*, Fayard, 2000 (second edition).

Misha Glenny, *The fall of Yugoslavia*, Penguin Books, 1996 (third edition).

Roy Gutman, *Witness to Genocide : the first inside account of the horrors of 'ethnic cleansing' in Bosnia*, Element Books, 1993.

Roy Gutman and David Rieff (ed.), *War Crimes, what the public should know*, Norton, 1999.

John Hagan, *Justice in the Balkans, prosecuting war crimes in the Hague tribunal*, University of Chicago Press, 2003.

Florence Hartmann, *Milosevic, la diagonale du fou*, Denoël, 1999.

Pierre Hazan, *La Justice face à la guerre, de Nuremberg à La Haye*, Stock, 2000.

Yves Heller, *Des brasiers mal éteints, un reporter dans les guerres yougoslaves 1991-1995*, Le Monde Éditions, 1997.

Thomas Hofnung, *Désespoirs de paix, l'ex-Yougoslavie de Dayton à la chute de Milosevic*, Atlantica, 2001.

Louis Joinet (ed.), *Lutter contre l'impunité, dix questions pour comprendre et agir*, La Découverte, 2002.

Jean-Paul Jean and Denis Salas, *Barbie, Touvier, Papon, des procès pour la mémoire*, Autrement, 2002.

Eric A. Johnson, *Nazi terror, the Gestapo, Jews and ordinary Germans*, Basic Books, 1999.

Tim Judah, *The Serbs, history, myth and the destruction of Yugoslavia*, Yale University Press, 2000 (second edition).

Alice Krieg-Planque, *'Purification ethnique', une formule et son histoire*, CNRS Éditions, 2003.

Sandrine Lefranc, *Politiques du pardon*, PUF, 2002.

Primo Levi, *The Drowned and the Saved*, Abacus, 1991.

Peter Maass, *Love Thy Neighbour, a story of war*, Macmillan, 1996.

Noel Malcolm, *Bosnia, a short history*, Macmillan, 2000 (third edition).

Stjepan G.Mestrovic, *The Balkanization of the West, the confluence of postmodernism and postcommunism*, Routledge, 1994.

Aryeh Neier, *War Crimes,Brutality,Genocide, Terror and the Struggle for Justice*, Random House, 1998.

Elisabeth Neuffer, *The Key to my Neighbor's House, seeking justice in Bosnia and Rwanda*, Picador, 2002.

Dimitri Nicolaïdis (ed.), *Oublier nos crimes, l'amnésie nationale : une spécificité française*, Autrement, 2002.

Pierre Nora (ed.), *Les Lieux de mémoire*. Vol. I, Gallimard, 1997.

Jean Rolin, *Campagnes*, Gallimard, 2000.

Paolo Rumiz, *Maschere per un massacro*, Editori Riuniti, 2000.

Michael A. Sells, *The Bridge Betrayed, religion and genocide in Bosnia*, University of California Press, 1998.

Laura Silber and Allan Little, *The Death of Yugoslavia*, Penguin Books and BBC, 1996.

Christophe Solioz, *L'après-guerre dans les Balkans : appropriation des processus de transition et de démocratisation pour enjeu*, Karthala, 2003.

Wojciech Tochman, *Mordre dans la pierre*, Éditions Noir sur Blanc, 2004.

Tzvetan Todorov, *Les Abus de la mémoire*, Arléa, 1998.

Stéphane Yerasimos (ed.), *Le Retour des Balkans, 1991-2001*, Autrement, 2002.

Juli Zeh, *De stilte is een geluid, een reis door Bosnie*, Van Gennep, 2003.

Testimony of Survivors

Rezak Hukanović, *The Tenth Circle of Hell, a memoir of life in the death camps of Bosnia*, Abacus, 1998.

Kemal Pervanić, *The Killing Days*, Blake, 1999.

Documents

Helsinki Watch,*War crimes in Bosnia-Herzegovina*, volume II, 1993.

Justice, Accountability and Social Reconstruction :an interview study of Bosnian judges and prosecutors. Human Rights Center, International Human Rights Law Clinic, University of California, Berkeley and Centre for Human Rights, University of Sarajevo. May 2000. Available at website www.hrcberkeley.org

Mirko Grmek, Marc Gjidara and Neven Šimac (ed.), *Le Nettoyage ethnique, documents historiques sur une idéologie serbe*, Seuil, 2002.

Le Nouvel Observateur et Reporters sans frontières, *Le Livre noir de l'ex-Yougoslavie, purification ethnique et crimes de guerre*, Arléa, 1993.

Diane F. Orentlicher, 'Settling accounts : the duty to prosecute human rights violations of a prior regime', Yale Law Journal, June 1991.

Ni krivi, ni dužni. Opčina Prijedor, knjiga nestalih, 2000 (second edition) - (list of missing persons from the Prijedor region).

Ranko Pejić, *Istorija za osmi razred osnovne škole*, Zavod za udžbenike i nastavna sredstva Republike Srpske, Srpsko, 2002 - (history textbook for the 8th grade in RS schools).

Historija 8 razred osnovne škole, Bosna i Hercegovina, Federacija Bosne i Hercegovine, Ministarstvo Obrazovanja, Nauke, Kulture i sporta, Sarajevo, 1996 - (history textbook for the 8th grade in Federation schools).

Judgements of the International Criminal Tribunal for the Former Yugoslavia (ICTY)

Available on the Internet at website www.un.org/icty under 'cases and judgements'.

Opinion and judgement in the Prosecutor versus Duško Tadić, Trial Chamber, Judge Gabrielle Kirk McDonald presiding, 7 May 1997.

Judgement in the Prosecutor versus Duško Tadić, Appeals Chamber, Judge Mohamed Shahabuddeen presiding, 15 July 1999.

Judgement in the Prosecutor versus Miroslav Kvočka, Milojica Kos, Mladen Radić, Zoran Žigić, Dragoljub Prčac, Trial Chamber, Judge Almiro Rodrigues presiding, 2 November 2001.

Sentencing judgement in the Prosecutor versus Duško Sikirica, Damir Došen, Dragan Kolundžija, Trial Chamber, Judge Patrick Robinson presiding, 13 November 2001.

Sentencing judgement in the Prosecutor versus Dražen Erdemović, Trial Chamber, Judge Florence Mumba presiding, 5 March 1998.

Reports

The Prijedor Report. Final report of the United Nations Commission of experts established pursuant to Security Council 780 (1992). Annex V, the Prijedor Report. Prepared by Hanne Sophie Greve, member and rapporteur on the Prijedor Project, 28 December 1994. The entirety of this remarkable and exhaustive report, which gives a graphic picture of ethnic cleansing at Prijedor, is available on the Internet at the following website: www.ess.uwe.ac.uk/comexpert/ANX/V.htm

The Unindicted : Reaping the Rewards of 'Ethnic Cleansing', Human Rights Watch. This report, drafted in 1997 but still very relevant in its main lines, is available on the Internet at the following website: www.hrw.org/reports/1997/bosnia

Prijedor in the Bosnian Krajina : a background report, prepared by Robert J. Donia, Center for Russian and East European Studies, University of Michigan, USA, 22 March 2002. Expert witness testimony presented to the ICTY in the context of the Milomir Stakić trial.

Rapport sur le processus de purification ethnique dans la région de Prijedor. Document drawn up by Louis Joinet, chairman of the working group of the UN Human Rights Commission on arbitrary detention following a visit to 'southern Krajina', October 1992.

Évolution de la population à Prijedor de 1991 à 1997. Study report prepared by Helge Brunborg, Torkild Lyngstad and Ewa Tabeau in the context of the ICTY's consideration of Keraterm, 19 April 2002.

Serbian Nationalism in the Twentieth Century. Expert report for the Prosecution in the case against Slobodan Milošević, prepared by Audrey Budding, Harvard University. 29 May 2002.

Internet Sites

Official Websites
Website of the International Criminal Tribunal: www.un.org/icty
Website of the Office of the High Representative of the international community in Bosnia (OHR) : www.ohr.int
Website of the Prijedor town hall: http://city.prijedor.com
Website of the Truth and Reconciliation Commission (in Bosnian, Croat and Serb) : www.angelfire.com/bc2/kip
and in English: www.angelfire.com/bc2/kip/english/index.htm

Websites Providing Information
Website of *The Bosnian Institute* based in London :www.bosnia.org.uk
Website of the *Osservatorio dei Balcani* (in Italian), frequently updated thanks to a network of correspondents: www.osservatoriobalcani.org
Website of the *Institute for War and Peace Reporting* (IWPR), very informative, thanks to

a huge network of correspondents both throughout the Balkans and at the ICTY – see its *Balkan Crisis Reports* et *Tribunal Updates*: www.iwpr.net

Website of *Le Courrier des Balkans*, for French-language coverage of the Balkans: www.balkans.eu.org

Website of the Human Rights Center of the University of California, Berkeley – indispensable for everything concerning international justice, war crimes and postwar reconstruction: www.hrcberkeley.org

Website of Haverford College in Pennsylvania, USA, which provides a wealth of information, notably on the crimes committed at Prijedor: www.haverford.edu

Websites on Prijedor

The town's website, hosted by the firm Ki Sistemi, provides general and business information : www.prijedor.com

Survivors of the war and the camps have created a website devoted to the history and tragic past of the region and city of Prijedor, with numerous photographs: www.prijedor.ba

Finally, articles written by the authors of this book, together with information about Prijedor and its region relevant to the issues raised here, may be found on the website www.prijedor-bosnia.com

Visual Documentaries

Begunci-The fugitives, the case of Dr. Radovan Karadžić and General Ratko Mladić, by Mirko Klarin and Mina Vidaković, SENSE, 2003, 54 minutes, The Hague (can be viewed on www.sense-agency.com)

Calling the ghosts, by Mandy Jacobson and Karmen Jelinčić, 1996, 60 minutes. Produced by Women Make Movies, New York.

Justice Unseen, by Refik Hodžić and Aldin Arnautović, 2004, 58 minutes. Produced by XY Films Produkcija, Sarajevo.

Those who killed the light, by Maria Warsinski, 1994, 51 minutes, Oslo.

Viol, une arme de guerre, by Sabina Šubašić and Fabrice Gardel, 2001, 52 minutes. Doc en stock/Arte France.

Yugoslavia, death of a nation, by Brian Lapping, 1995–6, 5 hours, Brian Lapping/BBC.

Index